# SECULAR *faith*

# SECULAR *faith*

## *How* CULTURE *Has* TRUMPED

## RELIGION *in* AMERICAN

## POLITICS

Mark A. Smith

UNIVERSITY OF CHICAGO PRESS

*Chicago and London*

*Mark A. Smith is professor of political science and adjunct professor*
*of comparative religion at the University of Washington. He is the*
*author of* The Right Talk: How Conservatives Transformed the
Great Society into the Economic Society *and* American Business
and Political Power: Public Opinion, Elections, and Democracy.

The University of Chicago Press, Chicago 60637
The University of Chicago Press, Ltd., London
© 2015 by The University of Chicago
All rights reserved. Published 2015.
Printed in the United States of America

24 23 22 21 20 19 18 17 16 15    1 2 3 4 5

ISBN-13: 978-0-226-27506-2 (cloth)
ISBN-13: 978-0-226-27537-6 (e-book)
DOI: 10.7208/chicago/9780226275376.001.0001

Library of Congress Cataloging-in-Publication Data
Smith, Mark A. (Mark Alan), 1970- author.
   Secular faith : how culture has trumped religion in American politics /
Mark A. Smith.
       pages    cm
   Includes bibliographical references and index.
   ISBN 978-0-226-27506-2 (cloth : alkaline paper) — ISBN 978-0-226-27537-6
(e-book)  1. Christianity and politics—United States—History.  2. Politics and
culture—United States—History.  3. Christianity and culture—United States—
History.  I. Title.
   BR115.P7S57 2015
   261.70973—dc23
                                                            2014047941

♾ This paper meets the requirements of
ANSI/NISO Z39.48-1992 (Permanence of Paper).

# Contents

# Preface

Scholars and political commentators routinely assert that a "culture war" rages throughout American society. Sociologist James Davison Hunter popularized this term in an influential book he published in 1991. In Hunter's view two competing groups—the "orthodox" and the "progressives"—invariably clash in the political and social worlds because they embrace "different systems of moral understanding." The orthodox hold strong religious beliefs and derive their moral standards from an "external, definable, and transcendent authority." They confront progressives who ground morality in "the spirit of the modern age, a spirit of rationalism and subjectivism."[1] Lacking the basis for agreement that a shared worldview might provide, the two sides wage endless battles over schools, government, the family, the arts, and the entertainment media.

Political commentator Bill O'Reilly, among others, echoes Hunter in calling America's divisions a culture war.[2] According to *New York Times* columnist Ross Douthat, the culture war persists because "there's no common ground on which to call a truce." Although concerns over jobs and the economy often drive the news cycle, electoral campaigns, and government decisions, Douthat continues, "the arguments that we remember longest, that define what it means to be democratic and American, are often the debates over human life and human rights, public morals and religious freedom—culture war debates, that is, in all their many forms."[3]

These culture war debates expanded in the twenty-first century when the "new atheists" joined the fray. Various scientists, philosophers, and public intellectuals such as Sam Harris, Richard Dawkins, Daniel Dennett, Christopher Hitchens, and Victor Stenger attacked religious belief and sought to document its negative consequences for society.[4] While atheists used to pen obscure philosophical and academic tracts, they now wrote best-selling books, hosted public events, and attracted media attention. Harris, for example, stirred controversy by dismissing religion as the only domain in life where people bypass the need for evidence and accept claims purely on faith. In turn, Christian writers responded forcefully with books such as *The Last Superstition: A Refutation of the New Atheism* and *The Reason for God: Belief in an Age of Skepticism*.[5]

The atheist and Christian writers debated not only whether God exists but also how a society can promote and sustain moral behavior. To atheists, a blind allegiance to faith historically undermined morality by encouraging Christians to support warfare, repress women, engage in bigotry, and trample on the rights of religious minorities. We could improve society, atheists insisted, if people abandoned religion and formed their morals solely through the power of reason.[6] Christians, meanwhile, linked atheism with immorality and argued that no moral code could exist without a religious foundation. In this account compassion, charity, restraints on self-interest, and respect for the law all depend on religious convictions. A society without religion is therefore a society without morality.[7]

After witnessing disputes of this kind, observers might easily conclude that Americans are indeed fighting a culture war with religion at its center. Interestingly, however, many political scientists and sociologists argue that the general public does not participate in the culture war waged by intellectual, political, and religious elites. Through interviews with and surveys of ordinary Americans, some scholars have shown that people do not typically embrace the polarized positions that supposedly characterize the culture war. Instead, this research indicates, most Americans hold relatively moderate views but find themselves surrounded by politicians, activists, and interest groups who take extreme positions, use inflammatory rhetoric, and coarsen our political discourse.[8] Other scholars disagree, finding that the combatants in the culture war include not only elites but also the politically engaged members of the general public.[9] To Hunter, it hardly matters how far the culture war extends beyond elites, for they control the images, symbols, and narratives that guide our most powerful institutions. An active minority, he notes, can sustain the culture war without the majority's assent or even awareness.[10]

I take a different approach in this book by examining the culture war through a historical lens. Analyses of the culture war typically presume that participants keep fighting over the same issues, but in reality controversies ebb and flow. People often revise their moral beliefs, causing an issue to be contentious in one period but not the next. I show in the upcoming chapters that Christians have openly or tacitly accepted many modern ideas by either changing their long-standing positions or refraining from political action. Christians are part of society, not separate from it, and they often fail to realize how much they absorb from the surrounding culture. Their political stances often resonate with contemporary opinions, values, and behaviors but clash with the moral commitments and biblical understandings that Christians held in previous eras. Christians of earlier centuries would be shocked and appalled if they knew about some of the beliefs and practices of Christians today.

In short, by examining how issues develop over time, we will see just how narrow the culture war's boundaries really are. Focusing on a handful of current disputes has caused many scholars and journalists to overlook the principles and policies on which most Americans, regardless of their religious affiliations, actually agree. Religion in America seems less divisive once we learn how and why the prevailing culture causes people to adjust and update their values. By charting the political development of several important issues, this book shows that religious diversity need not lead to moral and political conflict. As we will see, Christians agree with non-Christians—and even atheists—far more often than the metaphor of a culture war would predict.

To sustain these claims, I explore some of the most prominent controversies in which religion and politics have intersected in America. In the same way that biographers normally write about major rather than minor historical figures, I searched for the religious issues that have sparked the most intense and sustained political conflict. Across American history, slavery attracted nearly two centuries of religious mobilization on all sides and, along with the Civil War it helped inspire, created especially deep political divisions in the 1800s. Slavery would make anyone's short list of topics for this book to cover, and so I give the issue the attention it deserves. As the two most prominent contemporary issues where religion and politics intersect, homosexuality and abortion must also be included in a book of this kind. Beyond those issues, one could investigate many others that citizens, religious leaders, and politicians have framed and understood in moral terms. The issue of divorce is a prime example because it relates to family values, receives explicit condemnation in the Bible, and created political controversy earlier in American history. Owing to the long-running debates over women's roles in American society, I also examine the broad cluster of issues connected to women's political and economic rights. Slavery, divorce, homosexuality, abortion, and women's rights represent a wide range of issues, and yet—as I will demonstrate—the connections between religion and politics were similar in each case.

For each issue I analyze not only the evolution of public opinion, social practices, and government policies but also the shifting positions and biblical interpretations of various Christian groups. Broadly speaking, Christian leaders have responded to cultural developments on these issues with one of three strategies. Sometimes Christian leaders have held firm and insisted that the Bible and Christian tradition reject a moral and political position gaining support in society. At other times these same leaders have accommodated cultural trends by preserving a moral teaching while declining to press for government laws and regulations that reflect it. Finally, some Christian leaders have openly changed their moral and political stances on an issue by offering a new biblical interpretation that matches the prevailing spirit of the age.

Throughout the book I mainly analyze how Christian individuals, denominations, and lobbying organizations have employed these three strategies. I focus on Christianity not from any conviction that it is the only religion worth studying, but rather because Christians—a large majority of the population throughout American history—have wielded much more political power than members of other religions. To be sure, various Jews, Muslims, Buddhists, Hindus, Sikhs, Scientologists, New Agers, and others have left a political mark as individuals through their work as politicians, activists, or intellectuals. In terms of group power, however, no other religion in America comes close to Christianity. Of course, Christianity in America has always been diverse, and the upcoming chapters explicitly incorporate and analyze that diversity.

Armed with the insights gained from studying how Christians have engaged prominent historical and contemporary issues, readers will come to see the culture war in a new light. Once we understand how issues develop, it becomes clear that the supposed culture war does not live up to its name—even among elites. The processes of cultural change and religious accommodation, I show, lead Americans to agree with each other much more frequently than observers of our polarized politics would expect. In fact, we all take for granted certain values and beliefs that we share with other members of our society. For example, hardly any Americans call it immoral to charge interest on loans, but their predecessors in earlier centuries often disagreed. As we will see in the first chapter, the history of collecting interest illustrates the central claim of this book: religion, politics, and morality evolve together, thereby limiting the scope of the culture war and offering a hopeful message for the future. Despite what currently seems to be unceasing conflict on particular issues, history shows that Americans often forge agreements on contentious moral and political questions.

# Strategies of Adaptation

1

When I was accepted into the Massachusetts Institute of Technology, my parents nearly choked upon seeing the price tag. My father's income as a pharmacist, combined with my mother's earnings as a legal secretary and church organist, could not possibly cover the enormous costs for tuition, fees, and room and board, especially since my parents were already paying most of my brother's college bills. What was a middle-class family like mine to do? Short of winning the lottery, we took the only course available to us: we applied for loans and other forms of financial aid.

Back when I went to college, students borrowed from banks rather than directly from the government. As a bright-eyed student signing the loan paperwork, I did not for a moment pause to consider whether, by paying interest to a bank, I was participating in an immoral transaction. Believing that the bank's actions were normal and proper, I took it for granted that the loans would include interest. Even as an eighteen-year-old, I understood that banks are profit-seeking businesses, not charities, and that they earn money by charging interest. Like any rational consumer, I would have preferred lower interest rates, just as I would rather pay six rather than twelve dollars to see a movie. But it never crossed my mind to question the very concept of interest. Without it, how could someone like me borrow the hefty sum required for my student loans?

My parents, too, found nothing unusual or unethical about the bank collecting interest from me, and they would have dismissed as ludicrous any suggestion that the government should prohibit the transaction. Indeed, they had followed a well-traveled path to the middle class by using bank loans like mine. Few Americans could afford to pay cash for a house or even a car, 1 and the Smiths of Pickerington, Ohio, were no different. My parents accepted interest as the price one pays to finance major purchases, and I—just like everyone else in America—accepted this assumption without much thought.

How is this story relevant to the larger themes of this book? To grasp the story's significance, we must recognize that people living in earlier times and other places, including ancient Israel, did not always share our society's beliefs about the propriety and necessity of interest. Several biblical passages condemned the practice of collecting interest and led generations of Jews and Christians to call it sinful. In Exodus 22:25 and Leviticus 25:35-37, Moses relayed God's command that Israelites not charge interest to any of their neighbors who had fallen into poverty. Deuteronomy 23:20 expanded this rule, stating, "You may charge a foreigner interest, but you may not charge your brother interest."[1] Among later Old Testament books, Ezekiel 18:5-9 forbade collecting interest from anyone, regardless of the person's nationality or economic status, and Psalms 15:5 said that a righteous person "does not put out his money at interest."

Statements against charging interest continued in the New Testament. Luke 6:34-35 presupposed lending without interest as the requirement for ethical behavior—a standard, Jesus said, that even sinners meet. Jesus asked people to go even further, for true generosity requires lending without expecting repayment at all. The New Testament mentioned interest in one other place, the parable of the talents in Matthew 25:14-30. In that parable, the master rebuked his third servant, who buried the master's talent (a unit of currency in the Roman Empire) instead of working to multiply it as the first two servants did. The master seemed to approve earning interest when he cried out, "You ought to have invested my money with the bankers, and at my coming I should have received what was my own with interest."

When contemplating these passages from the Old and New Testaments, what should a Christian conclude about the morality of interest? If Christians restrict themselves to the literal meaning of the verses, several interpretations seem possible, the first of which, following Ezekiel 18:5-9, Psalms 15:5, and Luke 6:34-35, judges harshly any attempt to charge interest. Alternatively, Christians could read the parable of the talents in Matthew 25:14-30 to indicate the acceptability of moneylending at interest. Although parables create a wider range of interpretive possibilities than do direct commands, Christians could conclude that the code of conduct implied in Matthew clarifies or overturns the Bible's other standards regarding interest. Between these two categorical interpretations, Christians could infer that God permits lenders to collect interest only from certain people, such as foreigners (Deuteronomy 23:19-20) or anyone who is not poor (Exodus 22:24 and Leviticus 25:35-37).

For the first fifteen centuries of Christianity, strong voices in the Church, including theologians, popes, and ecumenical councils, found no ambiguity in these verses and took a hard line against interest. St. Jerome and many other writers explained that the Hebrew prophets and Jesus had generalized the understanding of "brother" such that Moses's protections for Jews now applied to Gentiles as well. Hence, lenders could not demand interest from anyone, foreigners included, despite appearances to the contrary in Deuteronomy.[2] In 1139 the Second Lateran Council placed a heavy penalty, extending through life and a bit beyond death, on anyone making a living by charging interest: they should be "held infamous throughout their whole lives and, unless they repent, be deprived of a Christian burial."[3] Other ecumenical councils and papal decrees expanded these themes. St. Thomas Aquinas appealed to both natural and divine law to undercut the concept of interest, fashioning a philosophical argument about the nature and definitions of money, selling, and renting to explain why interest was unnatural and thus impermissible.[4]

But the financial needs of merchants and manufacturers were changing, which put pressure on traditional beliefs about the immorality of charging interest. Despite the Church's history of clear and authoritative statements, some theologians eventually responded to this pressure by allowing exceptions for certain financial dealings. Through one such transaction, which was similar to a modern mortgage or annuity, the borrower paid the lender each year a certain amount of money or an equivalent value in goods. While these practices initially raised the ire of Church authorities, over time many theologians creatively shifted definitions to conclude that lenders were not assessing interest even when the total value of the borrowers' payments exceeded the original loan.[5] In certain periods and regions, secular rulers allowed Jews to earn interest openly, though Christian leaders usually refused to sanction this exception.[6]

Even without lending by Jews, who often faced persecution and expulsion, and whose small and scattered numbers prevented them from meeting the full demand for credit, Christians could sometimes obtain short-term and long-term loans in other ways. During the late Middle Ages international merchants increasingly used bills of exchange through which they redeemed payments from banks in one country, at a future date, at banks in another country. Bankers did not explicitly charge interest but profited by using a deflated exchange rate to calculate repayment for the loans, and many theologians held that this process did not amount to collecting interest.[7] By stating that "an infinite number of decent Christians" were using bills of exchange and that he could not countenance a rule that would "damn the whole world," the Spanish theologian Martín de Azpilcueta acknowledged that the Church's traditional opposition to interest must be modified by generously defining what did and did not qualify.[8]

The increasingly popular "triple contract" demonstrates even more clearly that theological understandings gradually accommodated common business practices. As commercial society expanded during the late Middle Ages and the Renaissance, individuals who needed additional capital for their businesses often turned to outside investors. The first part of a triple contract specified a passive investor's contribution, the second part insured the passive partner against loss, and the third—of special relevance here—guaranteed a particular rate of return. These contracts frequently promised 5 percent per year, leading to centuries of controversy over whether the investors were, in fact, flouting long-established doctrines by collecting interest.[9] Many Church authorities answered yes, and during the Reformation popes continued to issue strict decrees forbidding interest. Yet the theologians who involved themselves in the details of lending softened the Church's teachings by approving the fixed rate of return in the triple contract.[10] Martin Luther followed his Catholic counterparts by endorsing interest rates of 5 percent and 6 percent, along with 8 percent for investments based on land holdings, and John Calvin established 5 percent as the maximum interest rate in Geneva.[11]

By accepting modest interest rates, these theologians contributed to an evolution in the definitions of key terms. The English word *usury* derives from the Latin *usura* and the medieval Latin *usaria*, both simply meaning "interest."[12] The Church's original positions, then, referred to lenders demanding any interest at all from borrowers, and the practical questions required determining which types of financial exchanges constituted interest and thus violated the edicts. As Christian writers and society at large began embracing the triple contract and other kinds of investments, usury gradually came to refer only to charging exorbitant interest. Anyone who consults a modern English dictionary will find *usury* defined in this narrow sense. Like the faded dye of an old garment, the term's current meaning preserves only a trace of the Church's formerly stark denunciation of interest.

Contemporary attitudes toward moneylending thus reveal the full extent to which Christians accommodated an important underpinning of modern economies. Christian leaders no longer make fine distinctions about whether bills of exchange, mortgages and annuities, and the triple contract include interest, for those distinctions are pointless when people view interest as morally permissible. In fact, the Catholic Church now unapologetically earns interest from its own investments, and so do Protestant institutions. Individual Christians rarely stop to consider whether God approves the interest they collect as depositors and investors or pay as borrowers. Members of most other religious groups in America, and people unaffiliated with any religion, act in a similar manner.[13] Regardless of their religious beliefs or lack thereof, Americans almost always treat interest the same way I did with my college loans: they unconsciously accept it as a central component of a modern economy.

This societal consensus on interest affects our contemporary politics. From the Middle Ages to as late as the seventeenth century, European rulers often responded to the perceived immorality of interest payments by outlawing them.[14] In contemporary America, by contrast, interest seldom becomes a political controversy. When the subject does reach the political agenda, the discussion focuses only on whether people are paying exorbitant rates (for example, to payday lenders), not the mere existence of interest. Thus an issue that theoretically could incite a prolonged moral and political struggle—in short, a culture war—instead creates only an occasional skirmish. Because Americans have reached a consensus about the acceptability of interest, any Christian leaders who called for banning it would sound hopelessly naïve about basic economics.

### *Religious Leaders as Political Advocates*

Clearly, Christians over several centuries changed their beliefs about the morality of collecting interest, thereby recasting the politics of whether and how to regulate the practice. An educated observer might assume that this is an isolated case, perhaps reflecting people's need for borrowing and lending in any economy that advances beyond the subsistence level. A shift in the Christian response to interest would then represent a unique development that teaches no broader lessons about the interplay of religion, morality, and politics. Yet the research presented in this book shows that many other issues, both historical and contemporary, underwent similar metamorphoses that transformed the scope and meaning of the culture war. For a wide range of issues, I document a clear evolution of American values and practices, religious beliefs and doctrines, and political activism and public policy. Affecting not just the periphery but the core of American politics, moral evolution redefined the political issues that have attracted the most concern from religious groups.[15]

What patterns do these issues follow as they unfold over decades or centuries? The processes of moral evolution begin with the relationship between religious leaders and their constituencies. Consider the case of Protestant ministers, who provide leadership to their congregations and sometimes their local communities. In principle ministers can take stands on political issues, if they so choose, in sermons or other forums. Scholarly research based on interviews with pastors, however, finds that they hesitate to express from the pulpit political opinions that significant segments of their congregations oppose.[16] This reticence should not surprise anyone familiar with religious trends in America today. In a country with many different churches, denominations, and religious traditions, and where people choose which religious community, if any, to devote their time, money, and energy, clergy who espouse divisive political views risk alienating some of the laity. Pastors are all too aware that members who object to the political messages they hear from the pulpit may reduce their rates of giving or attendance and may even exit the church altogether. In the words of one minister who explained why he did not clearly address a controversial issue affecting the local community, "I guess I'm afraid that if I'm too clear, everyone will leave."[17]

Besides potentially causing a mass exodus from the church, pastors who make unpopular political statements could also endanger their own employment and careers. Achieving success in the ministry, just like any other profession, requires hard work, personal convictions, and obeying certain norms, one of which says that clergy should avoid offending their parishioners. Mark Driscoll, the influential and sometimes polarizing founder of a megachurch in Seattle, laments the fact that congregations can sometimes oust clergy who become too outspoken. "In most churches," Driscoll observes, "the sermons are short, the pastor doesn't get to say anything controversial, and if he does, he's quickly no longer the pastor."[18] Driscoll might have exaggerated slightly to make his point, but he accurately conveyed that pastors depend on continuing support from their congregations. Indeed, Driscoll himself eventually resigned his post while facing a litany of charges, though these involved his managerial style rather than any political statements.[19]

What can pastors do when they disagree with some or most of their members on a political issue? Must they become hypocrites who say things they do not believe? Pastors can often manage these difficult situations by simply remaining silent on the relevant subject. During the civil rights movement, for example, white clergy sympathetic to the cause commonly kept quiet unless they had backing from their congregations.[20] Ministers who differ with parts of their congregations can also choose to work outside the formal church setting for their favored causes.[21] When they do make political statements to their congregations, pastors face incentives to stay within the broad range their members would find acceptable.[22]

Similar agreement between leaders and members occurs at a denominational level. At annual conventions or other venues, leaders can pass resolutions or write documents that commit the denomination to a particular political statement. If these decision-making bodies include representatives from different states and regions, leaders stay abreast of the range of opinions in the denomination. Absent rough agreement among various members and congregations, leaders may choose not to put the denomination on the record one way or another. By contrast, when a stance under consideration enjoys widespread assent, leaders can adopt it without jeopardizing the ties binding the group together. In this way formal denominational positions usually reflect the sentiments prevailing in the membership at that time.[23] The turmoil that arises when denominations take stands many of their members resist, which occurred in earlier decades when mainline denominations began ordaining gay ministers and bishops, shows why leaders work so hard to find common ground.

R. Albert Mohler Jr., president of the Southern Baptist Theological Seminary, described how his denomination remains responsive to its members: "At last week's annual meeting in Orlando, we reaffirmed our beliefs in our traditional way—democratically. . . . Our conservatism comes from our members and remains dominant through their determination. The Southern Baptist Convention really is a convention. Messengers elected by local congregations debate and vote in a setting that is part New England town meeting and part sawdust revival."[24] Resolutions in the Southern Baptist Convention, which must be submitted in advance, require approval from a resolutions committee appointed by the organization's president and then a majority vote by attendees at the annual meeting.[25] Through this two-stage process, resolutions need to garner backing throughout the denomination before taking effect.

The processes work differently in the Catholic Church, though with a similar need to satisfy a membership. Since the Catholic Church is organized much more hierarchically than Protestant churches, there are fewer opportunities for perspectives from Catholic laity to bubble up through participatory forums and thereby shape the authoritative positions of the Church.[26] Bound by tradition and canon law, Catholic leaders have historically been more willing than their Protestant counterparts to take stands unpopular with their membership. This difference does not mean, however, that popes, cardinals, bishops, and priests can ignore the views and concerns of the laity. The Pew Forum on Religion and Public Life's comprehensive survey shows that ex-Catholics (or lapsed Catholics) are one of America's largest religious groupings, and the Church hierarchy cannot compel parishioners to attend mass, give tithes and offerings, or maintain their identity with the faith.[27] Catholics who continually hear objectionable political statements from their leaders may react by dropping their affiliation with the Church. Later in the chapter, I explain how the Catholic Church can maintain its traditional teachings while minimizing the political fallout in cases where lay members oppose its doctrines.

The founders and managers of religiously influenced interest groups such as the Moral Majority, Christian Coalition, and Family Research Council face, if anything, more serious constraints from their members than do the leaders of Catholic, Protestant, Mormon, Jewish, or Muslim bodies. Whereas religions can give their members spiritual comfort, a community of like-minded believers, and insights about eternal salvation, lobbying organizations offer only their political stands. People do not voluntarily affiliate with a lobbying organization unless they embrace its political agenda and activities. Although the groups need not enroll a majority of their target population to become a significant political force, they still require an active minority who will contribute financially, participate in the organization's events, and respond favorably to letters or e-mail appeals. Without memberships giving them a financial base and democratic legitimacy, interest groups would lose much of their vitality and perhaps cease to exist at all. From the full set of political stances organizational leaders might want to express, then, they must be careful to select only those that will retain the allegiance of current members and attract others in the future.[28]

## The Bible and Politics

Rank-and-file members thus influence the political positions that their religious leaders publicly embrace. This influence, exerted within congregations, denominations, and religiously based lobbying groups, makes it important to understand the means through which ordinary members form their political attachments. The United States has a long tradition of an institutional separation of church and state, but individual believers have often connected their religious and political views. From colonial Puritans to today's Pentecostals, people have sought to use their religious convictions to inform their political commitments. How can believers determine the best ways to apply the tenets of their faith to the political issues of the day?

Many Christians regard the Bible as a crucial source of guidance on how to think and act politically. Especially for evangelicals who view the Bible as inerrant, but to some extent for all Christians, the Bible is the fountainhead for their doctrines, rituals, and practices. To learn the policies they should advocate to government and their fellow citizens,

Christians can search their scriptures for relevant stories, messages, and commands. The challenge for believers is that the Bible is primarily a religious rather than political text. The Bible contains many passages and themes that can inspire political action, to be sure, but this material must be extracted from the much greater amount of biblical narrative with religious but not political significance.

Even when the politically relevant content scattered throughout or implied in the Bible has been identified, Christians still need to interpret it. If the Bible offers general principles for how people should relate to each other, how can those principles guide responses to the concrete problems facing government today? Do exhortations to turn the other cheek and show compassion for the poor apply only to what individuals should do, or are the Bible's messages binding for national policies involving war and peace, the domestic welfare state, and international trade, foreign aid, and economic development? Should Christians use the Bible to press their governments to prohibit or allow a practice, or do the historical circumstances in which the biblical authors were living affect the political inferences drawn from their writings? When two biblical passages give different political advice, which one should Christians follow?

Christians resolve these dilemmas not in the abstract but rather within particular cultural environments.[29] People's backgrounds, presuppositions, and social contexts influence the ways they interpret a text, and Christians are no different when they try to learn political wisdom from the Bible.[30] Sometimes the factors shaping biblical interpretations are shared throughout the entire society, with most Christians deriving the same political meanings from their scriptures. In these instances a society's taken-for-granted beliefs, values, and ways of viewing the world constrain the dominant biblical interpretations to a narrow range. When members of a society largely or entirely agree on a certain political question, readers usually see the words of the Bible through this consensus.

An illustrative example can be found in the principles of pacifism, which are difficult to maintain in America or, for that matter, anywhere else. Most people can envision circumstances under which war would be necessary, such as when their country faces invasion or a great evil must be combated. Political leaders throughout history—chiefs, kings, emperors, dictators, presidents, and prime ministers alike—have rallied their populations to war when aggressive foes put the country's security and interests at risk. Shrewd (or, to their opponents, manipulative) leaders can sometimes whip their people into a war frenzy on just the pretext of a foreign threat.

People's acceptance of war under certain conditions stands in some tension with biblical passages and themes that seem to condemn violence of any kind. In the Sermon on the Mount, for example, Jesus instructs his followers to turn the other cheek, love their enemies, and pray for those who persecute them (Matthew 5:38–44). In the beatitudes Jesus states, "Blessed are the peacemakers, for they shall be called sons of God" (Matthew 5:9). When a companion attempts to use violence to prevent Jesus's arrest, Jesus rebukes him and proclaims, "All who take the sword will perish by the sword" (Matthew 26:52). According to the apostle Paul, "If your enemy is hungry, feed him; if he is thirsty, give him something to drink. . . . Do not be overcome by evil, but overcome evil with good" (Romans 12:20–21).

What conclusions do Christians draw when they encounter these and related messages in the Bible? Some Christians do, in fact, respond with calls for pacifism. In the early centuries of the Church, writers such as Justin Martyr, Origin, and Martin of Tours condemned warfare and military service. After the Reformation, the denominations known as the historic peace churches, including Quakers, Mennonites, and the Church of the Brethren, enshrined pacifism as a central tenet. Within the larger Christian community, however, pacifism remains a minority position. Dating back to Augustine's principles for a just war, various theological approaches cite material from the Bible, along with reason and experience, to reject pacifism. At several places in the Old Testament, for example, God instructs the Israelites to take arms in either seizing or defending their lands, and the recorded narratives glorify the successful warriors. In the New Testament, Jesus makes "a whip of cords" to drive money changers from the temple (John 2:13–16), and he states in another passage, "Do not think that I have come to bring peace to the earth. I have not come to bring peace, but a sword" (Matthew 10:34).[31]

So which interpretation is correct? Does the Bible condone warfare under certain circumstances, or does it demand pacifism? Given the vast body of Christian writings and reflections on war and peace, any attempt to resolve the dispute here would reach well beyond the scope of this book. For present purposes we can simply note that one side of the debate resonates with most Americans, while the other, in the context of American and world history, sounds idealistic and potentially foolhardy. We should not be surprised to discover that few Christians in America derive pacifist principles from the Bible. On this and other subjects, personal experiences and cultural assumptions influence Christians' political views and the meanings they glean from their scriptures.

The potential for an issue to spark a culture war shrinks when Christians and non-Christians absorb the same values from their society. Sometimes the cultural pull is so strong that society maintains a consensus on how government should handle a certain subject. A consensus does not require complete unanimity, just a strong majority—and in politics strong majorities tend to see their desires become law. Public policy usually aligns with the consensus; if there was any deviation between the two, politicians could win favor from constituents by fixing the discrepancy. Because government policies already embody the consensus, the issue in question seldom appears on the political agenda. Lawmakers, activists, interest groups, and other participants in politics give their limited time and attention to issues marked by conflict, not consensus. Religious groups nevertheless sometimes affirm their agreement with the consensus and record their positions in resolutions, reports, pamphlets, articles, and books. But such agreements do not always persist: new ways of thinking and acting often emerge in society, and religious leaders must decide how to respond.

## Responding to Cultural Trends by Holding Firm

When a long-standing consensus begins to unravel, the matter typically rises on the political agenda as a topic for discussion and action. Similarly, evolving values, institutions, and economic realities can bring entirely new political issues to public attention. Practices formerly considered unobjectionable can later become controversial, while behaviors that previous generations scorned and outlawed (like charging interest) can become morally neutral and legally permissible. Depending on the historical circumstances, moral rules on a given subject can become either tighter or looser. During these periods of transition, several examples of which appear in later chapters, political conflicts focus on whether public policy should change and, if so, in what ways. How can a religious group respond when its current or former leaders are on record supporting a position that was once consensual but now faces opposition?

Similar situations in the secular world help explain why religious leaders often choose to hold firm, maintain their political stances, and continue expressing them to members and the larger society. Reliant on perceptions of their credibility and trustworthiness, secular individuals and organizations risk being dismissed as crass opportunists when they change their positions.[32] A politician who switches positions on a policy invites criticism from opponents, who will relish the chance to score political points. As Democratic presidential nominee John Kerry learned in the 2004 election, getting labeled a "flip-flopper"—whether accurately or not—puts any candidate or officeholder on the defensive. In unusual situations, politicians can benefit from revising their stance on an issue, but they must proceed with great care. A political organization also needs strong reasons to shift a stance, because such a move might alienate its base and suggest that it lacks any steadfast principles.[33]

If changing positions is risky for secular individuals and organizations, the dangers are even greater for religious groups. Besides potentially getting labeled unprincipled or hypocritical, thereby compromising their credibility in the political world, religious groups must worry that changing their political outlooks will undercut their fundamental religious teachings. Religions typically ground their teachings in timeless truths discovered through revelation or tradition, and they use these truths to develop orientations toward political issues. What does it mean for core doctrines when a religious group changes its stance on a political issue? If the political implications of religious truths shift from one period to another, an onlooker might conclude, then perhaps the truths were not so timeless after all. Needless to say, no religious leader wants to get boxed into that corner.

Religious leaders therefore find themselves caught between competing pressures. On the one hand, modifying political stances in an open and explicit manner poses major risks. On the other hand, failing to adapt to political circumstances carries risks, too. When norms and values in a society evolve, the rank and file of religious groups often change alongside the rest of the population. Religious groups that aspire to grow often see their distinctiveness erode over decades or centuries as they increasingly resemble the societies from which they draw their flocks. Large and expanding groups are, almost by definition, replenished by new members who carry with them the ways of thinking and acting found in society. Small sects such as the Amish can sometimes protect their autonomy by creating barriers around their way of life. If a group can minimize its contact with other people through marriage, friendship, schooling, the workplace, and the local community, it can preserve distinctive mores and political views, but few religious groups exist for long in such an insular bubble. Far more commonly, members of religious groups drink from the same cultural fountain that sustains the rest of society.[34]

The issues of war and peace mentioned earlier offer a striking example of this phenomenon. As American national identity solidified in the twentieth century, citizens sought to show their patriotism during wartime by serving in the military or supporting the war in other ways. Many Quakers, who increasingly entered the mainstream of American life, absorbed these social norms and gradually lost their distinctive character as pacifists.[35] The best-known study of this development, based on archival records of Quakers in Kansas, documents the intermediate steps.[36] Only three Kansas Quakers fought in the Civil War, compared to many others who refused to take arms. From the founding of Quakerism through the nineteenth century, individuals who participated in warfare were "read out of the meeting" — that is, banished from the equivalent of a congregation in other denominations.[37] Facing such intense pressure from their peers, Quakers refused to fight in the Civil War.

By the outbreak of World War I, pacifist beliefs among Quakers had weakened somewhat, and local meetings softened their policy of banishing members who fought in wars. Still, the pacifist legacy continued, and Kansas Quakers who faced the draft opted, by a two-to-one margin, for alternative forms of civilian service over combat duty. But when the United States entered World War II, Quakers typically bypassed the noncombat roles constitutionally available to them. During World War II, the number of Kansas Quakers who asked for civilian service totaled only one-fourth the number who chose military service. The transformation of Quaker pacifism was nearly complete by the time of the Korean War, when only a handful of Kansas Quakers requested noncombat jobs.[38]

The Quaker experience is far from unique, for the social factors that affect the general population also affect people within particular religious groups.[39] In the midst of changing beliefs and behaviors, religious leaders can find themselves saddled with a political position that no longer suits the group's constituency. In theory, religious leaders could ignore the pressure to address it, but most leaders are practical as well as spiritual. They are mindful, possibly at an unconscious level, of religious pluralism and competition among religious groups. Parishioners who hear too many unacceptable political messages in church might choose to leave their congregation or denomination. Alternatively, the leaders may not agree with their predecessors' position, which makes it easier to consider a different one. After all, the leaders live in the society too, and they see and experience similar cultural trends as the people filling pews, joining denominations, and contributing to lobbying groups. Putting all these pieces together, we see that religious leaders do not necessarily maintain a fixed viewpoint across generations.

### Responding to Cultural Trends by Separating the Private from the Public

Fortunately for religious leaders, they can sometimes choose a strategy that acknowledges cultural transformations affecting their own members without modifying any doctrines. By separating the private from the public, leaders can accommodate the new realities and practices of everyday life. Through this approach, leaders affirm an established belief, grounded in tradition or revelation, about moral behavior. Because members continue to receive the same instruction their parents and grandparents heard at similar ages, leaders cannot be accused of abandoning any core doctrines. God presumably does not change his mind about how people should behave, and groups that maintain their teachings over time gain the benefits of consistency and stability.

The creative part of the strategy comes through a deliberate attempt to deemphasize the relevant issue politically. To implement the strategy, leaders of local congregations, national denominations, and affiliated interest groups stop talking about or seeking political action on the subject in question. The leadership no longer lobbies government officials, publicizes a political position through the media, or urges group members to vote on the basis of the issue. By declining to promote government policies that write the religious stance into law, leaders avoid the political backlash from their membership and the larger society that might ensue if they took a divisive political stance. In this way they defuse an issue that otherwise might instigate a culture war.

The Catholic Church's response to birth control over the last half century illustrates this approach of separating private morality from public policy. The Church had to address the question of birth control in the 1960s when technological innovations, most importantly the development and refinement of the Pill, brought new forms of contraception into widespread use in Western countries. In the wake of the Second Vatican Council, many observers expected the Catholic Church to reverse its long-standing position and embrace artificial forms of birth control as compatible with canon law. Instead Pope Paul VI in 1968 issued his *Humanae Vitae*, which restated the traditional teaching holding that sex was permissible only within marriage and married couples must not artificially exclude the possibility of procreation. While many Protestant denominations once agreed with Catholics on the immorality of contraceptive use, they had dropped their opposition by the 1930s.[40] In the decades since the landmark encyclical of 1968, the Catholic Church has not revised its doctrine in any fundamental sense. During an interview published in 2010, Pope Benedict XVI offered a minor qualification in saying that male prostitutes could take what he called a "first step" toward moral responsibility by using condoms to prevent the spread of AIDS, but he defended the comprehensive body of Catholic teachings on sexuality as a far better solution.[41] Reinforcing the Church's established theology, Pope Benedict XVI continued to instruct parishioners to forego any artificial means of birth control.

Of course, Catholics in America and other Western countries honor their Church's teachings in the breach. During her stand-up comedy routine in the 1980s, Lizz Winstead won many laughs with her joke, "I'm Catholic. . . . My mother and I were unpacking and she found my diaphragm. I had to tell her it was a bathing cap for my cat."[42] The joke relied on the tension between young Catholic women who flouted their Church's teachings and their elders who often believed that using birth control was sinful. A few decades later, the joke would not elicit much laughter because the rebellious Catholic youth of the 1960s, 1970s, and 1980s could hardly criticize their children and grandchildren for following in their footsteps. With recent data from the Centers for Disease Control and Prevention showing that 99 percent of sexually active women in

America aged fifteen to forty-four have used birth control at least once, Catholic mothers of today would have to be willfully ignorant to think their daughters of reproductive age reject all forms of contraception.[43] Popes since Paul VI have chosen to live with the contradiction between what the Church says about birth control and the actual practices of its Western members.

Despite that well-known contradiction, the Catholic Church has handled birth control more deftly than most people assume. Over the last half century, the Church quietly shifted its political goals on birth control, even as it resisted calls to reform the teachings it conveys to the laity. From the end of the nineteenth century through much of the twentieth, state laws limited or even forbade the sale and use of contraceptives, and Catholic leaders fought to protect these laws.[44] States with the most Catholics, in fact, typically enacted the toughest policies.[45] Prompted by shifts in public attitudes and behaviors, legislatures often weakened or repealed their laws until the issue met its final resolution in a pair of Supreme Court decisions, *Griswold v. Connecticut* in 1965 and *Eisenstadt v. Baird* in 1972. These two decisions ruled that government restrictions on contraceptive use by married and unmarried couples, respectively, violated the Constitution.

How did the Catholic Church react to losing the political struggle over birth control in legislatures and eventually the courts? It conceded defeat and made no significant attempt afterward to outlaw the use of contraceptives, an approach that differed from how the Church engaged other issues. In recent decades, the US Conference of Catholic Bishops publicly advocated changing many government policies, including those relating to abortion's legality and availability, immigration reform and justice for refugees, nuclear disarmament and international conflict, and support for the poor in America and around the world.[46] On these other issues, the bishops do not hesitate to press for government policies that align with Catholic principles. No Catholic officials in America today, however, call for reinstating the birth control laws of the twentieth century that their predecessors defended.

Interestingly, attempts to enlist the government to limit or outlaw birth control, which would necessarily require marshaling legal arguments and working through the courts, could complement the Church's goal of winning a government ban on most or all abortions. Because the

Supreme Court developed the right to privacy in *Griswold v. Connecticut* and then used that right to decide *Roe v. Wade*, overturning the former ruling could help the Church undercut the latter one. While the Catholic Church has repeatedly called for overturning *Roe v. Wade* and giving states full legal authority to restrict abortion, it has stood silent for several decades on *Griswold v. Connecticut*. Instead the Church has treated birth control within America as a moral question for individuals rather than a political matter for governments to address through legal and regulatory bans.

After many decades during which the Catholic Church in America gave birth control little political attention, it resisted the mandate in the Affordable Care Act for employers' health insurance plans to cover contraceptives. The requirement exempted all churches but applied to businesses owned by ordinary Catholics and—in its original form—to Catholic schools, hospitals, and charities. Catholic bishops denounced the initiative as a gross violation of religious liberty, and the Supreme Court forced the government to grant a wider range of religious exemptions in the 2014 case of *Burwell v. Hobby Lobby*. Despite the heated controversy the episode created, it bore little resemblance to the debates of the 1900s. The Catholic Church once supported state laws criminalizing the sale and distribution of contraceptives to anyone, Catholic and non-Catholic alike. Now it merely asked that the government not require employer health insurance plans to cover contraceptives. Within the legal rules the bishops preferred, employees would still be free to use the money they earned from employers, including Catholic employers, to purchase contraceptives on their own.

The fact that Catholic leaders in America do not seek to outlaw contraceptives makes the Church's teachings easier for lay members to swallow. It is one thing for popes and bishops to declare that using birth control is immoral because, after all, ordinary Catholics can and do ignore those statements. It would be another matter altogether for the Church to advocate banning contraceptives. Without the power of law to enforce the Catholic teachings, they have little practical effect on people's behavior. In countries like America where people commonly use contraceptives, separating private morality from public policy allows the Church to uphold its traditional doctrines without threatening the laity or members of other religious groups. In some African countries with greater support for Catholic teachings, by contrast, bishops in recent decades have often sought government policies to limit the availability of contraceptives.[47]

The Catholic Church actually builds this country-by-country flexibility into its standard ways of operating. Reflecting the Church's global reach, popes and councils establish doctrines for the entire body of believers. The responsibility then falls to bishops within each country to determine how to apply the Church's doctrines to their local circumstances. Varying conditions often lead to differences between countries in the policies that bishops advocate to governments.[48] Even within a country, one area's bishops might choose different emphases than another's, and bishops can shift their political goals over time. Although popes and councils rarely modify the Church's official doctrines, bishops can accommodate their parishioners' changing values and behaviors by moving issues up or down the list of Catholic political priorities for that area. By deemphasizing an issue politically, bishops retain the Church's moral guidance for the rank and file while declining to press for government policies embodying that morality.

In 2013 Pope Francis encouraged those bishops to help him adjust the Church's political priorities. In describing the messages the Catholic hierarchy conveys to parishioners and the general public, Francis stated that "we cannot insist only on issues related to abortion, gay marriage and the use of contraceptive methods." Bishops in the West had already deemphasized contraception as a political issue a half century earlier, but he was the first pope to ask Catholic leaders to talk less about abortion and homosexuality. Reaffirming traditional doctrines on all three issues, he explicitly denied that he was offering any innovations in Catholic teachings. Instead he attempted to reform his Church's political agenda, stressing that "it is not necessary to talk about these issues all the time."[49] Protestant leaders also sometimes preserve their moral instruction while moving an issue off their list of political priorities. When Catholic or Protestant leaders shift their focus away from divisive political issues, the culture war loses some of its intensity.

### Responding to Cultural Trends by Changing Positions

Amid shifts in prevailing values, beliefs, and behaviors, religious leaders sometimes go even further by changing not only their political emphases but also their moral teachings. Such a process need not involve any one leader retracting a previous statement and thereby admitting, whether directly or indirectly, "I was wrong." As new moral and political orientations gain support from a group's membership, younger leaders may step forward to endorse them openly. When older leaders die or retire, their replacements often possess a contemporary mentality, which makes it easier to revise the group's moral and political stances. Even if leaders simply follow their own preferences rather than respond to their members, the result is a change in the group's positions. A saying among Quakers highlights the occasional need for this kind of generational replacement. Changing a custom or practice, the saying goes, sometimes requires waiting for "a few good Quaker funerals."

Generational replacement might be the underlying sociological mechanism that allows morality to evolve, but leaders still need to justify the new position to critics inside and outside the group. Believing in the wisdom and authority of their scriptures, Protestant leaders can rebut accusations of flip-flopping by citing biblical passages that imply or require the position the group now holds. If current leaders can claim that earlier generations misinterpreted the Bible, the case for switching positions becomes not just optional but mandatory. To win wide acceptance from lay members, the new interpretations must resonate with their opinions and values. Fresh ways of interpreting scripture thus work hand in hand with social and cultural trends affecting the membership.

Earlier in Western history, the laity did not exert this much influence on the formation and expression of biblical interpretations, partly because lay members did not understand what the Bible actually said. Before Martin Luther initiated a split in Christendom, secular and religious authorities persecuted anyone who attempted to give the common people access to the Bible by translating it into vernacular languages. Groups of heretics during the Middle Ages had expounded unorthodox interpretations, and leaders within the Church believed that people would be vulnerable to false teachings and the Christian community would splinter if the scriptures circulated widely. With the Bible read only by people who spoke Latin, religious elites could limit interpretations to those consistent with Church tradition.[50]

The Reformation ended the Church's tight control over the Bible. Led by Luther himself, Protestants translated the Bible into almost every

European language during the 1500s and 1600s, making it available to any literate person. Combined with the refinement and spread of the printing press, which greatly lowered the cost of books, translations gave more people the opportunity to buy and read a personal copy of the Bible.[51] Not surprisingly, people who undertook their own study often reached conclusions differing from the traditional ones, and they also disagreed with one another on both minor and major theological points. Putting the Bible into the hands of ordinary people thus ensured proliferating interpretations over the following centuries well beyond what Luther could have anticipated. By now there are, according to the best estimates, over thirty-three thousand different Protestant denominations.[52] When comparing Protestant individuals within the various denominations, the differences on points of interpretation become too large to count. Like their forerunners in earlier centuries, modern Protestants who read the Bible for themselves cannot help but use their own backgrounds, experiences, and worldviews to extract the Bible's wisdom. As a society changes, then, so do the perspectives Protestants bring to their scriptural interpretations.

Modern Catholics are not immune from these processes whereby broader trends in society affect how people interpret the Bible. Although perhaps not as commonly as Protestants, ordinary Catholics now read the Bible too, whether individually or within study groups, and their cultural environments influence the spiritual and political meanings they discern from their scriptures. On some questions Catholic lay members might not know the authoritative teachings of their Church, forcing them to rely on their own efforts to understand the Bible. When they are aware of official Catholic doctrines, they might nevertheless form their own interpretations.[53]

### *The Possibilities and Limits of Religious Leadership*

We have now seen how the evolving norms and customs of secular life encourage Christians to revise and sometimes overturn their doctrines. Several basic facts and processes lead to this result. The Constitution forbids the US government from establishing an official religion, and the country's religious diversity both within and outside Christianity forces the different groups to compete for members. Amid the resulting pluralism, religious leaders need continuing support from their constituencies to maintain their legitimacy and accomplish their aims. In their roles as clergy, denominational officers, and heads of lobbying organizations, religious leaders must be careful not to take political stands that alienate their members; otherwise, those members could take their commitments elsewhere. These constraints, in turn, make it crucial to understand how rank-and-file members develop the opinions and values that shape the positions their leaders publicly embrace.

Over the course of their lives, religious believers spend most of their time in the secular world. Unless they join a monastery, even the truly devout cannot allocate all of their waking hours to prayer, scripture reading, worship services, and other religious behaviors. Most children, for example, watch television, play games, attend public schools, participate in sports, music, or other activities, and interact with peers who are also socialized within the secular world. These childhood experiences affect how people think and act later in their lives. Sociologist Christian Smith and his research team, for example, document the extent to which young adults in America have internalized the values of consumerism, moral relativism, and unrestrained sexuality.[54] As they age, people continue to be socialized through the processes of earning a living, purchasing goods and services, and consuming news and entertainment media. During childhood and adulthood, people learn the prevailing beliefs, norms, and values of their society.

Without any conscious intention, people then bring these secular ideas into their religious communities. As the secular culture changes, people gradually embrace new moral and political positions that sometimes clash with the traditional teachings of their religion. Shifts in the secular culture, however, do not necessarily create turmoil within religious groups. The scope of the potential conflict shrinks if cultural changes simultaneously influence a group's leaders and members. When values and behaviors in society evolve, leaders and members often respond to the same forces at a given moment, leading them to move along parallel tracks in updating their political outlooks. Conflict is avoided when leaders, who live in the society and experience its trends, embrace the same innovations as their members. In these instances the leaders can work cooperatively with the rank and file to modify the group's political stands.

The leaders face a greater challenge if they adhere to older views that their members now reject. Alarmed by such a situation, the leaders might nevertheless continue to teach the religion's historical positions. The leaders thereby fight a rearguard battle — often a losing one — against the cultural changes sweeping through their constituencies. To manage the actual or potential backlash, the leaders alternatively might preserve a moral teaching but deemphasize the issue within the group's political priorities. By declining to press the government to enact the teaching into law, the leaders effectively give members a choice on whether to obey.

These processes unfold in a system where the secular culture is, in the language of social science, an "exogenous variable" — something religious leaders respond to but do not create. Can the leaders step outside this dynamic such that they proactively shape the culture rather than simply react to it? Can leaders exercise a kind of "prophetic leadership" that jumps ahead of the culture and instills new ideas about the social and political worlds?

To examine these possibilities, we will find it helpful to consider a concrete instance when leaders made such an attempt. In one noteworthy example, Catholic bishops in America tried to move their members and the country toward a new economic system after World War I. Signed by a committee of bishops within the National Catholic War Council, the "Program of Social Reconstruction" advocated federal policies to set a national minimum wage, fund vocational training, establish and protect the right to unionize, and tax incomes, inheritances, and excess profits. Rounding out their comprehensive package of policy proposals, the bishops sought to create public housing and provide social insurance to workers for sickness, disability, unemployment, and old age.[55]

Back in the nineteenth century, no influential religious leaders made these kinds of proposals. With few responsibilities for most of the 1800s, the federal government normally did not affect people's daily lives. But by 1919 the federal government had not only managed the war effort but also had undertaken initiatives to break up monopolies, regulate the railroads, form the Federal Reserve System, and protect consumers from impure food and drugs. A minority of the American population, along with certain intellectuals and parts of the labor movement, could now contemplate a more extensive government of the sort the Catholic bishops envisioned. These bishops pushed the boundaries acceptable to many of their own constituents in outlining a program that would depart from the nation's political history.

Unfortunately for the bishops, most of the country rejected their proposals and instead chose the "return to normalcy" Warren Harding offered during the 1920 presidential campaign. A decade later, however, the Great Depression opened up possibilities for departures from traditional policies. Franklin Roosevelt campaigned for president in 1932 by promising Americans "bold, persistent experimentation" and what he called a "New Deal."[56] President Roosevelt worked with Congress to enact policies similar to those the Catholic bishops had sketched more than a decade earlier. The bishops' economic program has interesting parallels on issues such as slavery and homosexuality, which I discuss in more detail in later chapters. As happened with the "Program of Social Reconstruction," some Southern religious leaders moved in front of their members in trying to outlaw slavery after the American Revolution. In seeking to legalize sodomy in the 1970s and same-sex marriage in the twenty-first century, mainline Protestant leaders similarly risked opposition from their memberships.

In all the examples above, religious leaders were slightly but not radically ahead of their members in embracing a particular cultural development. These examples thus give insights into the possibilities for prophetic leadership. If religious leaders endorse truly radical ideas to which their members object, they will jeopardize the group's vitality. If the leaders are only slightly ahead of their members, by contrast, they just might succeed in winning more adherents to their cause. Timing often determines the difference between prophetic and radical leadership. The "Program of Social Reconstruction" would have been radical if Catholic bishops had offered it during the 1800s. By 1919 its policies and principles had already gained minority support among ordinary Catholics and the general public. The bishops thus exercised prophetic rather than radical leadership.

Mainstream religious leaders rarely take genuinely radical or countercultural positions with no support among their members or the broader population. With so many secular influences on how people think and act, leaders of large, mainstream groups face an uphill battle if they want to confront single-handedly a culture that evolves largely for nonreligious reasons. Political scientists Benjamin Page and Robert Shapiro show that when public opinion changes, different subgroups in the population—including those based on religious affiliation—update their positions in the same direction and at the same time. Through exposure to shared ideas in schools, neighborhoods, the media, and other institutions, people of different religions generally move together in their beliefs and opinions.[57]

Over time this socialization can lead people to approve a practice, such as collecting interest, that their predecessors condemned. Similarly, a practice that earlier generations accepted as permissible can later face both moral opprobrium and legal restrictions. Religious leaders sometimes contribute to these developments but only as one factor among many. In driving long-term changes in the culture, material forces such as demography, technology, and the economy are more important than religious leadership. The culture also evolves through the ideas, grounded in reason, philosophy, science, and public debate, that people use to understand and explain the problems, conditions, and events in society. In a modern country such as the United States, values and behaviors change largely for nonreligious reasons. Surrounded by religious pluralism and unable to force anyone to accept their teachings and traditions, religious leaders occasionally influence but seldom control cultural developments.

### The Place of This Book

Having examined the responses religious leaders can take to cultural transformations, we are now ready to address in detail several prominent issues. My analyses, I hope, will add to the understanding of American religion that other scholars in political science, sociology, religious studies, and history have contributed. Alan Wolfe, for example, shows how religious groups in America have adapted their worship styles, theological doctrines, and moral teachings to the secular culture.[58] Robert Putnam and David Campbell, meanwhile, demonstrate that most Americans can count members of other faith traditions among their friends and family, which reduces the amount of intergroup conflict.[59] My book complements these and other studies by explaining what happens as people of different religious persuasions evolve together in their moral and political beliefs.

Given that my analyses center on English-speaking Christians in

America, I must choose one or more English translations when examining how Christians have interpreted the Bible. In an attempt to maintain an ecumenical spirit, I use a variety of translations favored by American Protestants and Catholics of different theological orientations. For my investigation of slavery in chapter 2, the King James Version—by far the most prominent Bible in the American colonies and states from the seventeenth to the nineteenth centuries—serves as the obvious choice. Elsewhere I quote from several contemporary translations including the English Standard Version (in the current chapter), the New International Version (chapter 3), the New Revised Standard Version (chapter 4), the New American Bible (chapter 5), the New King James Version (chapter 6), and the New Jerusalem Bible (chapter 7).[60] In cases where biblical inferences depend on the translation used, I quote and compare multiple translations.

# Slavery

2

People derive their morals, we are often told, from their religion. On first glance the American experience of slavery and its abolition appears to confirm that assertion. In the decades immediately preceding the Civil War, abolitionists often cited the Bible and their Christian faith to justify their opposition to slavery. There is no reason to doubt the sincerity of these Christians in thinking that their religion compelled their antislavery stances. Their testimony seems to show that religious doctrines and beliefs determine people's moral judgments, at least among the devout.

But we should hesitate before drawing conclusions too quickly. To understand the relationship between Christianity and slavery in America, we must examine the entire two and a half centuries of the "peculiar institution," not just its final decades. The earlier periods of American slavery yield important facts to consider. When the colonies began practicing slavery in the 1600s, for example, Christian resistance was nowhere to be found. If there was some inherent contradiction between Christianity and slavery, why did the conflict take so long to emerge? The earliest systems of slavery in the colonies, we will see, can be better explained by secular rather than religious influences.

Secular influences continued to shape the later development of American slavery. The first wave of emancipation occurred during the era of the American Revolution, when many colonists refined their conceptions of liberty and denounced the king as a tyrant. Northern states proceeded to abolish slavery for violating the principles of liberty for which they were fighting. Through this connection to the Revolution's animating ideas, the timing of Northern emancipation suggests that secular rather than religious forces were the primary causes. 27

Once the ideas of liberty spread widely, many Christian leaders subsequently discovered that they had a religious objection to slavery. Quakers, who condemned slavery even before the American Revolution, were now joined by many evangelicals and other Christians.

To learn how slavery relates to the themes of this book, however, we must also consider the people who defended the institution. These defenders—almost all of them Christians—pointed to biblical passages explicitly endorsing the principle that one human being could own another. Despite their confidence that they were simply following the Bible, slavery's defenders encountered serious opposition. Refusing to accept a literal reading of the Bible, abolitionists countered with creative interpretations based on other verses to justify their own positions. With both sides appealing to the Bible for support, scripture alone could not determine a person's stance.

Meanwhile, denominational leaders struggled to manage the related divisions among their members. Rather than leading the debate by taking a strong stand one way or the other, the heads of major denominations instead expressed moderate positions designed to alienate as few members as possible. These leaders acted more like politicians seeking votes than prophets trying to follow God's revealed word. From the inception of American slavery until its end, then, secular forces overshadowed religion in shaping how most people formed their moral and political commitments. To see how the parts of this story fit together, we can begin with the very founding of the colonies.

## From Unquestioned Order to Political Debate

When Queen Elizabeth I considered colonizing North America, her advisers pointed to several potential benefits for England. In the economic realm, outposts across the Atlantic Ocean could create a new market for English manufacturers, absorb some of the country's unemployed and underemployed young males, and possibly lead to finding the Northwest Passage to untold riches in the Far East. Among the religious motivations, backers thought settlements would spread Protestantism to the indigenous populations and provide an outlet for Puritans chafing under the authority of the Church of England. Perhaps most compelling of all to the Crown, the political benefits included strengthening the monarchy, establishing a base for raiding Spanish ships, and boosting England's international power and prestige.[1]

Elizabeth's advisers did not intend for English settlers to enslave anyone, whether Africans, Native Americans, or other peoples, and yet the English mindset was compatible with slavery. The initial settlers held the values of a hierarchical society with a rigid class structure, where the higher orders expected and received deference from the lower ones. Markers such as clothing, manners of speech, and even seating at church reflected a person's status, and people could be punished for violating the norms. Imbuing hierarchy with the authority of divine will, the English, like other Europeans, believed that God had cast each person into a distinct and permanent order.[2] Slavery could be justified within that mentality as just one more division allowing some people to lord over others.

Still, it was no coincidence that English colonists made slaves of Africans, not each other. When slave ships arrived at Jamestown and other colonies in the early 1600s, the settlers felt no qualms about purchasing the Africans offered for sale. The English people, along with continental Europeans, held negative stereotypes of Africans that made enslavement seem desirable, even natural. During the previous century, various forms of literature portrayed Africans as barbaric heathens, a kind of intermediate group between humans and apes. Reinforcing these negative images, the Elizabethan period linked colors and morality, with white connoting goodness, kindness, and purity, while black indicated evil, sin, and Satan. When fair-skinned Englishmen encountered people with a darker pigmentation, it was not difficult to project onto the outsiders moral qualities that made them suitable for enslavement.[3] English colonists thus accommodated slaveholding with little difficulty.

In subsequent generations, colonial leaders such as Cotton Mather explicitly defended the morality of slavery, but his predecessors apparently accepted the rightness of one person owning another without giving the matter much thought.[4] Consequently, during the first few decades of American slavery, the colonists left no record of lengthy debates, angst-filled writings on both sides of the question, or appeals to authority, reason, or tradition as the means to settle the question. Instead slavery was taken for granted, its existence so obvious that no one challenged it, and therefore no one else needed to mount a systematic defense. That silence characterized both the earliest years, when colonists treated the Africans they purchased as indentured servants, and the middle of the seventeenth century, when slavery developed into a hardened system with rigid rules and limits. The Puritans of Massachusetts, who in 1641 described the reasons for which a person could become a slave, offered the only written consideration of these larger concerns.[5]

The absence of explicit Christian advocacy either for or against slavery persisted throughout most of the seventeenth century. The two main branches of English Protestants, along with the Catholics who settled in Maryland, accepted largely by default the presence of slavery in the colonies. To the extent that they considered the question at all, different religious groups deemed slavery a natural part of God's created order. In the initial decades of North American slavery, then, religion followed the social consensus that already existed. The first inklings of the issue's future transformation appeared when Quakers, a group outside the religious and cultural mainstream, began settling in Pennsylvania in the 1680s.

## Quakers and the Beginnings of Abolitionist Stirrings

Quakers in the twenty-first century enjoy a benign if not favorable public image, rarely getting labeled as strident, fanatical, dogmatic, or extreme. Such was not the case in the seventeenth century, when the general public in England and the colonies viewed Quakers as ill-mannered and disrespectful at best, heretical and dangerous at worst. English authorities persecuted and jailed George Fox, the group's founder, and his followers for offenses such as blasphemy, disturbing the peace, holding illegal religious meetings, and refusing to swear oaths.[6] The name "Quakers," in fact, originated not from within the group but from a hostile judge whom Fox told to "tremble at the word of the Lord."[7] By standing far outside the mainstream of English society, Quakers were the kind of group that could challenge many of the prevailing norms and conventions.

Their theological commitments encouraged some Quakers to oppose one of the most important institutions in the colonies: slavery. As religious dissidents who pressed to its logical limits Martin Luther's doctrine of the priesthood of all believers, Quakers brought radical innovations to their worship services (which they called "meetings"). From their founding in the 1640s, Quakers rejected status differentials among believers and insisted that all members could speak in meetings, with decisions reached by consensus rather than any sort of hierarchical procedure. By emphasizing the direct experience of God, an "inward light" each individual must follow to attain salvation, Quakers bypassed the need for clergy, sacraments, creeds, or structured worship services. To Quakers, all believers must feel God inwardly and let his presence guide their consciences in meetings and in their daily lives.

Following the inward light meant that Quakers broke from the Protestant doctrine of *sola scriptura* ("by scripture alone"), which held that the Bible is the only authority for Christian faith and practice. Believing that the Bible reflected the hand of God but was insufficient by itself, Quakers insisted that God's will cannot be grasped through written texts. People should be led by the spirit of God rather than scripture alone, with the Bible nonetheless placing boundaries around the personal revelations someone could disclose. Seen as accurate in describing historical events and proclaiming Christian principles, the Bible thus played an important but secondary role to the spirit in leading believers to the proper faith and practice. Although this relationship to the Bible changed over time, with some Quakers coming to view it as authoritative, almost all Quakers from the seventeenth to the early nineteenth century maintained an unorthodox approach to the Bible.[8]

Their distinctive beliefs prompted some Quakers to develop a strong antipathy toward slavery. The act of owning slaves established differences in social rank between slave and master and also between different Quakers, thereby imposing the very kinds of hierarchy they opposed. Moved by their religious commitments, a group of Pennsylvania Quakers drafted in 1688 the first statement in America opposing slavery. Initially unrepresentative of their own communities, these antislavery Quakers eventually won additional adherents. As late as the 1750s, Quakers were as likely to own slaves as were members of other religious groups in Pennsylvania, but within two decades, Quakers had nearly eliminated the practice from their membership.[9] By 1775 this small religious sect had created the first antislavery organization in America, the Society for the Relief of Free Negroes Unlawfully Held in Bondage, and Quakers dominated many of the like-minded societies that formed across the country in the subsequent decades.

From 1775 through the Civil War, Quakers wielded influence in the abolitionist movement far beyond what their small numbers would predict. Despite their moral fervor and leadership by example, though, Quakers could not sustain the abolitionist cause by themselves. Prioritizing the inward light over the Bible, a choice other Protestants considered bizarre and perverse, cast doubt on everything the Quakers believed. With Protestant denominations growing throughout the nation, Americans of the nineteenth century cherished the proverbs, stories, and teachings of the Old and New Testaments.[10] To gain a hearing in a society where the Bible represented the single book many households owned, opponents of slavery needed to ground their claims in scripture.

Fortunately for the abolitionist cause, new leaders emerged who granted full authority to the Bible. Some of the most influential abolitionists of the antebellum period, such as Charles Grandison Finney and Theodore Weld, were faithful evangelicals who could cite chapter and verse to explain their positions. As the morality of slaveholding came under scrutiny, however, defenders of the practice countered with their own biblical interpretations. In the first three-quarters of the seventeenth century, when all religious groups in the colonies accepted slavery, colonists did not need to develop and publicize a biblical justification. When slavery's opponents invoked the Bible for rhetorical assistance in later centuries, the institution's defenders responded in kind. Thus ensued a back-and-forth debate within the Christian community over how to interpret the Bible's passages relating to slavery.

To unravel the threads connecting religious beliefs, public opinion, and the slave system in America, we need to understand the contours of this wide-ranging debate. Especially during the height of antebellum tensions, public argumentation on slavery often proceeded through appeals to the Bible. As it turned out, advocates on both sides found plenty of biblical material that seemed to validate their positions. With the public and religious arenas awash in contending arguments about whether the Bible endorsed slavery, Christians could not avoid exposure to one or both sets of claims.

By examining this debate closely, we will learn how difficult it was for Christians desiring to base their opinions solely on the Bible to arrive at a definitive position. Many biblical passages directly supported the institution of slavery, but abolitionists used verses and themes drawn from elsewhere in the Bible to build a contrary case. Depending on the parts of the Bible they emphasized and the methods of interpretation they employed, people could argue for either side of the question. As we will see, the Bible's malleability allowed both supporters and opponents of slavery to project into their scriptures the opinions they already held.

### The Debate over the Bible and Slavery

The Curse of Ham, perhaps more accurately called the Curse of Canaan, provided the opening salvo for religious defenders of slavery. The story appears within the larger account of Noah and his family, who follow God's commands, endure the flood, and accept God's promise to never again destroy the world through water. As explained in Genesis 9:20–27, Noah then plants a vineyard and becomes inebriated from the wine he produces.[11] Noah is naked, drunk, and asleep in his tent, where-upon his son Ham chances to see him. Ham tells his brothers, Shem and Japheth, who walk backward to cover Noah's naked body with a blan-ket. Upon waking, Noah discovers what has happened and curses Ham's son, declaring that Canaan shall henceforth become the servant of Shem and Japheth.

Sunday school classes ignore this awkward part of Noah's appear-ance in the Bible, focusing instead on the more uplifting account of his obedience to God in preparing for and then surviving the flood. The Curse of Ham nevertheless proved useful to proponents of slavery, who deemed the prophesy a clear sign of God's will. Centuries before English settlers planted their first crops in North America, various Muslim, Jew-ish, and Christian interpreters inferred that Canaan was black.[12] Colonial defenders of slavery such as Cotton Mather recycled the myth to explain why God ordained the enslavement of Africans.[13] The story had the ad-vantage of being simple and straightforward, thus making it easy to tell and retell, all the while implying that Africans — as the descendants of Canaan — deserved their fate as slaves.

Sophisticated readers of the Bible had little trouble dispatching this particular defense of slavery.[14] The Curse of Ham contained unusual moral, historical, and geographic elements that made it a thin rod on which to rest a biblical rationale for slavery. For example, the text of Genesis never explained why Canaan should be punished for Ham's actions. Even if the reader came to understand why Ham's behavior con-stituted a sin, the punishment of perpetual servitude for Canaan seemed wildly disproportionate to the offense. Most important, no one could find textual evidence, either in Genesis or elsewhere in the Bible, that Canaan or his descendants settled in Africa. To the contrary, the very next sec-tion of Genesis stated that the assorted Canaanite clans occupied an area bounded roughly by Sidon, Gaza, and Lasha, cities in modern-day Lebanon, the Palestinian territories, and Jordan, respectively. God prom-ised that same area to Abraham and later instructed the Israelites to anni-hilate the Canaanites and other peoples living there, and the Old Testa-ment contained no record of the Canaanites fleeing to Africa. Centuries of tradition, not scripture itself, allowed the casual observer to read into the Curse of Ham the crucial detail of Canaan's connection to Africa.[15]

Besides undercutting the probative value of the Curse of Ham, oppo-nents of slavery argued that that Bible demands that people eliminate, not perpetuate, the practice. Through narratives, poetry, and the teach-ings of the prophets, the Bible condemns oppression and injustice — the very basis of the slave system — and instead conveys God's mercy, benevolence, and compassion. According to this line of reasoning, God made his message clear by calling forth a leader, Moses, who would de-liver the Israelites from four hundred years of bondage in Egypt. Pha-raoh decided to free the Hebrew people after God cast a series of plagues on the Egyptians, most powerfully a mysterious illness that killed every first-born son. The fickle Pharaoh later changed his mind and pursued the Israelites to the sea, after which God again saved his people through miracles allowing their escape. In the eyes of abolitionists, the story of how God heard his people's cries for help and relieved their suffering showed his intense hatred of slavery.[16]

Proslavery advocates countered by observing that the Exodus story conveyed nothing about God's will on slavery per se and instead merely reflected his covenant with his chosen people. As evidence for this alter-native interpretation, the Israelites brought slaves of their own to the Promised Land and acquired more upon arriving. The patriarch of the Jews, Abraham, was himself a slaveholder, as was his wife, Sarah. When Sarah proved unable to conceive a child, she gave her slave girl Hagar to Abraham as another wife so that he could father the great nation that would become the Jews. God instructed Abraham to circumcise all males, both those born in his household and those "bought with thy money" (Genesis 17:13). Abraham obeyed these and other commands, proving willing even to sacrifice his own son. The apostle Paul later upheld Abraham as a model for Christian faith. To slavery's defenders, Abraham's lifelong status as a slaveholder demonstrated God's approval of the institution.[17]

Backers of slavery claimed that the Bible legitimized it in other places too. Far from forbidding the practice, the Old Testament prophets and the New Testament apostles presumed slavery's existence, regulated it through specific rules, and defined the duties of masters and slaves. The words of the apostles drew particular notice. In Ephesians 6:5, Paul gave these instructions: "Servants, be obedient to them that are your masters according to the flesh, with fear and trembling, in singleness of your heart, as unto Christ." If the act of slaveholding was a sin, Paul surely would not require slaves to consider their masters "worthy of all honour" (1 Timothy 6:1). Paul preached that people should not worry about their temporary status in this lifetime, for believers share equally in eternal salvation through their faith in Christ. The churches founded by the apostles welcomed slaveholders into their inner circle, indicating that the early Christian church saw nothing wrong with one person owning another.[18]

Opponents of slavery challenged these points at every turn. One argument held that slavery, as described in the Bible, was voluntary and hence contrasted with its later development in America. In the words of one abolitionist, people under the Mosaic code became servants "of their own accord" and were paid for their labor. People who chose to be servants, typically to relieve massive indebtedness or protect themselves or their children from poverty, voluntarily agreed to undergo circumcision, abandon idolatry, keep the Sabbath, and receive instruction in the Hebrew law. Servants possessed rights and privileges, including protection from abusive treatment, participation in all festivals and holidays, and freedom—should the servant so desire—after six years. Paul's commands, too, referred not to slavery, but to what one abolitionist called the "ordinary free relation of master and servant."[19]

Americans who consulted their Bibles to examine the specific wording of relevant passages might have found this line of reasoning compelling. In the period between the inception of American slavery in 1619 and its nationwide prohibition in 1865, scriptural interpretations relied on the King James Version (KJV), the translation of the Bible that predominated throughout the English-speaking world. Remarkably, the KJV uses the word "slave" only twice: in Jeremiah 2:14, where the prophet asks whether Israel as a collective people should be considered a slave, and in Revelation 18:13, where the narrator of a heavenly vision mentions slaves among the items that merchants buy. The forty-seven scholars who completed the KJV in 1611 chose English words such as *servant, bondman, bondservant,* and *manservant* to translate the related Greek and Hebrew terms transliterated as *doulos* and *ebed.* Those two words are the most commonly used designations in the ancient biblical manuscripts that could refer to a slave. Scholars agree that the Greek word *doulos* carries the clear meaning of "slave," making "servant" in the KJV an imprecise and thus inaccurate translation.[20] The situation is more complicated for the Hebrew Old Testament, for a writer calling someone an *ebed* could be referring to a paid laborer, an indentured servant, a forced laborer who works without pay, or a chattel slave that owners could sell in the marketplace or pass to descendants. Biblical interpreters must draw from their knowledge of ancient Jewish society, as well as the context of the relevant passage, to understand each reference to an *ebed.*[21]

Proslavery writers found textual support of that kind to show that references to "servants" in the KJV went beyond just voluntary servants and forced laborers to include chattel slaves. For example, in Deuteronomy 20:10–16 God commands the Israelites to turn captives of war into slaves. Such individuals can be said to submit themselves "voluntarily" only because the other option available to them, according to Deuteronomy, is mass slaughter. Similarly, the books of the Old Testament require fair treatment for servants, such as release during the seventh year and jubilees, but restrict these rules to fellow Hebrews. The section describing the regulations begins with the crucial qualifier "If thou buy an Hebrew servant . . ." (Exodus 21:2). Different standards apply for people outside the covenantal community, and Leviticus 25:44–46 describes how heathens and strangers can be bought as slaves, held as property, and then passed to the buyer's children:

> Both thy bondmen, and thy bondmaids, which thou shalt have, shall be of the heathen that are round about you; of them shall ye buy bond-

men and bondmaids. Moreover of the children of the strangers that do sojourn among you, of them shall ye buy, and of their families that are with you, which they begat in your land: and they shall be your possession. And ye shall take them as an inheritance for your children after you, to inherit them for a possession; they shall be your bondmen for ever: but over your brethren the children of Israel, ye shall not rule one over another with rigour.

Reflecting on this passage, one commentator remarked that "the distinction here made, between the temporary servitude of the Israelite and the perpetual bondage of the heathen race, is too plain for controversy."[22] Scholars of the twentieth and twenty-first centuries have amassed additional evidence from inscriptions, Rabbinic sources, and written law codes to demonstrate that slavery existed in Jewish communities in Palestine and the Diaspora in both Hellenistic and Roman times.[23]

Believing that their case did not hinge on it, some of the antislavery writers of the nineteenth century were willing to concede that the ancient Israelites practiced slavery.[24] Abolitionists turned instead to specific proof texts that, they explained, opposed slavery. Prominent among these was the requirement in Exodus 21:16 of capital punishment for "manstealing," an old-fashioned English name for a heinous offense: "And he that stealeth a man, and selleth him, or if he be found in his hand, he shall surely be put to death." Slaves that existed in America, these writers asserted, had either been kidnapped or were the descendants of those originally victimized. Either way, current slaveholders were morally implicated in the crime even if they were not the actual kidnappers.[25] Paul reinforced the prohibition by placing "menstealers" among the ungodly sinners whose ranks included murderers, whoremongers, liars, and perjurers.[26] By denouncing the means by which slavery originates, Paul gave the rationale through which later generations could abolish it. Abolitionists also noted that Paul told slaves to gain their freedom if possible, thereby indicating his disapproval of the institution (1 Corinthians 7:21).[27]

Those who believed that the Bible justified slavery doubted that the manstealing references implied anything consequential for the slave system in America. The Exodus verse on manstealing, for example, appears within a more general description of how the Israelites should treat each other, thus raising questions about its relevance for other peoples. To slavery's defenders, a straightforward reading of Deuteronomy 24:7 showed that its similar prohibition on manstealing applies only to fellow Israelites: "If a man be found stealing any of his brethren of the children of Israel, and maketh merchandise of him, or selleth him; then that thief shall die; and thou shalt put evil away from among you." The reference in 1 Timothy, too, failed to convince slavery's supporters. The Greek word translated in the KJV as "menstealers" refers literally to slave traders. These people sometimes violated the law and kidnapped someone in order to reduce that person to slavery, and Paul was not alone in disparaging the practice of illegal slave trading.[28] Roman law rested on clear distinctions between free persons and slaves, with most slaves during Paul's lifetime acquiring their status either because they were born into it or because they were captured during the numerous wars the Romans fought against neighboring groups. Some people also became slaves because they were abandoned as children, could not pay their debts, or committed serious crimes.[29] While manstealing was illegal in the Roman Empire, both law and culture approved these other means of becoming a slave. According to slavery's defenders in America, Paul merely confirmed and reinforced the existing morality of his society.

Given that Paul cast no aspersions on slavery in general yet declared manstealing sinful, what conclusions follow for the later enslavement of Africans? Military conflicts during the nation building in Africa from the sixteenth to the nineteenth centuries yielded a steady supply of slaves. Paralleling common practice in the Roman Empire and ancient Israel, the winners enslaved and sold people from the losing groups. These tribal wars between African kingdoms and chiefdoms yielded the majority of the slaves shipped to the Americas.[30] The international slave trade also ensnared people who were sentenced for crimes. Other African slaves, it is true, were free persons kidnapped for profit, making them the victims of manstealing. European slave dealers either conducted raids themselves or worked with African brokers who captured people from the interior, transported them to the coast, and sold them for profit. Does the fact that some Africans suffered this fate implicate the later generations of slaveholders who did not participate in the original crime? What about the majority of owners who acquired their slaves directly or indirectly not through manstealing but through means that Paul accepted? In short, did the biblical denunciations of manstealing undermine the morality of the slave system in America? Proslavery writers answered no.[31]

They found additional support in Paul's letter to Philemon, where the apostle asks his "dearly beloved" correspondent to receive back a runaway slave, Onesimus. Paul had apparently converted Onesimus to the Christian faith and now asked Philemon, a leader in the church at Colossus, to treat the returning slave kindly. Had Paul intended to pronounce as sinful the entire institution of slavery, regardless of how a person became a slave, this moment offered him a golden opportunity. Paul could have demanded that Philemon set Onesimus free, repent of his sins, and work to eliminate slavery. Instead Paul merely requested that Philemon consider Onesimus a brother in the Lord.[32]

Antislavery interpreters of the Bible rejected this evidence of Paul's beliefs. Although the Greek word that Paul uses to describe Onesimus normally refers to a slave, in this instance it could mean a debt servant. The text hints at this interpretation in Philemon 1:18, where Paul promises to repay any debt that Onesimus owes: "If he hath wronged thee, or oweth thee ought, put that on mine account."[33] Reading between the lines of the preceding verses, Paul may be asking Philemon to release Onesimus as a personal favor. Judged in its entirety, opponents of slavery argued, the short letter to Philemon cannot yield any inference that Paul approved of human bondage.[34]

These advocates also turned to the words and deeds of Jesus to make their case. While acknowledging that much of the Bible appeared to permit slavery, they criticized the other side of the debate for quoting only "isolated passages" and ignoring "the spirit of the Scriptures."[35] Abolitionists relied on Jesus's teachings to uncover that spirit. Although Jesus never spoke directly on slavery, he affirmed principles that, if applied fully and honestly, would lead to its rapid abolition. For example, he made all people equal in their personal salvation, telling his listeners to regard as brethren individuals in unpopular groups like the Samaritans. He summarized the way we should treat each other in the Golden Rule, expressed in Matthew 7:12: "Therefore all things whatsoever ye would that men should do to you, do ye even so to them: for this is the law and the prophets." Jesus stated elsewhere in the Gospel of Matthew that the law and the prophets hang on two simple commandments, that people should love God with all their hearts, and they should love their neighbors as themselves (Matthew 22:36–40). As the abolitionists explained, what could be a greater violation of the Golden Rule than enslaving another human being? Since no one would want to persist in that abject condition, how can anyone justify ruling over another person as the slave owner?[36]

These antislavery arguments influenced two people—John Brown and Harriet Beecher Stowe—who shaped the events preceding the Civil War. On trial for murder, conspiracy, and treason after his failed raid at Harper's Ferry, Brown, as if reading from the abolitionist script, declared to the court that Jesus had taught him to do unto others as he would have them do unto him.[37] Some of the characters in *Uncle Tom's Cabin* expressed similar sentiments. In a memorable scene where Senator Bird and his wife, Mary, are discussing the morality of returning a fugitive slave, she invokes the spirit of the scriptures to explain her opposition: "I can read my Bible; and there I see that I must feed the hungry, clothe the naked, and comfort the desolate; and that Bible I mean to follow."[38]

As convincing as this line of reasoning seemed to some people, it rang hollow to others. Proponents of slavery noted that Jesus claimed no originality for the Golden Rule, presenting it as a summary of "the law and the prophets" (Matthew 7:12; see also Matthew 22:40). Jesus stated elsewhere that he came to fulfill the law, not overturn it—thereby implying that the Mosaic code on slavery and other topics remained in force. In spreading Jesus's message to the Gentiles, Paul wrote in 1 Timothy 6:1, "Let as many servants as are under the yoke count their own masters worthy of all honour, that the name of God and his doctrine be not blasphemed" and then two verses later Paul stated that he is teaching "the words of our Lord Jesus Christ." Paul understood the doctrines that Jesus had taught, the reasoning went, and instructed Timothy to preach them far and wide.[39] Had Jesus intended the Golden Rule to prohibit slavery, Paul would have known this and taught it to his followers. Paul instead accepted the institution, instructing masters to treat their slaves kindly and slaves to obey and respect their masters. He told slaves to not be concerned about their status, for people should retain the same condition they held, whether slave or free, when the Lord called them.[40]

Put back on the defensive, abolitionists countered with a solution to the dilemma Paul's letters posed. According to one interpretation, Paul secretly abhorred slavery but could not express those beliefs publicly and explicitly for fear of jeopardizing the nascent Christian movement. As a nonresident missionary in the lands where he traveled, he held no authority over lawmaking. Slavery was embedded in Roman society and could not be easily removed, regardless of what Paul said on the subject. Had he demanded abolition, Roman authorities would have persecuted him as a threat to law and order. Paul and other apostles instead simply preached the gospel, thereby changing the moral foundation of society. Once they had achieved that goal, their descendants could eliminate practices such as slavery that contradicted Christian principles.[41]

Paul's letters, the abolitionists continued, made his position clear even though he did not condemn slavery outright. Besides denouncing man-stealing, he told masters to give their slaves what is "just and equal" (Colossians 4:1). A slaveholder could not follow that command while holding another person in bondage, and so the verse contained an implicit appeal for manumission.[42] As recorded in the book of Acts, Paul announced at Areopagus that God "hath made of one blood all nations of men for to dwell on all the face of the earth" (Acts 17:26). Slavery, which typically involves enslaving foreigners, would not exist if everyone accepted this appeal to "one blood."[43]

Supporters of slavery viewed these assertions as perversions of scripture. In each church he founded, Paul allowed slavery to continue—a fact, they argued, that could not be papered over by appealing to certain verses that supposedly unveiled his "true" beliefs. The writers of the New Testament used slavery as a model to explain the workings of Christian faith; had they viewed the institution as sinful, they surely would have chosen a different metaphor. Many prominent clergymen feared that the abolitionists' methods of interpretation, especially appeals to the spirit of the Bible, degenerated into a posture of dismissing scriptural authority altogether.[44] Overriding his personal desire for a gradual end to slavery, a leader of the Congregationalists in Connecticut lost patience with the abolitionists, alleging that they "torture the Scriptures into saying that which the anti-slavery theory requires them to say."[45]

Serving as the first bishop of the Episcopal Diocese in Vermont, John Henry Hopkins echoed the reasoning of his contemporary from Connecticut. Hopkins stated that God's approval or disapproval of slavery "can only be settled by the Bible. . . . From his Word there can be no appeal." "If it were a matter to be determined by my personal sympathies, tastes, or feelings," the Vermont bishop continued, "I should be as ready as any man to condemn the institution of slavery; for all my prejudices of education, habit, and social position stand entirely opposed to it. But as a Christian . . . I am compelled to submit my weak and erring intellect to the authority of the Almighty."[46] Hopkins then proceeded in the rest of his book to explain through careful and patient biblical exegesis that God's moral laws permitted slavery.

Twenty-first century readers who delve into the exhausting debate over the Bible and slavery could be forgiven for becoming confused rather than enlightened. Christians who regularly prayed, read the Bible, and tried to lead a moral life were prominent on both sides, and yet the two groups disagreed over whether God's revealed word authorized slavery. Determining the truth about the Bible and slavery without preconceived notions of the answer, using only the Old Testament, the New Testament, and the library of available pamphlets, essays, and books on the subject, is indeed a difficult challenge. Reading the assembled literature would lead many observers to feel like they are watching a never-ending tennis match. One combatant cracks a powerful serve and rushes the net, only to see the opponent pivot, swing, and return service with equal force. The server follows with a crisp volley that the opponent tracks down and turns into an offensive lob to the back corner. The other combatant retreats and hammers the shot back, and so the match continues. When one tries, to the extent possible, to assume the mentalities and mindsets prevailing in eighteenth- and nineteenth-century America, the contest seems to forever evade a decisive "match point."

In the real world, nobody enters this debate on the Bible and slavery with a truly open mind. Readers use their experiences, beliefs, and values to assess the Bible's meaning for not just theological but also political matters—a point that applies both now and in earlier periods. To decide what their scriptures say about slaveholding, Christians do not merely read the Bible—they interpret it, carrying with them predispositions about what they will find. Working within a modern value system that abhors slavery, today's Christians invariably find the biblical arguments of the abolitionists persuasive. In the context of the eighteenth and nineteenth centuries, however, many Christians read the Bible differently.

Of course, slavery was never a fixed and static institution in American society, and neither were people's normative evaluations of it. The interpretive filters people applied to the issue varied from one person to another at a given point in time and changed for the entire population over hundreds of years. Drawing from their cultural backgrounds, English colonists during the earliest decades of settlement had no reason to doubt the morality of slaveholding. Succeeding generations of Englishmen and then Americans found themselves within a different cultural milieu, and they responded accordingly when forming their judgments. The first large-scale reevaluation of slavery occurred as cries for liberty filled the air during the period of the American Revolution. That newfound prominence of concerns about liberty, in turn, developed in reaction to English policies that upended the relationship between the colonies and the Crown in the 1760s and 1770s. We will see in the next section that secular forces — not religion or the Bible — prompted Northern states to consider whether slavery should be legal.

## *Liberty, Slavery, and the American Revolution*

The English development of North America initially proceeded under a policy that historians have called "benign neglect."[47] Lacking natural resources easy to extract or Indian empires to conquer and plunder, North America offered few financial rewards for the Crown. English kings therefore felt little need to govern directly the settlements along the Atlantic Seaboard and in the Caribbean islands, instead largely leaving the colonies alone to administer their own affairs. The Crown maintained firm control over external affairs, notably by regulating trade, but the colonies developed vibrant traditions of self-government over local matters. With North America and the Caribbean islands serving as a safety valve for religious and economic discontents, the Crown thereby relieved tension at home without having to pay for governing the colonies.

The policy of benign neglect no longer sufficed once the Crown began expending large sums to defend its colonies during and after the French and Indian War. To force colonists to bear some of these costs, Parliament approved a variety of revenue-raising measures in the 1760s and 1770s. Through the Sugar, Stamp, Townsend, and Tea Acts, Parliament used excise taxes on sugar, paper products, glass, paint, and tea to raise money from the prosperous colonies. Many colonists, as every American schoolchild knows, resisted those measures using strategies such as pamphleteering, smuggling, and dumping tea into Boston Harbor. A strong contingent of colonial residents came to believe that King George III, from his ascent to the throne in 1761 to the official Declaration of Independence in 1776, had conspired to deprive them of their liberty as English subjects.

Dramatizing this infringement of their liberty, leaders of the resistance movement frequently used the words *slave* and *slavery* to describe the relationship between the colonists and the king. Never one to mince words, Pennsylvanian John Dickinson affirmed that "those who are taxed without their own consent, given by themselves, or their representatives, are slaves." Other colonists took political self-determination equally seriously, viewing its violation as tantamount to human bondage. Summarizing the wrongfulness of the mother country's actions, John Adams stated that colonists who "have no way of giving or withholding their consent to the acts of this parliament" necessarily lose their status as freemen, becoming "the most abject sort of slaves." On the eve of the American Revolution, James Cannon rallied the colonists for independence with his charge that "Liberty or slavery is now the question."[48]

These writers did not mean that the colonists had literally become slaves, reduced to mere chattel by the king. The metaphor was nevertheless powerful in extending the meaning of slavery and connecting it to its binary opposite, liberty. To actual slaves, the meaning of slavery was obviously much more tangible. During the Revolutionary War, the British promised asylum to slaves who fled their masters, and nearly one hundred thousand slaves seized the opportunity to run away and seek shelter behind British lines.[49] Others used the newfound contrast between slavery and liberty to make legal arguments for their emancipation. Immediately before and during the Revolution, slaves in New England submitted petitions to courts that used the colonists' language of self-determination to demand a similar freedom for themselves.[50]

Although most petitioners did not win immediate freedom, the contradiction between slavery and the motivating beliefs and rhetoric of the American Revolution was impossible to miss. The Whig ideology that nourished the colonists, developed most thoroughly by John Locke, emphasized the contractual basis of political authority and the consent of the governed. Slaves were obviously denied the opportunity to consent to their own status or to society's social and political arrangements. This denial undermined the persuasive force of revolutionary writings based on Enlightenment notions of universal equality and fundamental rights. When the Declaration of Independence stated that all men had the inalienable right to life, liberty, and the pursuit of happiness, the presence of slavery could not help but create dissonance for colonists who pressed the revolutionary arguments to their logical conclusion. Benjamin Rush made this case explicit: "Ye advocates for American liberty, rouse up and espouse the cause of humanity and general liberty. . . . The plant of liberty is of so tender a nature, that it cannot thrive long in the neighborhood of slavery."[51]

The sudden emergence of this antislavery sentiment during the revolutionary era deserves careful attention, for it illustrates how religious groups live within a cultural environment that shapes, often without their conscious awareness, the values, attitudes, and beliefs they apply to political issues. Except among Quakers, a group with few members in the colonies, slave-owning stood virtually unchallenged until George III ascended to the throne in 1761. Christians had immigrated to America, established farms and other businesses, and passed property to generations of descendants, all the while either participating in slavery or tacitly accepting its existence around them. If Christianity was incompatible with slavery, the conflict would have manifested itself sometime during that earlier period.

When slavery finally did encounter serious resistance, secular rather than religious ideas were the driving force. Believing that the king's actions and policies from 1761 to 1776 had usurped their rights, colonists expounded the principles of liberty and subsequently initiated a movement to curtail or eliminate slavery. The timing of these events shows that the main causes were secular, not religious. Christian beliefs and institutions enjoyed a revered place in colonial society from the very beginning, and yet major antislavery pressures did not emerge until colonists reacted to the Crown's tariff and taxation laws of the 1760s and 1770s. To justify and explain their initial resistance to those laws and later their armed rebellion that finally succeeded in 1783, colonists articulated and developed the concept of liberty — a concept that, many leaders soon realized, undercut the legitimacy of slavery.

The secular language of liberty was not just idle talk, for it brought concrete changes in the peculiar institution. The Northwest Ordinance of 1787, enacted unanimously by the Congress established under the Articles of Confederation, illustrated the power that antislavery ideas could exert in areas containing few slave owners. The Northwest Ordinance created in the Great Lakes region the nation's first organized territory, from which new states could form and then join the union. With only scattered outposts of white settlers already living in the area, Congress was not constrained by an entrenched political and economic system there. With the revolutionary rhetoric of liberty still ringing in their ears, the legislators outlawed slavery in the Northwest Territory. To protect existing slaveholders whose slaves attempted to flee from other states to the newly organized territory, however, Congress included a fugitive slave provision.[52]

The drafting of the Constitution revealed similar conflicts between the antislavery beliefs of many political leaders and the need to accommodate current slaveholders. In a crucial decision over allocating seats in the House of Representatives, the framers determined that each slave would count as three-fifths of a person for the purposes of representation. Aware of the precedent from the Northwest Ordinance, the framers also included a fugitive slave clause stipulating that all states, regardless of the legality of slavery within their own borders, must return runaway slaves. Antislavery delegates succeeded in gaining federal power to prohibit the international slave trade, but the Constitution forbade Congress from exercising that power until 1808. Hinting at some framers' embarrassment over these compromises, the word *slaves* never appeared in the document, replaced instead by euphemisms such as *other persons*.

With the Constitution having established the framework for federal policy, attention to slavery shifted back to the state level. Many people today assume that slavery was a uniquely Southern problem, which was true in the nineteenth century but not the eighteenth. When colonial minutemen fired the first shots of rebellion at Lexington, slavery existed in all thirteen of the colonies that would soon join together in a new union. Slaveholders in the North were typically artisans, tradesmen, and dock owners in the cities and occasionally prosperous farmers in the countryside. Limiting the profitability of slavery, Northern crops such as wheat were not as labor intensive as their Southern counterparts of tobacco, indigo, and rice. The growing season was also shorter in the North, making it less profitable for farmers to house and feed slaves during the winter, and families were normally large enough—supplemented if necessary by cooperative efforts and short-term hiring—to tend the fields. The particular features of climate and economy, not any principled opposition to slavery grounded in the morality or religion of earlier generations of colonists, left the North as of 1776 with few slaves as a percentage of its population.[53]

This accident of geography allowed antislavery ideas, once they emerged immediately before and during the Revolutionary War, to re-shape states' policies. Within a year after Britain conceded defeat, most Northern states had enacted gradual emancipation, typically with laws keeping current slaves in bondage while freeing their offspring when those children reached a specified age. The close connection between the war for independence, whose fighting lasted from 1775 to 1783, and the movement to abolish slavery can be seen in the dates of the emancipation laws: Vermont, 1777; Pennsylvania, 1780; Massachusetts, 1783; New Hampshire, 1783; and Connecticut, 1784. The only two Northern hold-outs were New York and New Jersey, which passed gradual emancipation in 1799 and 1804, respectively.[54] Slaveholders in the North naturally did not want to see their property reduced in value, but their voices were a minority within state legislatures. By setting a timetable for slavery to end, states prioritized liberty over the competing claims of slave owners for protecting legally acquired property. The decision of most legislatures to make emancipation gradual, and to include compensation in New Jersey, made the pill easier for slaveholders to swallow.[55]

This compromise solution proved untenable in Southern states, which relied on slave labor as the backbone of their economies. The planter class was large and powerful enough to block any form of mandatory emancipation. Still, times were changing, and many of the Virginia leaders who had defined the Revolution as a defense of liberty recognized the hypocrisy of proclaiming "all men are created equal" in a land that permitted slavery. In a key move by the South's most influential state, Virginia in 1782 overturned its law prohibiting manumission. Within a decade Maryland and Delaware had followed suit in making manumission easier.[56] By placing the emancipation decision in the hands of the individual rather than the state, these laws allowed slaveholders to satisfy a personal belief in liberty by choosing manumission.

Acting under the authority of these laws, planters set free thousands of slaves, and in written records the owners often traced their motivations to beliefs in liberty, equality, and human dignity. George Washington took the rhetoric of the Revolution to heart, disparaging slavery in his correspondence and then using his will to free his slaves after he and his wife died.[57] Thomas Jefferson may well have done likewise had he not run up a lifetime of debt, thereby forcing his estate to liquidate his slaves in order to repay his creditors. Through private manumissions, the proportion of free blacks living in the Upper South increased in the decades following the Revolution.[58] The manumissions offered hope that private action would soon prompt a public and permanent solution that would forever end slavery in the United States.

As these political events were unfolding, many evangelical churches jumped aboard the emancipationist train. Missionary work to convert slaves to Christianity, which planters initially opposed, had already led some evangelicals to question the entire slave system. Beyond the eye-opening experiences of missionary activity, evangelical doctrines, like those of Quakerism, eventually led many believers to declare slaveholding a personal sin. The notion that no one should be enslaved was a logical outgrowth of the egalitarian doctrine that all people, regardless of their station in life, could receive salvation through Christ. Compared to those of Catholics, Puritans, and mainstream Anglicans, evangelicals' beliefs more easily fostered an opposition to slavery.

Even for evangelicals, however, there was no necessary linkage from theology to positions on slavery—a point made clear by the timing of evangelical hostility to the peculiar institution. Before the outbreak of colonial resistance to English rule, the evangelical impulse usually manifested itself not in social reform but rather in revivalism, preaching the gospel, and efforts to achieve personal holiness. George Whitefield, a key instigator of the Great Awakening and the most prominent evangelical leader before the American Revolution, rebuked slave owners for their abuses yet felt no unease about slavery per se. In fact, Whitefield owned slaves who worked at his orphanage in Georgia. Living in a cultural environment that upheld the morality of slavery, evangelicals prior to the Revolution sought to reform rather than abolish the institution.[59] Evangelicals were part of the culture, not separate from it, and they could not escape its unreflective acceptance of slaveholding.

Evangelicals' quiescence did not last indefinitely, for the animating ideas of the American Revolution encouraged many of their leaders to declare slavery immoral.[60] Organizations representing Methodists and Baptists, the two most prominent evangelical denominations, jumped past their members by taking forceful stands during and after the war. Methodists, who would famously shift their practices and doctrines to mainline Protestantism in the 1900s, were the fastest-growing group of evangelicals up through the nineteenth century. John Wesley had founded Methodist societies in the eighteenth century as a reform movement within the Church of England, and for several decades he directed his organizing zeal to the British Isles. Methodist activities in the colonies occurred later, when nonordained preachers began evangelizing in New York, Virginia, Pennsylvania, and Maryland in the late 1760s. Wesley soon sent Methodist missionaries from England, most notably Francis Asbury, to the colonies.[61]

Wesley developed his well-known antislavery views during this same period. His journal entry of February 12, 1772, noted that he had just read a book "by an honest Quaker, on that execrable sum of all villainies, called the Slave Trade."[62] The next year Wesley offered his own contribution to the slavery question in a short essay, "Thoughts upon Slavery," in which he condemned slaveholding as contrary to the principles of liberty.[63] Reflecting the influence of Wesley and his disciples, a Methodist conference in America passed in 1780 a resolution requiring itinerant preachers to release any slaves they held and to encourage other Methodists to do likewise. The difficulty of enforcing the requirement notwithstanding, Methodists pushed an even stronger resolution four years later when they split from their parent body, the Church of England, and formed a separate denomination called the Methodist Episcopal Church. Upon its official founding, the Methodist Episcopal Church gave each member twelve months to "legally execute and record an instrument, whereby he emancipates and sets free every slave in his possession" on a specified schedule. Methodists who refused would be denied communion and excluded from membership until they complied with the requirements.[64]

Their Baptist contemporaries took parallel actions in condemning slavery. Analyzing the behavior of Baptists can be difficult because, unlike Methodists, they spurned hierarchical organization in favor of a congregational model where local churches were autonomous. Baptists did unite through state and later national conventions, and the statements of those larger bodies reflected the sentiments prevailing in their constituencies. Virginia contained far more Baptists than any other state in the 1780s, making the resolutions of its statewide committee particularly important for understanding the thinking of Baptist leaders. After the drive for independence brought attention to the principles of liberty, antislavery beliefs grew sufficiently strong that by 1785 Virginia's Baptist General Committee could declare hereditary slavery "contrary to the word of God." Five years later the same body demanded that Baptists "make use of every legal measure, to extirpate the horrid evil from the land."[65]

## Antislavery Activity in the Antebellum Period

Despite its initial promise, within a few decades the spirit of 1776 lost its ability to create momentum for emancipation. A slave rebellion in Richmond in 1800 terrified planters large and small, who feared not only property destruction but also the loss of their very lives. Emanating from concerns about a free black population that might foment such rebellions or harbor runaways, laws in Virginia in 1806 began requiring any manumitted slave to leave the state within one year. States in the Lower South revised their laws to force planters desiring manumission to win special permission from the legislature, a move that kept the population of free blacks to a bare minimum. South Carolina restricted the movement of all African Americans, free or slave, and banned any gatherings among members of the race after sundown. Across the South the number of private manumissions plummeted in the nineteenth century as controls over slavery tightened.[66]

Economic innovations complemented the reaction to slave rebellions in further entrenching slavery. While living on a Georgia plantation in 1793, Eli Whitney built an improved cotton gin that multiplied the yield planters could produce from each acre of cotton. The future of slavery had seemed doubtful during the long slump in tobacco prices in the late 1700s, but Whitney's invention made cotton, previously of little significance to the nation's economy, the new cash crop. Textile factories in Britain and the industrializing part of the North absorbed as much cotton as the states in the Cotton Belt could grow. Production of cotton bales increased tenfold during the 1790s and then more than doubled during the first decade of the nineteenth century. The emergence of cotton, a labor-intensive crop ideally suited to plantation agriculture, made slavery more profitable and dampened the calls for private or public emancipations.[67]

Even before these political and economic developments revived the institution of slavery, Methodist and Baptist leaders had already bowed to pressure from their members and backed down from their antislavery stances. As sometimes happens when values are in flux, the leaders had moved too far in front of their constituencies by embracing emancipation before rank-and-file members were ready. Slaveholders, an important constituency for any denomination proselytizing in the South, repudiated the Methodists' 1784 rule requiring manumission. Backed by Southern preachers, who feared that Methodists could not spread the gospel in such a contentious environment, a conference the next year suspended the rules "until the deliberations of a future Conference."[68] The Methodists' General Conference in 1796 returned to the issue, this time limiting the manumission requirements only to persons holding official positions in the church and stipulating that the rules take effect "as the laws of the States respectively and the circumstances of the case will admit." Furthermore, a slaveholder would not be accepted as a lay member until "the preacher who has the oversight of the circuit has spoken to him freely and faithfully on the subject of slavery."[69] These rules proved ineffective in practice, for "the circumstances of the case" allowed individual preachers to keep their slaves, and slaveholding laity joined Methodist churches with little remorse.[70]

Baptist leaders showed no more ability than Methodist leaders to resist pressure from their members. After the Baptist General Committee of Virginia in 1785 and 1790 issued antislavery statements, slaveholding members articulated contrary positions through local associations. Faced with the mounting opposition of crucial members of its community, the statewide body soon relented. At the 1793 meeting of Virginia's Baptist General Committee, representatives voted overwhelmingly to table any discussion of slavery, declaring it a political matter for legislatures to decide. In the following decades, certain Baptist individuals and groups objected to slavery, but no such expressions prevailed in the denomination at large.[71]

The Methodist and Baptist retreat from strong antislavery stances reflected, and likely contributed to, a dampening of reformist pressures throughout the country. After attracting attention during the period of American independence, slavery later faded from the national agenda. Politics in the early republic revolved instead around tariffs, westward expansion, internal improvements, the national bank, and the scope of federal powers. Except for banning the international slave trade in 1808, Congress rarely considered bills addressing slavery, and presidential campaigns largely ignored the issue. The Federalist and Democratic-Republican Parties did not take distinct and competing stands that would force voters to confront the issue.

During the muted political discussions over slavery in the opening decades of the nineteenth century, what was the state of public opinion? Some people considered slavery immoral but did not press for political action. As gradual emancipation thinned the already small population of slaves in the Northern states, Northerners became increasingly unlikely to encounter an actual slave. Given how important the issue would later become to American politics, modern observers might mistakenly assume that whites were consumed by disputes over the morality of slavery and its potential to split the union. On the contrary, with slavery far removed from their daily existence, white farmers, merchants, and factory workers in the North could earn a living, raise their families, and conduct their lives without giving the matter much thought. Missouri's petition to join the union as a slave state in 1819 threatened to bring the issue new prominence on the national stage, but Congress passed the Missouri Compromise the following year and defused the latent tension by simultaneously allowing Maine to enter as a free state.

But the issue never fully went away. In contrast to the white majority whose political priorities lay elsewhere, a smaller number of whites and blacks engaged the issue of slavery by drafting petitions, circulating pamphlets, and delivering speeches. This activity gained new visibility when the American Colonization Society (ACS), founded with considerable fanfare in 1816, began promoting an idea that various politicians, writers, and slave owners had advanced in the preceding decades. With the number of private manumissions having dropped precipitously, and public emancipation seeming impossible due to planters' resistance, gradually colonizing free blacks and former slaves, most likely in Africa, seemed to many the only realistic solution to ending slavery. Backed primarily by opponents of slavery, colonization also managed to win support from Northerners who were not necessarily antislavery as well as some Southern slave owners. Owing to racial prejudice and a fear of competition for jobs and land, whites in states such as Ohio, New York, and Massachusetts did not welcome the free blacks already living there and recoiled at the prospect of ex-slaves moving north and west en masse. Sending free blacks to Africa would eliminate the nation's "racial problem" once and for all. Such a strategy also appealed to some slaveholders, who worried about free blacks inciting slave rebellions, could not imagine an integrated society, and welcomed the opportunity to receive monetary compensation for their slaves.[72]

Colonization therefore steered a middle course between immediate emancipation, a political nonstarter, and perpetual slavery, an option also viewed as untenable even by many slave owners. Among the minority of Americans who gave political attention to the peculiar institution, colonization represented an attractive solution. Many of the nation's most prominent statesmen, including James Madison, James Monroe, Henry Clay, Daniel Webster, and a young Abraham Lincoln, either endorsed colonization or served as officers of the ACS during its three decades of national prominence. By allowing Christian groups to satisfy their antislavery members without alienating slave owners, colonization also bridged the religious divisions over the issue. Having avoided taking formal positions on slavery since the end of the eighteenth century, the nation's largest Protestant denominations endorsed the ACS plan, and religious weeklies conveyed to their readers the colonization message. So long as the resettled blacks were Christians committed to proselytizing for the faith, colonization carried the added benefit of spreading Christianity to Africa.[73]

Embraced at first by free blacks in Virginia, who believed they were unlikely ever to receive fair treatment in America, colonization later aroused intense opposition from the African American population in Northern cities such as Philadelphia and Boston. Resenting the assertion that they should abandon their homeland for distant shores, African Americans believed they had just as much right as anyone else to remain in America. William Lloyd Garrison, among other white abolitionists, flirted with colonization in the 1820s but later followed free blacks in rejecting it.[74] Garrison began publishing *The Liberator* in 1831, and his brand of unadulterated abolitionism soon attracted a loyal band of followers. He cofounded the American Anti-Slavery Society (AASS) in 1833, and within five years the organization had expanded to include nearly 1,350 local chapters and approximately 250,000 members.[75]

With a membership including many passionate evangelicals who linked their antislavery stances to their religious values, the AASS and its chapters initially sought to enlist organized religion in a crusade for nationwide emancipation. Abolitionists pressed churches to disavow fellowship with slave owners, a move that could be achieved if denominations expelled congregations that included them or if individual congregations denied them membership. The abolitionists also pleaded with churches to call slaveholding a sin, an important means of denying any moral legitimacy to the practice, and then embrace the goals of immediate emancipation and slaves' entry into American society as free citizens. The major denominations refused these demands, leading many abolitionists to believe that churches aided and abetted slavery. Deep disappointment in the religious response fractured the abolitionist movement into a prochurch faction, which continued to advocate reform within denominations; a Garrisonian wing focusing on moral suasion within the larger society; and an electoral branch seeing the formation of a new political party as the best strategy for vanquishing slavery.[76]

By spurning the abolitionists' appeals, denominations allied themselves with the majorities who filled the pews every Sunday. Most Americans would have preferred to avoid taking any definitive position on such a divisive issue; if national action proved necessary, they might have been persuaded to accept a moderate solution such as colonization. The white majority viewed the abolitionists as self-righteous fanatics who wanted racial equality, an unacceptable idea at the time. Fearing "amalgamation" of the races through intermarriage and other forms of social integration, angry mobs often destroyed the abolitionists' literature and printing presses, vandalized their buildings, and shut down their meetings with actual and threatened violence.[77] In a nod toward public opinion, most clergy refrained from endorsing what was perceived as the radical stance of abolitionism. Congregationalist preacher Amos Phelps nevertheless urged his fellow ministers to "lead the way" on slavery and other issues, saying that they "ought ever to be ahead of public sentiment."[78] Social theorist Harriet Martineau put the matter more negatively, saying that a cowardly desire to avoid offending their parishioners meant that clergy "do not bring what may be disturbing questions before their people."[79]

As they were resisting the demands of abolitionists, the nation's two largest denominations, the Methodists and Baptists, found themselves whipsawed from the other direction. Many Southern members insisted that their national organizations certify the morality of slavery by accepting the appointment of a slaveholding bishop (for the Methodists) and slaveholding missionaries (for the Baptists). The governing bodies refused in both cases, opting instead to revive their long-standing positions of calling the slave system evil while declining to propose emancipation, condemn slaveholding as a sin, or take actions against slave owners.[80] These moderate and measured responses avoided the perceived extremism of both abolitionists and slavery's defenders. The heightening sectional tensions meant that Southerners found even a moderate stance unacceptable, and they withdrew in 1844 and 1845 to form new Methodist and Baptist denominations taking the formal names of the Methodist Episcopal Church, South and the Southern Baptist Convention.

Close observers might have predicted that the loss of Southern congregations would allow Methodists and Baptists in the North to advocate abolition. While some individuals and state-level organizations did become more outspoken after the schisms, the national groups did not budge. Both denominations continued to rebuff calls to declare slaveholding a sin, and they also refused to punish members and congregations who engaged in the practice. Each group still included border-state congregations that contained slave owners, and denominational leaders worried that accepting the abolitionists' pleas could split their memberships and create national strife. Not until the eve of the Civil War would the Methodists' General Conference issue an advisory ruling stating that slaveholders could be denied membership in the church.[81]

That action came far too late to satisfy the abolitionists, who had long before lost faith in the leaders of various denominations. Having grown frustrated by the stalemate of the 1830s and 1840s, abolitionist members and congregations withdrew from the major denominations to form smaller sects that would reflect their views. These "comeouter" sects, as they came to be known, included the Wesleyan Methodist Connection, Free Presbyterian Church, American Baptist Free Mission Society, Frankean Lutheran Evangelical Synod, and Indiana Yearly Meeting of

Anti-Slavery Friends. In a sign that the large denominations had aligned themselves in the center of Northern opinion, the breakaway sects contained only 1–3 percent of the membership of their parent bodies.[82]

During this period of increasing pressure on churches, many of the arguments for and against slavery received their fullest expression. For example, Senator James Henry Hammond delivered his famous "mud-sill" speech, where he contended that every advanced civilization needs a subordinate class so that the enlightened few can make literary, artistic, and economic achievements. Especially relevant for this book is the connection between the Bible and slavery. Assertions that the Bible either did or did not justify slavery appeared repeatedly within sermons, pamphlets, articles, and books in the decades preceding the Civil War. Most of the interpretive claims advanced therein were not new, having been expressed in embryonic form in the competing essays of Samuel Sewall (1700) and John Saffin (1701).[83] Prominent works by the nation's leading theologians expanded the long-standing arguments and brought them additional visibility in the middle of the nineteenth century.

Torn by competing perspectives over whether the Bible allowed slavery, the nation's largest denominations remained in the middle of the road, albeit with differences reflecting their theological orientations. The national organizations of Methodists, Baptists, and New School Presbyterians took the strongest positions by exonerating individual slaveholders while criticizing the slave system.[84] The more liturgical denominations of Lutherans and Episcopalians rejected appeals from all sides and maintained strict neutrality on the intractable question. Drawing from Martin Luther's explanation of the "two kingdoms," Lutherans viewed slavery as a political rather than religious matter, and Episcopalian leaders saw the benefit of a similar posture for preserving harmony across different churches and regions.[85] Compared with the positions taken by abolitionists on the one hand and defenders of slavery on the other, the positions of major Protestant denominations, whether evangelical or liturgical, stayed within the mainstream of public opinion. The denominations thereby arrived at positions that did not reflect any coherent interpretation of the Bible but succeeded at the level of organizational maintenance, for they minimized the number of members and congregations they alienated.

Historian George Marsden, among others, recognized this important constraint on Protestant denominations, calling them "too democratic for effective social action." Marsden continued: "If the constituency is significantly divided, as is nearly bound to be the case on crucial social issues, effective denominational reform is impossible. Dissenters from the majority opinion . . . will simply leave" if the denomination takes an unwanted stand.[86] Methodists and Baptists in the South and the various comeouter sects in the North turned that possibility into a reality, and the prospect of a mass exodus narrowed the choices available to denominations. Of course, once the Civil War ended and states ratified a constitutional amendment prohibiting slavery, the issue would never again threaten denominational unity.

### Christianity, the Bible, and Slavery

In any narrative of the two and a half centuries of American slavery, religion will necessarily form a central part of the story, though in a surprising way. On a profound moral dilemma like slavery, one might expect people to derive their views from their religion. Dedicated to worshipping a timeless God through the right beliefs, practices, and rituals, churches theoretically might give firm and principled leadership to their members. While instances of such a process can be found, the more common pattern over hundreds of years shows the tail wagging the dog. The largest Christian denominations followed rather than led their members and the broader society.

When it first emerged in the colonies of the Atlantic Seaboard and the Caribbean, slavery fit easily within English worldviews. Englishmen carried cultural baggage that made slavery acceptable, with religious cleavages among Puritans, Anglicans, and Catholics irrelevant to how people approached the subject. Within a culture that assimilated slavery without significant discussion or debate, Christianity posed no barrier to the social consensus. With the exception of Quakers' objections, which began at the dawn of the 1700s, this pattern continued until the secular ideology of liberty clashed with slavery during the American Revolution. As the struggle for independence exposed the contradiction between republican ideals and the reality of slavery, Christian groups joined the growing movement for emancipation. Public opinion was a powerful force during the revolutionary era, bringing gradual emancipation in the North and laws making manumission easier in the South. Instead of creating these pressures, religious advocacy trailed behind the path secular ideas had already laid.

The counterreaction in the South during the late eighteenth century forced most churches to moderate their stances in the following decades. Methodist and Baptist leaders, who called slavery an intolerable sin during the heady years after the Revolution, backpedaled after many of their members objected. In the midst of hardening divisions during the antebellum years, people appealed to the Bible's wealth of relevant material for rhetorical support. Opponents of slavery seized on the verses involving manstealing, God's deliverance of the Jews from Egypt, and the spirit of the Bible exemplified by the Golden Rule. Defenders of slavery took their cues from Abraham, the Mosaic code, and Paul's letters to argue that God actually authorized slavery through the scriptures. Owing to different methods of interpretation, the plain words of the Bible could not be decisive in determining how people approached the issue.

Churches tried to manage an intractable situation, one that threatened to split not only the country but their own memberships. In the early 1800s, the major denominations first avoided the issue altogether and later backed colonization, thereby criticizing the slave system while refraining from labeling individual slaveholders as sinners. After the abolitionist movement gained adherents and visibility in the 1830s, denominations found themselves caught in a crossfire. Comeouter sects perceived the major denominations as too tolerant of slavery, while Methodists and Baptists in the South found them not supportive enough. The country had grown so polarized that any denominational actions would offend important parts of their constituencies. Like successful politicians who craft their positions to win the most votes, denominations took stands that kept the largest possible number of parishioners within the fold.

Now that plantation slavery is a distant memory, has public opinion lost its gravitational pull on churches? Can individual worshippers eliminate all economic, cultural, and political influences so that they can form a position on slavery that reflects only their religious commitments? On the one hand, these questions seem hypothetical because slavery has been illegal since 1865. In the United States and other Western countries, slavery still occurs through sex trafficking and other parts of the underground economy, but these practices persist despite government efforts to stamp them out. Unlike live issues such as abortion and marijuana use, for which debates revolve around whether and when certain behaviors should be legal, no one in America today lobbies the government to legalize slavery. On the other hand, we can conduct a thought experiment to demonstrate that religion, public opinion, and slavery are still tightly connected. Philosophers, along with a scattering of social scientists and historians, use thought experiments to complement other means of investigating conceptual and empirical questions.[87]

Suppose that we surveyed a random sample of Americans to learn what they thought about the morality of slavery. When asked for an evaluation, how would the Christians in the sample respond? They would surely call slavery a reprehensible evil. How about the non-Christians participating in the survey—what answers would they give? Without needing any time to ponder the question, they too would denounce slavery. In other words, people's religious beliefs do not distinguish their answers because everyone in America agrees on the moral response. As was true for hundreds of years, religious views are still in sync with public opinion; it's just that public opinion is now unified in condemning slavery.

What would happen if the survey asked Christians a follow-up question of whether God, through his revelation in the Bible, authorized the practice of slavery? In most cases the respondents would not have studied their scriptures to find guidance on that specific question. Nevertheless, many of them could reason, on the spot, that the answer must be no. Christians believe that God is omnipotent, omniscient, and benevolent, the source of all goodness in the universe. Particularly for conservative Protestants, but to some extent for all Christians, the Bible is the word of God and a blueprint for morality. Slavery is wrong; therefore—Christians reason—God could not possibly have endorsed it in the Bible. In the most remarkable aspect of this syllogism, no one actually needs to consult the Bible and consider its words before positing an answer. Because they accept their culture's starting assumption that slavery is immoral, Christians who have not grappled with the relevant passages nevertheless assume that they know the Bible's teachings.

The results of this thought experiment reflect more than just idle speculation, for we can observe similar processes among the Christians who do
engage the topic of slavery in a sustained way. Within short articles, blog
posts, snippets from sermons, and brief statements in books covering
other subjects, various Christian thinkers attempt to explain what conclusions follow from the biblical accounts of slavery.[88] These contemporary writings differ from those of the eighteenth and nineteenth centuries
in their publication frequency and average length. When slavery was legal
in America, thousands of advocates for and against the institution set pen
to paper in drafting sermons, pamphlets, essays, and full-length books.
Today the remaining pockets of slavery in the world operate in the shadows of national and international law. Now that no one in America argues
on behalf of slavery, the relatively few authors who assess the Bible's
teachings write shorter pieces than did their predecessors in the eighteenth and nineteenth centuries.

The current literature also differs in the variety of its conclusions. A
vigorous debate emerged in earlier centuries between the respectable,
God-fearing Christians who did and did not believe that the Bible endorsed slavery. Today's discourse, by contrast, is a monologue rather
than a dialogue, for Christian writers borrow interpretive methods exclusively from the abolitionists. Are these writers, unlike their predecessors,
somehow able to read the Bible objectively to learn its one true meaning?
No, of course not. As in earlier times, Christians in modern America
hold cultural predispositions; it's just that those predispositions now lie
all on one side of the debate. Regardless of their race, gender, political ideology, socioeconomic status, or religious beliefs, contemporary
Americans treat slavery as a moral outrage. Building from that shared assumption, Christians reason that God could not have condoned slavery,
and they interpret the Bible accordingly.

Beyond the unconscious processes through which cultural assumptions influence biblical interpretations, Christians hold another, more
conscious motivation for interpreting the Bible to oppose slavery. In the
twenty-first century, a group of atheist philosophers, scientists, and public intellectuals began writing powerful attacks on religion and its supposed role in creating social ills such as bigotry, war, and genocide.[89] As
the dominant religion of the West, Christianity draws considerable fire

from the new atheists. For example, Sam Harris attempts to undercut the moral foundations of Christianity by citing the Bible's support for slavery. If the Bible condones such a heinous institution, Harris reasons, it clearly cannot offer a moral code for people living in the modern world.

To sustain his case, Harris gives a straightforward, literal interpretation of the relevant passages. After dutifully quoting the verses in Leviticus allowing the permanent enslavement of heathens and foreigners, Harris notes that Jesus did not criticize slavery and Paul accepted its existence by commanding slaves to obey their masters.[90] To Harris, the conclusion is obvious: the Bible explicitly authorizes slavery. Needless to say, Harris rejects the various interpretations that have allowed the abolitionists of earlier centuries and myriad Christians today to reach different conclusions.

Aware of the claims that Harris and other atheists make, Christian writers often present their own interpretations as a direct response to help believers understand the truth of what the Bible says.[91] Despite their best efforts, these writers find themselves boxed into a rhetorical corner. Even if they could jettison their own cultural backgrounds, letting their interpretations go wherever the biblical evidence might lead, contemporary Christians would still possess a self-interested reason for finding antislavery messages in the Bible. Because public opinion in America now deems slavery repugnant, Christian writers need to interpret the Bible in a like manner to defend their religion against critics such as Sam Harris. If Harris and others could demonstrate that the Bible legitimized slaveholding, Christianity would suffer a major blow. Thus while no one in America advocates legalizing slavery, Christian perspectives on the issue continue to follow public opinion. William Faulkner was right when he gave one of his characters the lines, "The past is never dead. It isn't even past."[92] Four hundred years after merchants shipped the first Africans to North America as human cargo, public opinion still constrains Christian perspectives on slavery.

### Other Issues, Same Responses?

This history of American slavery answers some questions but raises others. Do issues besides slavery show a similar relationship between religion, politics, and morality? Is slavery unique in demonstrating that cultural developments prompt Christians to reinterpret the Bible? Have members' opinions, beliefs, and behaviors constrained the options available to Christian leaders on other issues? We can gain insights into these questions by investigating divorce, an issue that resembles slavery in the amount of attention it receives in the Bible.

# Divorce

3

You will almost never hear a political candidate utter words such as the following: "If elected, I will tighten our laws on divorce to eliminate this scourge that destroys families, harms children, and imperils our future." Many candidates pledge to enact conservative policies on other social issues, but they rarely make a similar promise on divorce. Why not?

You also won't hear of a Christian lobbying group that devotes significant attention to promoting legal restrictions on divorce. The Bible condemns divorce in no uncertain terms, which would seem to supply Christians with all the warrant they need to build a mass movement for reforming the relevant state laws. So why don't they mount a political effort to make divorce harder to obtain?

This chapter answers these questions. We will learn that, unlike today, divorce actually did create political controversy earlier in American history. In the eighteenth and nineteenth centuries, many people used the Bible to justify stricter divorce laws, and political debates often revolved around whether individual states and the nation at large were obeying God's revealed word. Over time, however, secular influences reshaped how Americans—Christian and non-Christian alike—think and act on this matter. In the world of public policy, the secular culture pushed religion aside as states increasingly granted each person the freedom to both enter and exit a marriage. Reflecting just how far the secular culture has spread, Christians in America today do not interpret the Bible's statements on divorce as binding on married couples or obligatory for deriving a person's political positions.

Because Americans' attitudes, beliefs, and behaviors cannot sustain a political struggle against divorce, the 63 subject rarely attracts sustained discussion during electoral campaigns or within state legislatures. Divorce thus forms part of what could be called the "missing" culture war. On first glance, divorce bears all the characteristics of a classic issue within the culture war: it involves personal morality, undermines traditional definitions of the family, and violates biblical teachings. It is therefore worth examining how and why we reached a point where the culture war does not include a political fight over divorce. We can begin by examining a group one would have expected to take a hard line on the matter: the Puritans.

## Divorce in the American Colonies

Chafing under the authority of the Church of England, many Puritans in the 1600s seized the opportunity to migrate to colonies in New England. Novelists, playwrights, and social critics in later centuries alternately denigrated or satirized these Puritans. Nathaniel Hawthorne portrayed them as zealots who resorted to any means to enforce the community's moral standards on wayward members.[1] H. L. Mencken went even further in defining Puritanism as "the haunting fear that someone, somewhere, may be happy," and secular writers continue to invoke the Salem witch trials as a warning against religious zealotry.[2] Even when explicit awareness of the Puritans fades from the American conscience, their legacy persists in the English language. Labeling people as "puritanical" is tantamount to calling them rigid, prudish, and narrow-minded.

In light of these common understandings, one might have expected the Puritans to enact strict laws on divorce. After all, their religious commonwealths demanded social conformity and respect for authority, using laws and customs to regulate sexual behavior and family life. Compared with today's permissive attitudes toward divorce, the Puritans do indeed appear strict. Within their own context of the seventeenth and eighteenth centuries, however, their approach seems downright loose. In fact, they contributed to historical processes that eventually culminated in high rates of divorce and public acceptance of the practice. The Puritan colonies thus offered the first, though far from the last, example of how people's theological orientations do not necessarily predict their beliefs, let alone their behaviors, regarding divorce.

Within England itself and the Southern colonies that initially relied on the Church of England as their guide for marital life, divorce was forbidden. People whose marriages failed, whether because of adultery, domestic violence, or mutual contempt, sometimes requested the Church's permission to live apart or, in extreme situations, simply abandoned their spouses. Remarriage in such cases was illegal, and those daring to attempt it could be prosecuted as bigamists. Reflecting the pervasive influence of the Church of England, divorce remained illegal in the mother country until 1857. In practice, some wealthy individuals obtained divorces before then through either private bills or complicated annulments, but the country's official policy did not permit divorce.[3]

The Puritan colonies, by contrast, deemed marriage a civil institution for political rather than religious officials to govern. Many marriages failed to achieve the Puritan ideal of companionship, love, and mutual respect, and the New England colonies struggled to address instances of marital breakdown. As the first course of action, family, friends, and ministers typically pressured the parties to resolve their differences amicably. Wives would be encouraged to reconcile with husbands who had committed infidelity, abuse, or other actions that jeopardized the couple's relationship. People who deserted their spouses, if found, would be forced to return to their domiciles, and abandoned spouses attempting to locate their partners sometimes resorted to posting announcements in newspapers. When a marriage had already crumbled beyond repair, though, couples could appeal to secular officials for a divorce.[4]

The first known divorce in the English settlements occurred in Massachusetts Bay Colony in 1639. Available records indicate that the colony subsequently granted at least thirty-one divorces up to 1692, the year that Parliament combined it with Plymouth Bay Colony into a single administrative unit. Other Puritan colonies followed similar practices. In the middle of the seventeenth century, New Haven became the first North American colony to codify through legislation the grounds for divorce, which included adultery, desertion, and impotence. Shortly after the American Revolution, Northern states passed statutes permitting divorce for reasons such as adultery, impotence, extreme cruelty, desertion of a specified number of years, and the failure of a husband to provide for his wife.[5]

Most of those allowances seemed to violate explicit biblical commands. Christians who believed that the Bible should guide political decisions could observe each reason for which people got divorced and compare it to what their scriptures permitted. Wondering how their society found itself in such a predicament, they frequently concluded that the legal code was more permissive than the Bible allowed. Benjamin Trumbull, a preacher and historian residing in Connecticut, penned a short book criticizing the prevailing approach to divorce. Trumbull declared that "divorces, as practiced in this state, are directly opposed to the authority of JESUS CHRIST." The teaching of Jesus, Trumbull continued, "demonstratively evinces the unlawfulness of divorces, in all cases whatsoever, excepting those of incontinency, when the marriage hath been legal."[6] As people used the term in the eighteenth century, *incontinency* referred to indulging improper sexual passions; in the context of marriage, those passions normally involved adultery.

Other learned clergymen, including the president of Yale College, shared Trumbull's theological position and preached it widely. Founded as an institution to train men for the ministry, Yale offered a platform from which its president, Timothy Dwight IV, condemned divorce in a series of lectures that his followers collected and published beginning in 1818. Pointing to the teachings of Jesus and the apostle Paul, Dwight declared that "divorces, for any cause except incontinence, are unlawful." Using public records available to him, Dwight calculated that "one out of every hundred married pairs" in Connecticut had divorced in a five-year period—a rate of divorce that led him to declare that "the progress of this evil is alarming."[7]

### *The New Testament and Divorce*

Did other Christians agree with Trumbull's and Dwight's interpretations of the Bible? In examining the history of Christian doctrines, I focus on the New Testament because, as we will see, Jesus overturns important parts of Moses's teachings on marriage and divorce.[8] Consider Luke 16:18, where Jesus decrees: "Anyone who divorces his wife and marries another woman commits adultery, and the man who marries a divorced woman commits adultery."[9] Note that in this quote, Jesus lists no conditions for a permissible divorce.

In the opening verses of the Gospel of Mark, chapter 10, Jesus gives a longer disquisition on the subject:

Jesus then left that place and went into the region of Judea and across the Jordan. Again crowds of people came to him, and as was his custom, he taught them. Some Pharisees came and tested him by asking, "Is it lawful for a man to divorce his wife?" "What did Moses command you?" he replied. They said, "Moses permitted a man to write a certificate of divorce and send her away." "It was because your hearts were hard that Moses wrote you this law," Jesus replied. "But at the beginning of creation God 'made them male and female.' 'For this reason a man will leave his father and mother and be united to his wife, and the two will become one flesh.' So they are no longer two, but one. Therefore what God has joined together, let man not separate." When they were in the house again, the disciples asked Jesus about this. He answered, "Anyone who divorces his wife and marries another woman commits adultery against her. And if she divorces her husband and marries another man, she commits adultery."

One can see that in Luke's and Mark's accounts, Jesus forbids divorce with remarriage. Jesus allows no exceptions, proclaiming that "what God has joined together, let man not separate." According to these passages, anyone who divorces and remarries thereby commits adultery. Given that the Ten Commandments prohibit adultery, and Jesus (Mark 7:22 and Matthew 15:19) describes adultery as one of the "evil thoughts" that come from a person's heart, this is a grave matter indeed. These words cannot help but give pause to any Christian who has ever received a divorce or even contemplated seeking one.

Determining the Bible's teaching is not so easy, though, because the Gospel of Matthew gives slightly different instructions. While Matthew 19:1–9 resembles Mark 10:1–12, in parts word for word, there is one key difference. In Mark's gospel, the Pharisees test Jesus by asking, "Is it lawful for a man to divorce his wife?" In Matthew's gospel, by contrast, the Pharisees ask, "Is it lawful for a man to divorce his wife for any and every reason?" At the end of the passage (Matthew 19:9), Jesus gives the answer: "I tell you that anyone who divorces his wife, except for sexual immorality, and marries another woman commits adultery." Matthew carves out the same exception for divorce in 5:31–32, where he records Jesus's words as, "It has been said, 'Anyone who divorces his wife must give her a certificate of divorce.' But I tell you that anyone who divorces his wife, except for sexual immorality, causes her to become an adulteress, and anyone who marries the divorced woman commits adultery."

Thus whereas in the Gospels of Mark and Luke he makes no exceptions, Jesus in the Gospel of Matthew identifies a partner's "sexual immorality" as the only acceptable reason to request a divorce. There is no obvious way to handle this discrepancy among the synoptic gospels. Like Benjamin Trumbull and Timothy Dwight, most Protestant theologians have emphasized the verses in Matthew permitting divorce in cases of marital infidelity. They typically reason that Matthew either recorded Jesus's words from a different occasion or, led by the Holy Spirit, Matthew added his own authoritative voice to resolve the matter.[10] A minority of Protestant theologians have concluded that Jesus taught the stricter rules in Mark and Luke, but either Matthew or subsequent scribes who copied his manuscript altered Jesus's original words.[11]

The apostle Paul adds other material to help Christians determine the proper stance toward divorce. In his first letter to the Corinthians, he writes:

> To the married I give this command (not I, but the Lord): A wife must not separate from her husband. But if she does, she must remain unmarried or else be reconciled to her husband. And a husband must not divorce his wife. To the rest I say this (I, not the Lord): If any brother has a wife who is not a believer and she is willing to live with him, he must not divorce her. And if a woman has a husband who is not a believer and he is willing to live with her, she must not divorce him. For the unbelieving husband has been sanctified through his wife, and the unbelieving wife has been sanctified through her believing husband. Otherwise your children would be unclean, but as it is, they are holy. But if the unbeliever leaves, let it be so. The brother or the sister is not bound in such circumstances; God has called us to live in peace. (7:10–15)

Paul begins this passage by relaying Jesus's command that wives must not separate from their husbands, and husbands must not divorce their wives. Paul then adds his own clarification that believers must not divorce their non-Christian spouses so long as those partners are willing to live with them. However, "if the unbeliever leaves"—that is, deserts the

Christian partner—then the Christian should "let him do so" and "is not bound in such circumstances."

What does Paul mean when he says that the Christian is "not bound" or, in other translations of his original Greek phrase, "not under bondage?" Once again, Christians over the centuries have been forced to make interpretations with little textual guidance. Led by John Calvin, many Protestant theologians have deduced that the "not bound" clause allows a deserted Christian partner to obtain a divorce and remarry.[12] Without this expansive reading, Christian partners would remain tied in law, if not in practice, to non-Christian spouses who abandoned them. A narrower Protestant interpretation uses the meaning and context of Paul's words to conclude that the "not bound" clause refers to separation rather than a complete divorce with the possibility of remarriage.[13] If both partners are Christians, the whole discussion is moot and Paul's exception no longer applies.

## Catholics and Protestants in the Nineteenth Century

Catholics have traditionally approached marriage and divorce differently. Following Augustine's lead, theologians of the Middle Ages regarded marriage as a sacrament, a channel through which—along with faith in Jesus—God granted the gift of salvation. Augustine emphasized Jesus's decree that man cannot break apart what God has brought together through marriage. Further limiting the possibility of divorce, Augustine echoed Paul's words in Romans 7:2-3 stating that only the death of a partner can dissolve the marital bond and thereby permit remarriage. Augustine drew on Paul's other letters to proclaim the superiority of celibacy to marriage, with matrimony a second-best alternative for those unable to control their sexual desires.[14]

Augustine's intellectual legacy was profound, but his theological pronouncements could not bind subsequent generations. During the Middle Ages marriage practices varied dramatically from place to place.[15] Over several centuries the Church solidified its doctrines and exerted control over marriages. As part of their response to the Reformation, Catholics codified their accumulated doctrines in the Council of Trent (1545-1563). To be valid, a marriage ceremony now needed to be performed by a priest and witnessed by at least two people. Most important for this chapter, the Council of Trent reinforced traditional Catholic teachings that marriage was inviolable and therefore divorce was impossible. Canon law allowed, for unusual circumstances, annulments stating that a proper marriage had never existed.[16]

The New Testament contains only a few passages about divorce, and so we have examined all of them in this chapter. As we have already seen, however, determining the authoritative reading of the Christian scriptures is much more difficult than merely quoting them. Given that the articles and books attempting this feat could fill entire bookcases, the glimpses offered here are only a small sampling of the debates.[17] Catholics and Protestants have differed, Protestants have argued among themselves, and many Catholics have tried to reform their Church's teachings. In the United States, Protestants have always outnumbered Catholics, especially during the eighteenth and nineteenth centuries, giving the various Protestant teachings a greater influence on American laws.

These Protestant teachings have clustered in four broad groups: forbidding divorce altogether, granting it only in cases of adultery, permitting it on grounds of adultery and desertion, and allowing divorce for reasons other than adultery and desertion. Benjamin Trumbull and Timothy Dwight fell into the second of these groups, and they lamented that Connecticut and other states granted divorces for causes besides adultery. To the dismay of Trumbull's and Dwight's successors, state legislatures loosened rather than tightened divorce laws in the subsequent decades. After America gained its independence from England, Southern states (with the exception of South Carolina) began allowing divorce, with the legislature itself serving as the grantor. By the middle of the nineteenth century, most of those states had moved the increasing workload of divorce cases into specially designated courts. Meanwhile, in the Northern states, the list of permissible reasons for divorce gradually expanded.[18]

For believers in lifetime marriage, the problems worsened as additional states joined the union with even more lenient laws. In 1824, shortly after passing from a territory to a state, Indiana added an omnibus clause to its laws whereby judges could grant divorces when the litigants brought "proper" grounds. Pioneered in other states, this provision allowed individuals to push beyond the legislatively specified limits and plead their specific case to a judge. In 1852 the state repealed its residency requirements, replacing them with a stipulation that one must reside in the specified county at the time of filing. With the loosest laws in the country, Indiana gained a reputation as a "divorce mill" servicing hordes of migratory couples from other states. Modern scholars doubt that many people moved to Indiana for a fast-and-easy divorce, but the state nevertheless became the first of many states to attract nationwide criticism for its laws and practices.[19]

Christian advocates continued to address the question of whether marriages could be dissolved and, if so, for what reasons. *New York Tribune* editor Horace Greeley, who had helped found the Republican Party in the 1850s, denounced Indiana as "the paradise of free-lovers" that "enables men or women to get unmarried nearly at pleasure."[20] Greeley viewed his own state's law as biblically sound in authorizing divorce solely on grounds of adultery, but his desire to base public policy on the Christian scriptures did not go unchallenged. His debating opponent Henry James Sr., a lecturer and writer whose two sons would achieve greater fame, argued that laws should reflect only secular considerations. "Jesus Christ may be an excellent practical authority for your and my private conscience," James wrote, "but in matters of legislation we are not in the habit of asking any other authority than the manifest public welfare."[21]

Notwithstanding the pleas of Henry James Sr. to separate divorce as a public issue from the dictates of private morality, opponents of easy divorce began winning modest political victories in the late nineteenth century. Several Western territories and states tightened their residency requirements to avoid either the appearance or the reality of serving as a magnet for couples seeking divorce. In 1878 Connecticut removed its omnibus clause that had given judges considerable discretion in granting divorces, and Maine followed suit in 1883. Other states, such as Vermont and Michigan, reformed their procedural requirements and limited the right to remarry.[22] The long-running campaign against lenient divorce laws appeared to be finally gaining traction.

## *Christian Resistance to Divorce Laws*

With marriages under strain due to geographic mobility, financial difficulties, and changing gender roles, several Protestant denominations joined the movement to pass tighter divorce laws. In 1880 the National Council of the Congregational Churches of the United States urged its ministers and churches "to do what lies in their power to put an end to the present widespread and corrupting practice of divorce for causes which find no sanction in the Word of God." The Presbyterian Church in the United States of America took similar measures in 1883, stating that "the action of the civil Courts, and the divorce laws in many of the States, are in direct contravention to the laws of God." [23] The Southern Baptist Convention later added its voice to the movement by calling on state legislatures "to discourage this great and growing evil by more stringent laws." [24]

Public perceptions of divorce as immoral contributed to this push for tougher laws. A judge in Colorado remarked that "divorce, in the estimation of all good people, causes ignominy and disgrace to fall . . . upon the party to be adjudged in the wrong." [25] Other people believed that scorn fell largely on the wife, regardless of whether her conduct played the greater role in breaking up the marriage. A book defending Christianity against agnostics and other skeptics mentioned the "stigma of immoral repute which attaches to the divorced woman of our day." [26] According to a writer in England, which had similar norms as America, "The social stigma incurred by the attempt to get a divorce is such that most women prefer to suffer in silence rather than bring a slur on their own and their children's name." [27]

Some women nevertheless proved willing to endure the stigma in order to end a troubled marriage, leading various Christian groups to seek legislative solutions to what an Episcopalian priest and writer called "the chief of all social abominations." [28] In 1887 Congress responded to this pressure by authorizing Commissioner of Labor Carroll D. Wright to conduct a comprehensive study of divorce in the United States. As the first systematic attempt to gather data from every state, Wright's report calculated that the number of divorces rose by 157 percent over the twenty-year period of its study, an increase far exceeding the population growth of 69 percent. [29] Wright's follow-up study in 1908 estimated that divorce ended between one in twelve and one in fourteen marriages, or about 7–8 percent, a figure that shocked and scandalized many of his contemporaries. States permitted divorce for many different causes, the report documented, and petitioners most often invoked desertion as the reason for their requests. With judges increasingly defining cruelty to include verbal as well as physical abuse, petitions also commonly cited cruelty as the grounds for a divorce. Analyzing state-by-state comparisons, Wright concluded that the stringency of the laws affected the number of divorces granted. At the same time, he also recognized larger economic and social forces as important contributors to divorce.[30]

Christian groups relied on these two Wright reports as the factual foundation for their movement to reform divorce laws. Realizing that separate efforts would be less effective than a united front, the General Convention of the Protestant Episcopal Church in 1901 passed a resolution demanding a new organization to represent denominations and to create uniform practices on divorce, both within churches and in the broader society.[31] The resulting Interchurch Conference on Marriage and Divorce met in 1903 and soon expanded to include representatives from two dozen Protestant denominations. Besides addressing the thorny pastoral issues, such as how to handle instances in which a person divorces in one denomination and then tries to remarry in another, the Interchurch Conference brought additional political pressure for stricter divorce laws.[32]

Legislators, church leaders, and other reformers moved along two parallel tracks in seeking to limit the availability of divorce. If individual states enacted varying and often lenient laws, then perhaps a representative body with delegates from different jurisdictions could recommend a single national standard for states to adopt. Pennsylvania Governor Samuel Pennypacker took the lead in organizing such a body, which became known as the National Congress on Uniform Divorce Laws. Meeting in 1906, the National Congress attracted considerable media coverage and included delegates from all but five states. These delegates asked states to approve no more, and ideally fewer, than the six permissible grounds most common in state laws: adultery, bigamy, cruelty, desertion, habitual drunkenness, and a felony conviction. The National Congress also recommended several procedural reforms along with legislation whereby states would refuse to recognize migratory divorces, which the delegates defined as divorces granted in any state other than the one where the causes of marital problems emerged. The practical obstacle to implementing these recommendations, as many observers noted at the time, was that states with lenient divorce laws were unlikely to enact reforms based simply on the advice of an interstate conference.[33]

Fortunately for the divorce reformers, they could turn to a second strategy that involved shifting authority from the state to the federal level. In congressional sessions beginning in 1884, members of the House of Representatives introduced a constitutional amendment to give Congress the power to regulate marriage and divorce. The amendment received a hearing in 1892, but a majority of the House Judiciary Committee voted against sending it to the floor for further action. For several decades members of Congress continued to introduce versions of the amendment, and the idea gained high-profile support when President Theodore Roosevelt endorsed it in 1906. Between 1911 and 1916 the legislatures of California, Illinois, New York, and Oregon all passed resolutions supporting the proposal. The constitutional amendment failed to advance in Congress, however, and achieved its last hurrah when a Senate committee held a hearing in 1924 to give its supporters and opponents a chance to voice their perspectives.[34]

## The Softening of Christian Resistance to Divorce

Divorce soon receded as a volatile political issue, but Christian groups still faced its reality as a social practice. With the underlying causes affecting Christians and non-Christians alike, the national divorce rate continued to rise in the 1920s as a tide of marital breakups moved over and around the barriers religious institutions had built.[35] Clergy could either change their rules on remarriage after divorce or else risk alienating growing numbers of their actual and prospective members. Protestant ministers recognized the quandary in which they found themselves, for couples that included a divorced partner proved ready and willing to leave one church for another that would bless their new marriage.[36] Under that kind of competitive pressure, most Protestant denominations found ways to accommodate the social trends.

Protestant denominations could, and often did, justify these accommodations by making theological claims that allowed a more flexible attitude toward divorce and remarriage. A new view held that the New Testament's passages on divorce did not give commands but rather established an ideal.[37] Evidence for this view appears in several verses within the moral code that Jesus elaborates in his Sermon on the Mount. Jesus declares, for example, that you will be subject to judgment if you get angry, that you should offer the other cheek to an attacker, and that you should gouge out your right eye if it causes you to sin. Needless to say, these rules are difficult, in some instances impossible, for anyone to follow. Since Christians believe that everyone sins, any attempt to adhere to the literal meaning of Jesus's words would lead to congregations comprised entirely of one-eyed people.

If people cannot follow each rule literally, then perhaps they should interpret the passages as creating ideals to which every person should aspire. By definition, no one can reach perfection, but believers can use the ideals to guide their actions. Within the Sermon on the Mount, for example, Jesus states that any man who divorces his wife, except for marital unfaithfulness, causes her and anyone she remarries to become adulterers. Since we cannot expect that people, under all circumstances, will refrain from anger, turn the other cheek, and gouge out their right eyes, can we realistically expect them to forego divorce when domestic violence, substance abuse, incompatible personalities, or other intractable problems have stripped all love and joy from a marriage?[38]

A related biblical interpretation offers lifetime marriage as a normative ideal, rather than a definitive command, by focusing on the definition of infidelity. By interpreting Jesus's statements expansively, Christians could permit divorce for reasons well beyond adultery. A commission of the Presbyterian Church in the United States of America took this stance in 1930 by defining infidelity broadly: "Anything that kills love and deals death to the spirit of the union is infidelity."[39] Although the commission did not specify which behaviors would constitute metaphorical infidelity equivalent to the more widely recognized sexual infidelity, this reasoning opened the gates to allowing divorce under more circumstances. A broad style of interpretation likewise might define desertion to include not only actual separation but also emotional or physical abuse. When one partner behaves in a way that undermines the trust necessary for a successful marriage, the other partner could justifiably request a divorce.[40]

Another interpretive approach considers the original Jewish context of Jesus's words when assessing their applicability to the modern world. Jewish law during biblical times held that only the husband had the legal right to obtain a divorce. In an age when Jewish men avoided marrying a divorced woman, and when women owned no property and could not easily find paid employment, divorce could doom a woman to lifelong poverty. By either prohibiting divorce altogether (as in Mark and Luke) or allowing it only for adultery (as in Matthew), Jesus's decrees therefore ensured economic security for women. Within this contextual approach to interpretation, Jesus's doctrines on divorce reinforced his larger message of protecting the poor, downtrodden, and disadvantaged groups in society.

In the modern age, however, the economic system no longer forces all women to depend on men for financial security. The principle behind Jesus's message—protecting the vulnerable—may therefore require a different application in our time. Some Christian writers have argued that broader grounds for divorce, at least in instances of genuine marital breakdown, serve Jesus's goal better than a literal reading of his words. Concerns about domestic violence point to a similar need for a more flexible means of terminating a marriage.[41]

These reinterpretations of Christian doctrines toward divorce and remarriage have not settled the matter for Protestant clergy and lay worshippers. Many theologians continue to insist that the Bible permits divorce only for the innocent partner in a case involving adultery.[42] For the purposes of this book, the key point is that envisioning inviolable marriage as an ideal rather than a biblical command grew more attractive as churches faced escalating numbers of divorces in their congregations. Although the revised biblical interpretations were not directly expressed from every pulpit, their background presence in theological debates helped justify denominational and pastoral moves to accommodate divorce. Clergy lost the desire to maintain a hardline approach to divorce once they saw how it could happen to upstanding members of their churches. Gradually, a practice formerly condemned on biblical grounds came to be accepted as a normal part of social life, even among the faithful.

The history of the Methodist Church demonstrates the intervening steps on the way to the acceptance of more liberal practices. "No divorce, except for adultery, shall be regarded by the Church as lawful," and divorced people may not marry someone else—or so the Methodists' governing body declared in 1884.[43] This statement followed traditional

Protestant understandings of permissible divorces from the Gospel of Matthew. After reaffirming the rule several times in the intervening years, Methodists in 1932 expanded the divorce and remarriage exception beyond adultery to include "other vicious conditions which through mental or physical cruelty or physical peril invalidated the marriage vow."[44] Methodists moderated their stance still further in 1964 to require merely that ministers counsel the parties and be convinced that a divorced person recognizes his or her previous failures and commits to a Christian marriage for the future.[45] Other Protestant denominations, such as the United Presbyterian Church in the United States of America, the United Lutheran Church of America, and the Protestant Episcopal Church, followed similar patterns in gradually bestowing legitimacy on remarriage for divorced persons.[46] Because Southern Baptists have long granted control over marriage to each congregation, their national association never officially adopted a permissive stance toward divorce and remarriage.[47] Given that the rise in divorce rates affected Southern Baptists just as much as other groups, however, their ministers clearly changed with the times as well.[48]

Roman Catholics have handled the matter somewhat differently. As the Protestant denominations loosened their requirements, Catholic doctrine remained fixed. The Catholic Church continues to prohibit remarriage for a divorced person whose former spouse is still alive. Prior to 1977 Catholic bishops in America threatened to excommunicate those who divorced and remarried outside the Church. While that doctrine no longer holds, the Church's canon law (updated in 1983) still officially forbids divorcées from partaking in the Eucharist, an important exclusion given that Catholics regard the Eucharist as a means through which they receive God's grace. At the same time, however, the Church has accommodated cultural realities by allowing what some consider a "backdoor" divorce and remarriage through annulments. Annulments can be granted only after a lengthy and expensive process, though, and every year several times more Catholics remarry than obtain annulments.[49] In other words, many Catholics ignore the canon law and simply divorce and remarry outside the Church.

Both Catholics and members of other groups have taken advantage of state laws passed during the second half of the twentieth century. New York, historically one of the most difficult states in which to obtain a divorce, began a new wave of reform in 1966 by expanding the permissible grounds beyond adultery to include cruelty, desertion, prison terms, and two years' separation. In 1969 California took the next step by enacting the nation's first no-fault divorce law. Legislators hoped that no-fault divorce would end the legal acrimony, and the accompanying incentive for litigants to impugn the character and behavior of their partners, by allowing either spouse to petition for divorce without citing a specific reason. The laws passed without much controversy and encountered little organized opposition. California's innovation gradually spread nationwide, and by 1985 all states had enacted some version of no-fault divorce, although some—such as New York—imposed requirements like mutual consent and a separation period before the legal proceedings could begin.[50]

Religious leaders of today often mistakenly believe that these laws created the era of marital instability.[51] According to this view, marriages used to last a lifetime. Then, under the sway of radicals who deemed marriage an oppressive and outmoded institution, state legislators decided to allow men and women to undo their vows for any reason whatsoever, thereby spreading divorce to all corners of American society. Its provocative name notwithstanding, no-fault divorce actually represented an evolutionary rather than a revolutionary change in the law. The stigma of divorce, which previously offered a powerful disincentive for marital breakup, faded during American history as more and more couples dissolved their marriages. Moving in fits and starts, colonies and later states for over three hundred years had responded to the pressures placed on marriages by loosening the laws regulating divorce.

Even if we focus solely on the twentieth century, no-fault divorce simply formalized in theory what already existed in practice for most people. After judges in most states began to interpret expansively the legal provisions for what counted as cruelty, partners who wanted a divorce could normally obtain one. Under the old fault-based system, some 90 percent of the divorce petitions nationwide went uncontested because the other partner did not mount a challenge, and even in the contested cases, people often subverted the rules through perjury or fraud.[52] With the enactment of no-fault provisions, laws caught up with social practices by minimizing the role of government and leaving the decision to divorce within the hands of each partner to a marriage. By signaling to families and churches that government would not force unwilling couples to remain together, no-fault laws formalized the tolerance of divorce that already existed. Blaming today's high rate of divorce on no-fault laws misses the extent to which they were a reflection of, not just a contributor to, American norms and practices regarding marriage.

Of course, no-fault laws could have caused the divorce rate, which had increased throughout American history, to rise still higher. By comparing rates of divorce across states and taking into account the timing of various no-fault laws, some researchers have found evidence for this effect.[53] Still, any realistic explanation of the frequency of divorce must consider not only public policy but also the reasons why people want to get divorced in the first place, and state legislators cannot make those reasons disappear. Restoring fault-based divorce would not eliminate the economic, personal, and cultural forces that push marriages to the breaking point. Under a fault-based system, many people would find legal grounds to terminate their union; others would rely on the fact that most partners would lack either the desire or the financial resources to challenge a petition for divorce.

### The Fading of Divorce as a Political Issue

Most Americans have heard someone assert that half of all marriages end in divorce. Because researchers must track marriages over a lengthy period to accurately calculate the divorce rate for couples marrying in a given year, actual estimates can vary. Using the most sophisticated calculations, many demographers doubt that the divorce rate in the United States ever quite reached 50 percent, but the figure stands as only a minor exaggeration.[54] In the twenty-first century, the divorce rate declined somewhat because the people most likely to divorce—those low in socioeconomic status—chose not to get married in the first place. Other people married at later ages and thereby increased their chances of maintaining a lifetime commitment. The best estimates project the divorce rate for couples currently marrying at about 40 percent.[55] By the standards of earlier centuries, America remains a land of rampant divorce.

The high percentage of broken marriages in America theoretically could have kept divorce in the public eye as a divisive political issue. From the late 1700s to the early 1900s, acrimonious debates about its legality filled legislative halls and galvanized Christian groups. Yet during the twentieth century, divorce ceased to motivate political action. To be sure, divorce continued to receive widespread attention within churches, families, advice columns, and self-help books, where people struggled to save troubled marriages and cope with those that fail. But after the last push for a constitutional amendment in the 1920s, divorce virtually vanished as a *political* matter. Today voters, journalists, and interest groups rarely press candidates for their stands on the issue, and once in office legislators spend their time on other matters.

Perhaps divorce fell off the political agenda in part because religious groups were poorly organized in the middle of the twentieth century. In particular, the Christian evangelicals who potentially could use the words of the Bible to demand stricter divorce laws were politically inactive. After the Scopes Monkey Trial of 1925, evangelicals retreated from politics and focused on redeeming society one soul at a time, outside the glare of public scrutiny. Their absence from politics obviously changed in the 1970s and 1980s. Since then evangelicals have built and employed the organizational capacity to articulate and defend their political views.

Rev. Jerry Falwell promoted evangelicals' political representation by cofounding the Moral Majority in 1979. With his background as a television evangelist and Baptist minister, Falwell possessed strong rhetorical and managerial skills that helped him turn the germ of an idea into a powerful national organization. On account of its size and influence, the Moral Majority assumed the mantle of leadership for the larger movement of Christian conservatives. Falwell himself penned the organization's mission statement, and the third item on his list of principles declared: "We are pro-traditional family."[56] The mission statement reminded the Moral Majority's staff, members, and supporters of its commitment to the traditional family.

Like any lobbying group, the Moral Majority had to decide how to translate the general principles in its mission statement into specific positions on political issues. Being "pro-traditional family" potentially could have led the Moral Majority to take a strong stand against the easy availability of divorce. After all, it is difficult to identify a greater threat to the traditional family than breaking it apart through divorce. During the ten years of its existence, Falwell's organization lobbied the government and sought media attention on many political issues, including abortion, pornography, gay rights, school prayer, the Equal Rights Amendment, and sex education in schools. Divorce failed to gain a place on that list, ranking so low on the group's agenda that books on the Moral Majority do not even give the issue an entry in the index.[57] In the 1980 presidential election, the Moral Majority used voter registration drives to promote the candidacy of Ronald Reagan, himself a divorced-and-remarried man who had signed the nation's first no-fault divorce law as governor of California in 1969. One could hardly imagine a stronger signal that the issue of divorce would not receive the Moral Majority's attention.

After the Moral Majority disbanded, leadership of the Christian right passed to other organizations. Building on the energy and donor list of Rev. Pat Robertson's presidential campaign of 1988, the Christian Coalition burst into the spotlight the next year and remained powerful through most of the 1990s. One of the group's early fundraising letters explained that it sought to outlaw abortion, restore school prayer, protect religious displays on public property, and resist messages and programs in the entertainment media that "defame our Lord."[58] With the addition of other issues like homosexuality, school choice, religious freedom, Darwinism and evolution, American support for Israel, and funding for the National Endowment for the Arts, the Christian Coalition pursued the agenda for which Christian conservatives are known.[59] The subject of divorce was noticeably absent from the group's priorities.

The Christian Coalition's telegenic and articulate executive director, Ralph Reed, helped attract funding and visibility to the group. At the height of his influence, Reed penned *Active Faith*, a best-selling book that discussed historical issues like temperance and slavery as well as the contemporary controversies bringing Christians into politics. Although he cited high rates of divorce as a sign of moral decay, Reed did not use the book to advocate legislation to tighten divorce laws.[60] Interestingly, the Christian Coalition finally elevated divorced on its political agenda in 1997 when it announced the Samaritan Project, an effort to address the concerns of blacks and Hispanics in the nation's urban centers.[61] The accompanying legislative proposals included a modest requirement that married couples with young children pass through a waiting period before obtaining a divorce. The Christian Coalition curtailed funding for the Samaritan Project later in 1997 amid the group's financial troubles, and the initiative did not change public perceptions of the Christian

Coalition's priorities and emphases.[62] Considering the entire record, from its founding to its virtual collapse in the late 1990s, the Christian Coalition devoted little attention to promoting stricter regulations on divorce. The group spent the vast majority of its time on the standard issues that galvanize the Christian right.

In recent years the Family Research Council (FRC) attained the visibility that groups like the Moral Majority and the Christian Coalition previously reached. Founded by Dr. James Dobson in 1983, the FRC existed as an initiative within Dobson's Focus on the Family before splitting off as a separate group in 1992. For many years its three-sentence mission statement announced: "The Family Research Council (FRC) champions marriage and family as the foundation of civilization, the seedbed of virtue, and the wellspring of society. FRC shapes public debate and formulates public policy that values human life and upholds the institutions of marriage and the family. Believing that God is the author of life, liberty, and the family, FRC promotes the Judeo-Christian worldview as the basis for a just, free, and stable society." Among the five "Core Principles" directing the FRC's operations, the third declared: "Government has a duty to promote and protect marriage and family in law and public policy."[63]

Some observers might expect that government's "duty to promote and protect marriage and family" would include restricting the availability of divorce. Judging from the materials it produces and makes available to members, supporters, journalists, elected officials, and civil servants, however, the FRC appears to hold a somewhat different conception of government's duty in regard to marriage and the family. Some critics have chastised the FRC and related groups for concentrating their marriage agenda on preventing same-sex marriage rather than limiting heterosexual divorce.[64] In an age where nearly half of all couples later break their wedding vows, the criticism goes, how does letting gays and lesbians into the club destroy the institution of marriage? For a group that defines its existence around marriage and the family, wouldn't it be better to address the massive numbers of heterosexuals ending their marriages rather than the same-sex couples wanting to join the institution?

From August 30, 2004, until nearly a decade later, the FRC used its website to present its standard response to this question. The text of the answer is worth repeating in its entirety:

Divorce causes tremendous devastation to families, children, and society. The issue of divorce reform has been an issue that FRC has dealt
with since we began in 1983. We have consistently called for the repeal
of no-fault divorce laws in all 50 states. We continue to promote the
sanctity of marriage, and we will not relent in our insistence to reform
divorce laws. Yet, the issue of divorce reform at the political level has
struggled to receive much attention.

Currently, FRC is faced with protecting marriage from being "redefined" so as not to include more than "just" one man and one
woman, and this is what we must deal with at the present time. With
our limited resources and staff number and considering the fact that
our nation is seriously threatened by the legalization of same-sex
"marriage," this is our current priority when it comes to public policy
about marriage.

We do, however, have a booklet that may be of interest to you, called
"Deterring Divorce." (The link is provided below.)

There are also organizations outside the public policy arena that
focus on strengthening marriages, such as Focus on the Family (www
.family.org), Marriage Savers (http://www.marriagesavers.org/), and
The Coalition for Marriage, Family, and Couples Education, L.L.C.
(www.smartmarriages.com).[65]

The text above contains four main points: first, the FRC supports divorce reform; second, the issue has failed to command national attention;
third, the FRC's limited resources and staff dictate that divorce must take
a lower priority than the fight against same-sex marriage; and fourth,
people interested in strengthening marriages can gain information and
join initiatives from outside the public policy arena. Each of these points
is worth examining in detail, and I will return to the second and fourth
later in the chapter. For now, I focus on the first and third points in which
the FRC explains that it supports divorce reform yet judges it less important than opposing same-sex marriage. Every organization involved in
politics must assess its resources and identify priorities, which necessarily leads to concentrating on certain issues. Setting priorities, however, does not force a political group to focus on one matter to the virtual
exclusion of another.

The FRC sends e-mail alerts to its members and supporters to inform, persuade, and reinforce their attitudes and beliefs about matters of interest to the group. Conveniently, I subscribed to the group's e-mail list in 2006–2007 and archived the messages. The FRC in those years dispatched hundreds of e-mails, most of which contained three paragraph-length items.[66] Surprisingly for an organization that structured its activities around marriage and the family, only 8 of the 1,366 items centered on divorce.[67] In its e-mails to members and supporters, the FRC rarely discussed divorce, and its limited mentions merely referenced the subject without pressing for new state laws to make divorce harder to obtain. Despite saying that "we will not relent in our insistence to reform divorce laws," the organization did not back its words with a sustained commitment of time or resources.

Perhaps the FRC's e-mails do not accurately reflect its priorities, meaning that analyzing a different facet of the group's activities would yield a different answer. Accordingly, I examined the messages the FRC expresses when it broadcasts its views through the mass media. As part of a larger strategy to influence both the mass public and political leaders, FRC staff write op-eds and seek to publish them in leading news outlets. During 2006 and 2007, the staff published op-eds on topics within the organization's mission, including abstinence programs in schools, gay rights and hate crimes, abortion laws in the states, and judicial activism regarding online pornography. Yet FRC staff also published op-eds that criticized wasteful government spending, warned against universal health care, and challenged the science behind global warming.[68] Certainly no one could deny that American citizens and political leaders should debate the subjects of government spending, health care, and global warming, but those issues fall outside the core mission of an organization whose self-definition centers on championing "marriage and family as the foundation of civilization, the seedbed of virtue, and the wellspring of society."

The FRC has stated that constraints of budget, time, and staff prevent it from engaging questions surrounding same-sex marriage and heterosexual divorce at the same time, and yet it allocated its scarce resources to addressing many other issues. Even if one could justify on practical or biblical grounds prioritizing gay marriage over divorce, such a view could hardly justify pushing divorce to the bottom of the pecking order, below issues with only a tenuous connection to marriage and the family. Of course, a comprehensive search of every FRC communication with members, the media, and government officials from 1983 to the present would probably uncover sporadic advocacy for changing public policy regarding divorce. Such a finding would not undermine the conclusions drawn here—namely, that the group does not prioritize divorce. Indeed, in the statement from its website quoted above, the FRC conceded that it allocates little political attention to the subject.

### The Modern American View of Divorce

Limited resources and staff time, then, cannot explain why the Family Research Council—along with its predecessors, the Moral Majority and the Christian Coalition—has devoted so little attention to reforming divorce laws. This omission seems difficult to understand for an organization dominated by evangelicals who try to derive their political commitments from the Bible. In earlier times conservative Protestants lobbied forcefully for laws that conformed to a literal reading of the Bible's prescriptions on divorce and remarriage. Within the context of modern American attitudes and practices, however, the FRC's actions make sense.

For most of Western history, marriage was not considered a personal matter best left to the couple's discretion. Instead marriage reflected and cemented social, economic, and political relationships between families. In an important sense marriage occurred between families rather than individuals, especially when dowries were given. With parents and family members engaged in finding suitable partners for children of marriageable age, social stability could be preserved and property could be passed to descendants in an orderly manner. Beginning with the Enlightenment, influential writers and thinkers articulated a new vision of marriage whereby men and women, guided by mutual affection and companionship, made their matrimonial vows of their own accord. With its emphasis on reason, individual rights, and the pursuit of happiness, the Enlightenment placed love at the center of the marriage ideal.[69]

This modern view of marriage brought the potential for greater happiness when, as the cliché goes, the partners find their soul mates. The earlier marriages driven mainly by economic needs kept both parties' expectations low from the outset. Although it could develop after the couple exchanged vows, love was not necessary for the marriage to survive. Marriages endured so long as the dependence of men and women on each other, combined with the ties between extended families, remained intact. Once people were granted free choice for entering marriage, however, it became hard to deny them any possibility of exiting it. Love, being fickle, proved a volatile basis on which to rest matrimonial vows.[70]

The Enlightenment ideal of marriage, now hundreds of years old, gradually spread from the pens of intellectuals such as John Stuart Mill and Mary Wollstonecraft into the minds of ordinary men and women. The biggest change in twentieth-century America, then, was not cultural norms about marriage but rather people's capacity to act upon them. Most important, the entry of more women into the paid labor force reduced — and in many cases ended — their need for men's wages in order to survive. Economic freedom allowed them to dissolve marriages marred by problems their grandmothers would have silently endured. New labor-saving devices and the ability to buy services on the open market made divorce easier on both the women and the men who now headed households without the assistance of a partner.[71]

The spread of divorce to virtually all segments of the population lessened the social stigma attached to it.[72] Over time people found it harder to maintain scorn for a practice to which they, or those around them, resorted when necessary. Many Americans are either divorced or were raised by divorced parents. People fortunate enough to have avoided these personal encounters with divorce nevertheless observe it among their friends, acquaintances, and family members. As with many other issues, the commonality of divorce makes it feel normal and acceptable.[73]

### Religious Orientation and Divorce Rates

Have people's religious commitments given them the means to resist the spread of divorce? To find out, I compiled evidence from a forty-year period. Using the complete set of data from the General Social Survey (GSS) from 1973 to 2012, I calculated the rates of divorce for different religious groups.[74] One clear advantage to pooling the different GSS surveys is that the data thereby yield sufficiently large sample sizes for

TABLE 3.1.

*Divorce rates for major religious traditions in America, 1973–2012*

| Group | Divorce rate (%) |
|-------|------------------|
| Evangelical Protestants | 38 |
| Mainline Protestants | 31 |
| Black Protestants | 48 |
| Catholics | 29 |
| Jews | 26 |
| Other religions | 38 |
| Nonaffiliated / no religion | 48 |
| National average | 36 |

*Source:* General Social Survey. The divorce rate for each group is calculated by dividing the number of people who have ever been divorced or legally separated by the number of people who have ever been married.

seven different religious traditions.[75] I calculated the estimates by dividing, for each group, the number of people who have ever been divorced by the number of people who have ever been married. Overall for the nation as a whole, the GSS data indicate a divorce rate of 36 percent. This figure falls below the frequently cited national averages because some of the people in the GSS data who were married at the time they were surveyed later got divorced. In other words, the lifetime incidence of divorce for people who participated in one of the surveys will necessarily be higher than 36 percent.

Table 3.1 shows that Jews have the lowest divorce rate (26 percent) among the seven major religious traditions. Catholics are the second least likely group to divorce, with 29 percent of them ending their marriages. Black Protestants and people unaffiliated with any organized religion tie for the highest divorce rate at 48 percent. One might expect evangelical Protestants, who hold theologically conservative views on a variety of religious matters, to divorce at lower rates than other Americans. But their divorce rate (38 percent) is slightly higher than the national average (36 percent).

The prevalence of divorce among the largest religious groups makes it unlikely that the issue will create significant political controversy in the near future. For the last several decades Americans have clashed over issues such as abortion, homosexuality, stem-cell research, teaching evolution in schools, and the role of religion in public life. Despite the conflict it inspired earlier in American history, divorce differs from these issues in that it has attracted little political attention. Even among people who hold conservative views on biblical authority, divorce has come to be seen as a matter of private morality, not a political question to be addressed in the public sphere.

Nothing prevents the Family Research Council and other groups that represent evangelicals from actively working to limit the availability of divorce, meaning that the FRC would move beyond just *saying* that they endorse divorce reform and would begin taking concrete action. Divorce reform need not occupy top billing on the FRC's agenda to qualify as a priority, but it would need to receive sustained attention in its communications with members, outreach through the media, and lobbying of government officials. With evangelicals' divorce rate on par with the rest of the country's, though, the FRC is unlikely to undertake such an effort anytime in the near future. Needless to say, it is not a winning political message to invite your divorced constituents to "join us in lobbying the government to prevent others from following you down the path of immorality." With no interest groups pushing for major policy changes, it is difficult to imagine how divorce could spark a culture war.

At the same time, divorce's absence from the culture war does not mean that Christian conservatives express indifference toward it. To the contrary, many of their most respected leaders take the subject seriously and blame many social problems partly on marital instability.[76] With the exception of scattered lobbying efforts by the Moral Majority, the Christian Coalition, and the Family Research Council, however, leading organizations representing Christian conservatives have treated divorce as a private matter that individuals, families, and churches must handle, rather than a political question requiring governmental action.

This distinction between private and political responses to divorce recurs in the history of Promise Keepers, a Christian men's organization that flourished in the 1990s and continues to exist today on a much smaller scale.[77] Best known for the stadium-packing rallies of its heyday, the group offers a means for men to affirm their commitments to God, each other, and their churches, children, and wives. Promise Keepers defines itself as "a Christ-centered organization dedicated to introducing men to Jesus Christ as their Savior and Lord, and then helping them to grow as Christians." The mission of Promise Keepers is, accordingly, broader than marriage and family but nevertheless includes those matters within a comprehensive set of principles intended to guide the thoughts and actions of Christian men. As stated in the fourth among the organization's seven promises, "A Promise Keeper is committed to building strong marriages and families through love, protection and biblical values."[78]

The group's messages and events found a receptive audience in the 1990s, as hundreds of thousands of men attended rallies across the country. A sizeable population of men proved willing to pledge support for long-lasting marriages as a crucial part of their Christian identity. But the group framed the matter as a personal decision, not a political question requiring legislative action. Even during its peak years, then, Promise Keepers represented a private rather than a political response to divorce. Instead of attempting to mobilize men to lobby for laws making divorce more difficult to obtain, the group took a voluntary and individualistic approach centering on the personal commitments of each Christian man.

Catholic leaders have resembled their Protestant counterparts, along with groups such as the Family Research Council and Promise Keepers, in seeking private rather than political solutions to divorce. In recent years the US Conference of Catholic Bishops issued statements, documents, and pastoral letters affirming the Church's historical support for lifetime marriage and opposition to divorce.[79] Priests teach these doctrines to parishioners and offer counseling services and other resources to protect and strengthen marriages. At the same time, Catholic bishops have declined to turn divorce into a political issue at the national or state levels. In 2011 the American bishops established political priorities in several broad areas including "Pro-Life Activities," "Migration and Refugee Services," "International Justice and Peace, "Domestic Justice and Human Development," and—most important for present purposes—"Marriage and Family Life."[80] This last item gave the bishops a platform on which they could have pressed the government to curtail access to divorce. Instead the bishops in this section focused exclusively on opposing civil unions and same-sex marriage.

## Public Opinion on Divorce

Public opinion polls offer evidence on the kinds of governmental actions that Americans will, and will not, accept to keep marriages intact. Given the fact that neither Protestant nor Catholic leaders have attempted to organize a political movement around divorce, an overtly religious appeal seems unlikely to convince most Americans to tighten the laws on divorce. As additional support for this point, consider Americans' responses to the following survey question posed in 2005. When asked whether they agreed or disagreed with the statement "Divorce is a sin," respondents disagreed by a margin of 69 percent to 22 percent.[81] Other surveys that used slightly different means of asking the same question—such as whether divorce is "morally acceptable or morally wrong"—yielded similar results.[82]

If Americans cannot be persuaded on religious grounds to limit the availability of divorce, perhaps they can be reached through other arguments. In the last three decades, several social scientists have conducted research suggesting that divorce harms children by making them more likely to experiment with drugs, underperform at school, face difficulties forming attachments, and run into trouble with the law.[83] Other studies have challenged these findings, though, and caution against couples staying married "for the sake of the children."[84] Whatever its merits from the standpoint of social science, this latter view commands greater acceptance from the American public. When responding to a survey stating that "for the children's sake, parents should stay together and not get a divorce even if the marriage isn't working," 62 percent of the people disagreed, compared to only 33 percent who agreed.[85] Note that the situation described in this question—"if a marriage isn't working"—does not mention instances where the partners hurl obscenities at each other on a nightly basis, the husband runs off with his secretary, or the wife suffers physical violence during her husband's drunken rages. Virtually no one thinks divorce should be prohibited in these kinds of extreme cases. In the most interesting finding from the public opinion data, a generic description of a dissatisfying marriage is sufficient for people to accept a divorce between a couple with children. The percentage believing divorce to be appropriate for parents rises still further when polls ask about situations in which "a marriage has serious difficulties" or the couple is "very unhappy."[86]

Do the public opinion data indicate that Americans now view marital breakup, like death and taxes, as something society must accept as inevitable? Actually, quite the contrary is true. Strong majorities believe that divorce is a "very serious problem."[87] About twice as many people choose "more difficult" as "easier" when asked, "Should divorce in this country be easier or more difficult to obtain than it is now?"[88] Similar results have appeared in survey after survey for several decades. This finding might seem to hint at public support for state legislatures and governors to pass laws making it harder for couples to untie the knot.

A closer examination of the question's wording, however, shows the hurdles that any prospective divorce reformers must overcome. The survey question quoted above, and others like it, simply asks whether divorce should be made harder or easier without mentioning *who* would be enacting these changes. When government is brought into the story as the agent that would promote and protect marriage, public support falls. Consider the following poll question from 2002: "A number of states are starting programs that seek to reduce divorce rates by offering 'marriage-education' classes. To what extent do you agree or disagree that marriage education is something that the state or federal government should be involved in?" Within the realm of possibilities, this is a modest proposal. It would not change the ability of couples to divorce but would simply involve the government in teaching people tools and strategies for staying married. Still, only 46 percent of Americans supported this proposal, with 55 percent opposed.[89] Qualitative evidence points to the same conclusion. In focus groups people express concerns about high rates of divorce, but they are uncomfortable with governmental involvement in regulating it.[90]

## Covenant Marriage as a Response to Divorce

As a prominent example of a limited policy reform that the public might accept, a new initiative in the late 1990s called "covenant marriage" offered couples the option of agreeing before the marriage begins that they can end it only for specified reasons. Laws authorizing covenant marriage establish a process through which couples sign an affidavit pledging their intention of a lifetime marriage. They agree to seek counseling before contemplating divorce and, should their attempt at reconciliation fail, that a fault-based system will govern any marital dissolution. Covenant marriage also includes premarital counseling in striving to solidify a lasting commitment from both partners.

In 1997 Louisiana enacted the nation's first law offering covenant marriage as an option, and Arizona and Arkansas followed suit within a few years. The three states differ somewhat on the grounds for which couples choosing to enter the new marital arrangement can later request a divorce. Louisiana's law resembles the common practice in many states prior to the 1960s in allowing individuals to file for divorce on charges of a partner's adultery, desertion, felony conviction, and physical or sexual abuse of the petitioner or children. Arizona's provisions are looser, allowing for additional grounds as well as ending the marriage through mutual consent, while Arkansas's law is stricter than Louisiana's in requiring a longer separation period before a divorce.[91] With its passage in these states, covenant marriage seemed for a time a realistic reform that might attract widespread support from families, churches, and politicians.

Despite the reformers' best intentions, covenant marriage failed to alter America's approach to marriage and divorce. After achieving a policy victory in three states, the movement for covenant marriage stalled. Legislators around the country introduced bills to establish the option, but no states since Arkansas have enacted it into law. Opponents marshaled counterarguments at every stage, including claims that covenant marriage inappropriately adds a religious dimension to marriage, traps idealistic young couples into marriages that could later turn dysfunctional, and fails to protect women from domestic violence. Advocates of covenant marriage could refute some of these claims; in Louisiana, for example, a wife facing physical or sexual abuse can end her marriage faster under a covenant marriage than a traditional marriage.[92] Still, the strong opposition to covenant marriage shows that curtailing the options for divorce, even when the parties voluntarily agree in advance, strikes many Americans as an unwarranted governmental intrusion into private lives.

A second and perhaps more important reason why covenant marriage failed to solve the divorce problem is that prospective couples did not embrace the new option. Researchers estimate that only 1–3 percent of marrying couples in Louisiana, Arizona, and Arkansas have opted for covenant marriages, a figure too low to shift the overall population in those states toward marital stability.[93] The effects on divorce rates might be even smaller than these figures suggest if covenant marriage disproportionately attracts the people least likely to divorce in the first place. Complementing and reinforcing couples' decisions to bypass covenant marriage, few clergy members have required it for the marriage ceremonies they perform.[94] Without a strong push from churches, covenant marriage is unlikely to transform domestic relations for society at large.

Churches' limited participation in covenant marriage sheds additional light on the reasons why divorce reform has failed to gain political traction. From the Moral Majority in the 1980s to the Family Research Council in the first decade of the twenty-first century, interest groups representing evangelicals have ranked divorce low among their political priorities. The plot thickens when considering that the Louisiana legislator who authored the nation's first covenant marriage bill, Tony Perkins, later became the president of the FRC in 2003. Because Perkins has established his credibility on the subject of divorce, the relative silence of his organization on the matter cannot be attributed to an apathetic leadership. The FRC's priorities instead appear to reflect straightforward political calculations. With divorce reform lacking strong support from any major constituency in America, including the FRC's, the group has chosen to allocate its time and resources elsewhere.

The possibility for reform made a modest comeback during President George W. Bush's second term. Bush's Healthy Marriage Initiative funded research and demonstration projects, incorporated marriage education into existing federal programs, and provided related grants to state and local governments. In constructing this policy, Bush operated under the same constraints as the FRC, and it is noteworthy that his Healthy Marriage Initiative did not seek to restrict in any way the availability of divorce. Instead his program focused on marriage education and research, attempting to persuade individuals to voluntarily commit to a stable, long-term marriage. By supporting the institution of marriage without constraining people's options for divorce, Bush kept his policy within the bounds of public acceptability.

## The Politics of Divorce Revisited

While the plain words of the Bible could provide sufficient motivation for Christians generally and evangelicals specifically to fight for antidivorce legislation, culture has trumped scripture in shaping public policy. More precisely, culture has influenced how the Bible is interpreted and used in politics—or, in this case, not used. Previous generations of Christians cited the Bible as justification for making a divorce difficult to obtain, but they abandoned those efforts early in the twentieth century.

No doubt some Christian leaders such as Tony Perkins would like to make divorce a prominent political issue today, but they cannot take vigorous action without jeopardizing support from their constituencies. Given the virtually unlimited ways that Christian beliefs could inform a person's political views, interest groups such as Perkins's own Family Research Council must choose the issues on which to lobby. Topics such as abortion, gay rights, school choice, Darwinism and evolution, and religious displays on public property have stood the test of time. Organizational positions and advocacy on those issues have attracted a mass constituency willing to contribute financially, attend protests and rallies, and express their beliefs to government officials. Divorce is a different matter altogether. From the Moral Majority to the Christian Coalition to the Family Research Council, organizations representing the Christian right have spoken mostly in whispers. These groups have occasionally raised their voices on the issue but never have made it a prominent part of their political agenda. Their leaders seem to recognize that a strong call to tighten divorce laws would alienate their own members and supporters.

Other Christian leaders lack even the desire to take a strong political stand against divorce. Within the value system prevailing in America today, both church leaders and their members have come to accept the unfortunate reality of divorce. From personal contact with people in their families, churches, and friendship circles whose marriages crumbled beyond repair, pastors and priests have come to see divorce as a choice that an upstanding, God-fearing Christian might make when necessary. Just as ordinary Americans no longer scorn divorcées as moral degenerates, neither do clergy members. After observing marriages that cannot be saved, few pastors or priests want to lead or otherwise contribute to a political campaign focused on new laws to curtail the options for divorce. In that respect they are fully in sync with their members. Because of the preferences of both Christian leaders and the rank and file, divorce is unlikely to emerge as a new front in the culture war.

Homosexuality might seem to follow different dynamics, for it has stood at the very center of the culture war in recent decades. Do the processes of accommodation I have described in this chapter apply to it? Can Christian leaders step outside the culture and maintain fixed, biblically grounded positions even as the society around them increasingly accepts homosexual behavior as morally neutral? To answer these questions, I need to situate recent developments in attitudes toward homosexuality in the context of long-term trends in public opinion, political activism, biblical interpretations, and public policy. Accordingly, I begin the next chapter by examining the public and political responses to homosexuality at the beginning of the twentieth century.

# Homosexuality

Americans of a certain age might remember the *Readers'
Guide to Periodical Literature*. In the days before the
Internet, Google, and digital library catalogs, generations of students used this index to find sources for their
reports and term papers. The *Readers' Guide* sought to
offer comprehensive coverage of American periodicals
by including subjects both well known and obscure.
From its inception in 1900, the *Readers' Guide* indexed
political and opinion journals such as the *Nation,
Harper's,* and the *New Republic*; general interest magazines such as the *Atlantic, Saturday Evening Post,* and
*Literary Digest*; scholarly journals such as *Political Science Quarterly* and *American Historical Review*; literary
reviews such as the *Southern Review* and *North American Review*; and other magazines such as *National Geographic* and the *Christian Century.*

The first bound volume of the *Readers' Guide*
spanned 2,491 pages and covered the years 1900–1904.
A researcher flipping through the middle of the "H"
section could scan successive entries on "homestead
law," "homeward bound," "homicide," "homiletics,"
and "Hommel, Fritz." "Homosexuality"—a term that
had recently entered the English language—could have
followed next, but it did not appear in volume 1. The
*Readers' Guide* also contained no entries for terms with
similar meanings at the turn of the twentieth century, including *inversion, sex inversion, perversion, sex perversion, sodomy, similsexualism, antipathic sexual instinct,*
and *the third gender.* By whatever name, homosexuality
attracted little interest from journalists, scholars, and
other writers.

The first five editions of the *Readers' Guide* had indexed over one million articles before homosexuality
finally received an entry in volume 6, covering the years

1929–1932.[1] To which of the many unexplored aspects of homosexual identities and lives did the initial articles refer? Did writers investigate the often strained relationships between homosexuals and their families, workplaces, and communities? How about political debates over civil rights protections for gays and lesbians, along with the resistance mounted by various religious groups? Did writers discuss competing theories about the origins of a person's sexual orientation and the difficulties of teenagers struggling with their sexual identities?

No, public dialogue would not address those questions until decades later, and we should not anachronistically project modern concerns into the earlier literature. The entry on homosexuality in the 1929–1932 edition of the *Readers' Guide* used three simple words — "see sex perversion" — to refer the reader to a meager two articles in a different section. That cross-reference speaks volumes about the cultural assumptions surrounding homosexuality in the 1920s and 1930s. On the rare occasions when an article mentioned same-sex desires and behaviors, the writer usually called them a reprehensible form of sexual perversion.

Cultural assumptions have clearly changed greatly in the decades leading up to today. Formerly discussed — if at all — behind closed doors, homosexuality now receives significant attention in households, workplaces, academia, and the media. A growing proportion of Americans — Christians included — fully accept the morality of homosexual relationships. Perhaps most interestingly, as we will see, many Christians have reinterpreted the Bible in ways that downplay or overturn its apparent denunciations of homosexual behavior. How did these transformations occur? How has the secular culture shaped the beliefs of clergy, denominational leaders, and the average person in the pews? To understand the processes at work, we can begin by tracking the information the reading public encountered in the 1950s. After examining the evolution in how homosexuality was viewed within the secular culture, we will be ready to analyze the religious responses.

### From Invisibility to Pathology

In the early 1950s homosexuality still attracted little coverage in the media, but a small uptick occurred during the middle of the decade. In volume 20 of the *Readers' Guide to Periodical Literature*, covering

March 1955 to February 1957, the entry on homosexuality for the first time listed articles instead of merely citing a cross-reference. Yet the content of the coverage had changed very little from earlier decades, and readers who searched under "sex perversion" were told to "see also homosexuality." The shift occurred in the amount of coverage rather than the tone, for enough articles now existed to warrant a new category. The articles' titles indicated that cultural perceptions had not budged: "Homosexuals played with dolls, not baseballs," "Idaho underworld," "Men only; homosexuals," "Sexually deviant student," and "Third sex, guilt or sickness?"[2]

For analysis, information, and quotes, the articles relied on two American institutions that dealt with homosexuals: the system of law and order and the psychiatric profession. Police forces, especially in major cities, treated homosexuality as a vice alongside racketeering, prostitution, drug running, and money laundering. Charged with keeping order and enforcing antisodomy statutes, police sought to prevent homosexuals from meeting together and forming communities. In some states a person arrested for soliciting gay sex could face a felony conviction and several years in prison.[3] Police officers in the 1950s routinely raided gay bars and the parks and beaches where gays congregated, and government officials were quick to take credit for the crackdowns. In 1960 the head of a division of the California Department of Alcoholic Beverage Control bragged to reporters—and, indirectly, to voters—that "a dozen undercover agents are at work gathering evidence to root out homosexual bars in the Bay Area."[4]

The national-security apparatus at the federal level worked hand in hand with city police by focusing on the threat homosexuals allegedly posed to the country as a whole. During World War II the US military refined its techniques for identifying and expelling gays and lesbians, and it gave dishonorable discharges to thousands of service members.[5] A few years later anticommunist agitators began asserting that communist subversives could blackmail homosexuals, making the need to purge the government of all gays and lesbians a Cold War imperative. After newspaper stories uncovered evidence of homosexuals working in various agencies and departments, the US Senate authorized an investigation in 1950 to determine the extent of the problem and offer solutions. The Senate report, "Employment of Homosexuals and Other Sex Perverts in the US Government," discussed ways to find the homosexuals already employed, fire them from their jobs, and prevent others from getting hired in the first place. "Since the initiation of this investigation," the subcommittee concluded, "considerable progress has been made in removing homosexuals and similar undesirable employees from positions in the Government."[6] Using the surviving records, historians estimate that thousands of people lost their jobs because of either the threat of discovery or formal allegations of homosexual activity.[7]

Treated as outcasts by the law-and-order systems at the local and federal levels, homosexuals might have expected more tolerance and understanding from psychiatrists. After all, these scientifically trained therapists and researchers sought to ground their knowledge in observations and evidence, not merely convention or cultural beliefs. Much like their counterparts in law and order, however, psychiatrists made pronouncements and established practices that confined homosexuals to the fringes of American society.

In 1952 the American Psychiatric Association discussed homosexuality in its *Diagnostic and Statistical Manual of Mental Disorders* (*DSM*), an attempt to codify psychiatric knowledge and standardize the diagnoses and treatments for mental illnesses. The *DSM* listed "sociopathic personality disturbance" as one of many mental disorders, noting that "sociopathic reactions are very often symptomatic of severe underlying personality disorder, neurosis, or psychosis, or occur as the result of organic brain injury or disease." "Sexual deviation" formed one kind of "sociopathic personality disorder," and the *DSM* stressed that a diagnosis should "specify the type of the pathologic behavior, such as homosexuality, transvestitism, pedophilia, fetishism and sexual sadism (including rape, sexual assault, mutilation)."[8] According to the best available medical knowledge, then, homosexuality was one of several kinds of deviant sexual behaviors, a group subsumed in turn within a larger category of sociopathic disturbances. Homosexuals who turned to psychiatrists for help received treatments such as Freudian psychotherapy, electroshock therapy, and hormone injections.[9]

## Initial Stirrings for Gay Rights

Before the long-established dynamics in the national dialogue *about* homosexuals could change, the voices *of* homosexuals had to be heard. As the first step, gays and lesbians needed to form communities and organizations to challenge the prevailing understandings. Such organizing had to be discreet, at least initially. In the social environment of the 1950s, people who publicly revealed their sexual orientation and became known as political agitators risked unemployment, police harassment, ostracism from family and friends, and violent retaliation from people who hated homosexuals. Given the difficulties for organizing, it should not be surprising that the gay rights movement developed slowly.

In 1950 several homosexuals in Los Angeles formed the first gay rights organization with staying power.[10] Taking the name Mattachine Society a year later, the group endured internal divisions during in its formative years over its tactics and leadership. One of the group's early documents stated that the Mattachine Society wanted to "provide a consensus of principle around which all of our people can rally"; to collect and conduct research "for the purpose of informing all interested homosexuals, and for the purpose of informing and enlightening the public at large"; and to establish a climate in which "the more far-seeing and socially conscious homosexuals provide leadership to the whole mass of social deviants."[11] In a sign of the times, the Mattachine Society seemed to accept the label of homosexuals as "social deviants" even as the organization worked to build a community, create a sense of shared purpose, and win over the public.

A few years after the Mattachine Society began its operations, a group of women in San Francisco founded Daughters of Bilitis, the nation's first lesbian organization. The group called itself "A Women's Organization for the Purpose of Promoting the Integration of the Homosexual into Society." In its mission statement, Daughters of Bilitis explained how it hoped to enlighten both lesbians and the general public, participate in wide-ranging discussions about homosexuality, support research by respected experts, and reform the criminal laws targeting homosexuals.[12] For a group representing a marginalized part of society and operating on a shoestring budget, those were lofty goals indeed.

Over the next decade the Mattachine Society and Daughters of Bilitis led the nascent gay rights movement, forming small chapters in a handful of cities. Despite achieving a measure of respect in the gay and lesbian subculture, these two organizations were unknown to most Americans, making them a sideshow to the cultural trends affecting the nation in the 1950s and 1960s. As one indicator of how hard it was to draw attention to their causes, the Mattachine Society and Daughters of Bilitis from their founding up through 1965 received a total of only six mentions, most of them fleeting, in the *New York Times*.[13]

While gay rights organizations failed to attract much interest from the news media, the general issues surrounding homosexuality rose in national prominence, eventually catching the eye of pollsters. Scientific polling gained popularity after World War II, when firms such the Gallup Organization, Opinion Research Corporation, and Roper Organization, along with academic operations like the Survey Research Center at the University of Michigan, asked Americans hundreds of questions about social and political issues. Yet before 1965 not a single poll inquired about homosexuality. When issues are absent from the national agenda, as was true for homosexuality until the 1950s, polling organizations feel little need to measure public attitudes. Furthermore, pollsters see their mission as quantifying the extent to which people disagree. The almost universal condemnation of homosexuality would have made a survey question a waste of time. But by 1965 increasing controversy over the subject encouraged Louis Harris and Associates, one of the largest polling firms of that period, to assess public attitudes for the first time through a scientific survey.

The question read, "America has many different types of people in it. But we would like to know whether you think each of these different types of people is more helpful or more harmful to American life, or don't they help or harm things much one way or the other?" The interviewer then presented the respondent with several groups, including "homosexuals," "prostitutes," "beatniks," "young men with beards and long hair," and "women who wear bikini bathing suits." When researchers tallied the results, only 1 percent of the respondents stated that homosexuals were "helpful" to American life, a figure well below the percentage of the population that self-identifies as gay, lesbian, or bisexual.[14] If homosexuals appeared within the Louis Harris poll at rates close to their population averages, most of them either did not say they were "helpful" to American life or else declined to answer the question. The rest of the public was no more favorable, with 70 percent of the respondents saying homosexuals were downright "harmful."[15]

Leading psychiatrists held similarly negative perceptions of homosexuals. In 1968 the American Psychiatric Association published *DSM-II*, an update of its original *Diagnostic and Statistical Manual* (which was now called *DSM-I*). Given the success of new medications for schizophrenia, manic depression, and other disorders, along with the fading influence of Freudian theories of mental health diagnoses, the profession's leaders revised their manual. The APA overhauled much of the content, and yet the section on homosexuality barely changed at all. Homosexuality was still classified as a "sexual deviation," along with fetishism, pedophilia, transvestitism, exhibitionism, voyeurism, sadism, and masochism. The compilers of *DSM-II* classified all these "sexual deviations" as part of the broad category of "personality disorders."[16]

When the APA released *DSM-II* in 1968, only a seer could have predicted that public dialogue about homosexuality would soon undergo a major shift. Historians and gay activists recall New York City's Stonewall riots of 1969 as the catalytic event that helped turn the small-scale organizing of the previous two decades into a major social movement.[17] For decades New York police had raided bars primarily serving a gay clientele, leading to arrests, intimidation, and disruptions to the flow of business. On June 27, 1969, patrons of the Stonewall Inn fought back, with the resulting melee destroying the interior of the bar and spilling out into the street. In the aftermath of the Stonewall riots, organizing for gay rights reached a new intensity. Gay pride parades commemorated the first anniversary of Stonewall in Chicago, Los Angeles, and New York before spreading to other cities in the following years.[18]

News coverage of homosexuality entered a third phase. For about half of the twentieth century, the subject rarely received any attention from news organizations. In the middle of the century, more stories in magazines and newspapers referred to homosexuality, but their messages were largely negative because journalists acquired most of their information from spokespersons from law enforcement and psychiatry. By organizing more vigorously at the end of the 1960s, gays and lesbians brought their own voices into the national dialogue and caught the notice of journalists. Although these voices still represented a minority position within the overall debate, straight people now had the chance to consider facts, perceptions, and arguments that might change their beliefs.

The new twists in the national dialogue accompanied and probably contributed to changes in public opinion. In 1970 a Louis Harris and Associates poll repeated in identical form the question previously asked in 1965, thereby allowing an apples-to-apples comparison of responses at the beginning and end of this five-year period. In 1970 only 2 percent of the public said homosexuals were "helpful" to American life, a tiny increase from 1 percent in 1965. While the pool of heterosexuals who viewed homosexuals favorably did not expand, the amount of overt hostility declined considerably. Whereas 70 percent of Americans said homosexuals were "harmful" in 1965, only 53 percent agreed with that assessment in 1970.[19] In public opinion polls, changes this large in only five years are rare, occurring only in special situations when people encounter new information.[20]

### The Revolution in Psychiatry

Psychiatrists played a key role in bringing this new information to the American public. DSM-I and DSM-II appeared to convey a unified stance of the psychiatric profession toward homosexuality, but dissent lurked just beneath the surface. A small body of research, much of it conducted by UCLA psychologist Evelyn Hooker, questioned the prevailing beliefs. For the seminal article she published in 1957, Hooker recruited samples of gay and straight men and administered tests of their psychological functioning. Independent experts who were blind to each subject's sexual orientation analyzed the results, finding no differences in levels of psychological adjustment between the two groups.[21] A few years later Judd Marmor published a collection of essays by mental health researchers, some of whom challenged the common view that people became homosexuals because of overbearing mothers and distant fathers.[22]

These and other scientific findings undercut the prevailing psychiatric assumptions, and political pressure forced the APA to respond. In 1970 gay activists picketed the APA's annual convention, disrupting one of the meetings and denouncing leading psychiatrists for their bigotry. More protests followed the next year, along with a formal panel session in which the APA allowed gay activists to make their case. The drama intensified further in a 1972 panel when a gay psychiatrist, who wore a mask to protect his anonymity and professional reputation, asserted that the APA's membership included more than two hundred homosexuals.[23] According to later accounts of APA insiders, many psychiatrists began doubting that homosexuality was a mental illness once they learned that some of their colleagues were gay.[24]

The association's most important action occurred in 1973, when the APA's Executive Board removed homosexuality as a personality disorder from the *Diagnostic and Statistical Manual*. In the revamped classification, homosexuality per se was not a disorder and became problematic only if someone did not want the sexual orientation he or she held.[25] The APA's membership affirmed the board's decision the next year through a referendum. Individual psychiatrists could dissent from the new approach to homosexuality, of course, and many continued to call it a sickness. Still, the APA's decision reverberated throughout its membership and influenced discussions in the rest of American society.

Scientific findings in subsequent decades further undermined the old view that poor parenting caused certain children to become homosexuals. Brain scans showed significant differences in the hypothalamus regions of gay and straight men, suggesting that sexual desire originated in (or at least could be understood through) neural activity in the brain.[26] Other studies, based on data from identical and fraternal twins, used standard methods of psychology to uncover genetic influences on a person's sexual orientation.[27] Additional research found that pregnant women help determine the sexual orientation of their offspring through the intrauterine hormones they secrete.[28] To be sure, many critics observe that biology has yet to offer a complete explanation of sexual orientation, and opponents of gay rights insist that people's behaviors, and possibly even their attractions, lie within their conscious control. Scientific research nevertheless has made it harder for the general public to dismiss homosexuality as a lifestyle choice.

The accumulated scientific research affected the tone of media coverage, with important implications for what people learned and how they formed their opinions. Consider a *Time* magazine article from the 1960s, when the APA still classified same-sex attraction as a mental disorder; at that time no major research documented the biological influences on sexual orientation. *Time*, one of the most prominent media outlets of the twentieth century, was considered moderate to somewhat liberal in the 1960s. A lengthy essay in the magazine on January 21, 1966, concluded that homosexuality "is a pathetic little second-rate substitute for reality, a pitiable flight from life. As such it deserves fairness, compassion, understanding and, when possible, treatment. But it deserves no encouragement, no glamorization, no rationalization, no fake status as minority martyrdom, no sophistry about simple differences in taste—and, above all, no pretense that it is anything but a pernicious sickness."[29]

Communication scholars note that journalists work within a cultural context that shapes their news coverage. When gathering information and soliciting quotes, journalists consult authoritative sources such as government officials, business leaders, scientists, and other experts. News stories thus capture the range of elite opinion on an issue at a given time, meaning that the content of the news changes when elites update their opinions.[30] When *Time* published its article in 1966, few psychiatrists or scientists considered homosexuals to be normal, functioning adults who differed from heterosexuals only in their sexual desires. By declassifying homosexuality as a mental illness in 1973, the APA signaled a major shift in elite opinion in a short period. Media coverage did not change overnight, but new scientific perspectives gradually seeped into news stories.[31]

## Public Opinion on Homosexuality

Amid the new scientific research and shifting media coverage, did ordinary Americans start changing their opinions—and if so, how? The General Social Survey (GSS), a long-running project of the National Opinion Research Center at the University of Chicago, contains data that document the evolving opinions.[32] Since 1973 the GSS has regularly asked a national sample of Americans the following question: "What about sexual relations between two adults of the same sex—do you think it is always wrong, almost always wrong, wrong only sometimes, or not wrong at all?" As it turns out, very few people during the lifespan of the GSS surveys (11 percent) took the middle two options of "almost always wrong" or "wrong only sometimes."[33] Most people believed that homosexual behavior is either completely immoral ("always wrong") or fully moral ("not wrong at all.")

Figure 4.1 plots for the general public the percentage saying same-

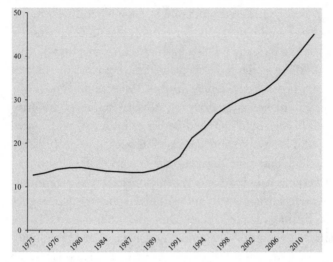

**Figure 4.1.** Percentage saying homosexual relations are "not wrong at all"
*Source:* General Social Survey. Data smoothed with LOESS.

sex relations are "not wrong at all."[34] In the US population as a whole, only 11 percent viewed homosexuality as moral in 1973.[35] Had pollsters asked Americans the same question in the 1940s or 1950s, when the social environment for homosexuals was more repressive, the level of support surely would have been even lower. With only minor and temporary movements, public support remained at roughly 11 percent until 1990 but rose thereafter. By 2012 a near majority of Americans (45 percent) said same-sex relations were "not wrong at all," nearly four times as many as the period from 1973 to 1990.

When interpreting these trends, we must keep two observations in mind. On the one hand, the American people shifted their views dramatically over the course of only two generations. On the other hand, roughly half of Americans still felt moral qualms about homosexuality in 2012. Because public acceptance of homosexuality began at such a low level in 1973, the immense changes had not, by 2012, produced a majority of Americans who deemed homosexual relations "not wrong at all."

The General Social Survey includes related questions tapping people's support for civil liberties. The introduction reads, "What about a man who admits that he is a homosexual?" The tone of this introduction—its reference to a man who "admits" to being a homosexual—reflects the prevailing sentiment when pollsters conducted the first iteration of the survey. We can nevertheless use responses to the questions following

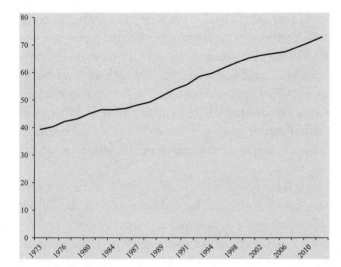

**Figure 4.2.**
Percentage
wanting
to protect
homosexuals'
civil liberties
*Source:* General
Social Survey.
Data smoothed
with LOESS.

the lead-in to examine how public opinion has changed. Participants in the GSS surveys answered the first follow-up question: "Suppose this admitted homosexual wanted to make a speech in your community. Should he be allowed to speak, or not?" After replying to that question, respondents heard the next query: "Should such a person be allowed to teach in a college or university, or not?" Finally, respondents were asked: "If some people in your community suggested that a book he wrote in favor of homosexuality should be taken out of your public library, would you favor removing this book, or not?"

Using answers to these questions, figure 4.2 graphs the percentage of people who would grant to homosexuals all three civil liberties in the survey. Unlike the pattern from figure 4.1, which showed stable opinions during the 1970s and 1980s but major changes thereafter, people's willingness to extend rights and liberties to gays and lesbians increased throughout the period represented in figure 4.2. The level of support among the American public stood at 38 percent in 1973 but rose to 54 percent in 1990 and 73 percent in 2012.

Why did public opinion change so much on both the morality of homosexuality and related questions involving civil liberties? Many scholars have studied the origins and development of public opinion on these issues, and research points to several driving forces. By no longer classifying homosexuality as a mental illness, the APA both signaled and contributed to a shift in how elites viewed the issue, and the media eventually conveyed those new understandings to the public. Americans became more aware of biological influences on sexual orientation, with a growing proportion of the public believing that attractions to members of the same sex lie outside a person's control. People who accept biological explanations of sexual orientation are much more likely to think homosexuality is moral and to support gay rights, and so the scientific research helped shape an environment in which people formed more tolerant beliefs.[36]

The lesbian, gay, bisexual, and transgender (LGBT) movement also helped foster a more tolerant public. The small-scale organizing of the 1950s and 1960s developed into a mature movement in the 1970s, spawning many organizations, activists, and supporting ideas. The movement encouraged homosexuals to come out of the closet to their family and friends, and over time larger percentages of straight people reported gay or lesbian acquaintances. Heterosexuals who don't know anyone who is openly gay or lesbian—generally the case in the 1950s and 1960s—can easily believe that anonymous homosexuals pose a grave threat to society. It is harder to maintain such beliefs when the unnamed social deviant is replaced with a flesh-and-blood friend, coworker, or family member. Research shows that knowing someone who is gay or lesbian correlates strongly with holding more tolerant views.[37] Along with these factors, generational replacement helped solidify the changes in public opinion. As younger people with more liberal views gradually replaced their more conservative elders, the population shifted toward greater acceptance of homosexuals.[38]

*Public Policy and Gay Rights*

Responding to these evolving views, governments at the local, state, and federal levels have revised their policies over the last several decades. The first major policy conflict involved the legality of sexual acts between persons of the same sex. At one time every state in the union criminalized sodomy, albeit with legal definitions that varied on whether the laws covered both oral and anal sex and whether criminal sanctions applied only to same-sex behavior or else included opposite-sex behavior as well. Although the laws were difficult to enforce, convictions often led to lengthy prison sentences and cast a pall of fear over the homosexual community.[39]

In 1961 Illinois reformed its criminal code, and one provision of the new law repealed the long-standing prohibition of sodomy. Discussion and debate occurred elsewhere, too, but no other states acted until the 1970s, when a succession of states either modified or repealed their laws. Twenty-four states had decriminalized sodomy by 1980, and that number rose to twenty-six by 1990 and thirty-seven by 2003, when the Supreme Court resolved the issue.[40] In *Lawrence v. Texas*, the Supreme Court declared antisodomy laws unconstitutional, a violation of the due process clause of the Fourteenth Amendment. After 2003 homosexual relations were legal in every American state.

Political conflict in recent decades expanded beyond antisodomy laws and addressed other issues important to gays and lesbians. In the 1970s some local governments banned discrimination in employment (hiring, promotion, and firing) based on sexual orientation. The conflicts soon spread to the state level, with Wisconsin passing a similar law in 1982, and twenty-one states plus the District of Columbia, covering 44 percent of the US population, enacting nondiscrimination laws by 2013.[41] Some city and county ordinances protected residents in the absence of a state-wide law, but advocates failed to win federal legislation. A proposed law finally passed the Senate in 2013 but died in the House of Representatives. Many localities and twelve states offer some protection from discrimination in the housing market based on sexual orientation, but again, there is no equivalent federal law.[42]

In the realm of military service, policymakers during most of the twentieth century offered no protection to homosexuals, for the goal was to exclude or expel them. Before and during World War II, the armed forces worked to purge homosexuals from their rolls, and in 1949 the newly created Department of Defense standardized the regulations in an effort to ensure prompt discharges.[43] For the next few decades, military recruiters used psychological screening to prevent homosexuals from joining the armed forces, though some evaded detection and advanced through the ranks. When located, often because another service member made an accusation and triggered an investigation, homosexuals were discharged from the military. The policies liberalized slightly in 1993 when Congress passed and President Clinton signed the famous "Don't Ask,

Don't Tell" policy, which forbade homosexuals from serving openly but allowed those in the closet to join and remain in the military. Recruiters and supervisors could not ask about a person's sexual orientation, and homosexuals could serve so long as they kept their sexual orientations private. If discovered, they were discharged, and some studies suggest that the policy did not decrease the number of these cases.[44] Gays and lesbians could not serve openly in the military until 2010, when Congress passed and President Obama signed a law repealing "Don't Ask, Don't Tell." Many commentators observed that the issue created much less controversy in 2010 than it did in earlier decades.[45]

The same could not be said of same-sex marriage, which continued to split the American public into competing camps. As early as the 1970s, gay couples unsuccessfully filed lawsuits to win in court the right to marry. The debate intensified in 1993 when the Supreme Court of Hawaii sent a case involving a gay couple back to the lower courts for additional analysis and clarification. The possibility that Hawaii or other states might authorize gay marriage led Congress in 1996 to pass the Defense of Marriage Act (DOMA), which prevented the federal government, for purposes such as estates and inheritance, social security benefits, and joint income taxes, from recognizing any same-sex marriage that a state certified. In 2013, however, the US Supreme Court declared unconstitutional Section 3 of DOMA, which defined marriage to include only heterosexual unions.

The battles continued in the states. Between 1998 and 2010, states voted a total of thirty-one times to pass a statute or amend the state constitution to declare marriage an institution between one man and one woman.[46] On every occasion but one, a majority of voters chose to prohibit same-sex marriage. The margins of victory steadily declined, though, and in 2012 supporters of same-sex marriage finally prevailed in all four states voting on the issue. Through a combination of legislative actions, court decisions, and initiatives and referenda, thirty-five states allowed same-sex marriage by the end of 2014.[47]

## Religion and Homosexuality in the 1960s and 1970s

As we have seen, many factors have influenced the politics of homosexuality since 1900, including the institutions of law and order, the psychiatric profession and other scientific and medical elites, the LGBT movement, the news media, and governments at the local, state, and federal levels. Together these forces form the context necessary to understand the factor most important for this book: religion. Indeed, if this book's thesis is correct, we cannot understand religious perceptions of homosexuality without first understanding the cultural environment—summarized in the preceding pages—that shaped them. How did religious adherents, especially those in the Christian majority, react to that environment at various points in the twentieth and twenty-first centuries? How did Christian leaders modify their positions in response to changing beliefs in society and among their members?

Given that many Christian leaders in later decades disparaged what they called the "gay lifestyle," readers may be surprised to learn that their predecessors said little about the matter. Before the late 1960s, religious leaders usually did not seek or receive media attention on topics related to same-sex attractions. It is striking, for example, that from the beginning of the twentieth century up to 1968, no Christian denomination in America passed a resolution or released a report that directly addressed homosexuality.[48] News stories about homosexuality quoted and referred to people working in government and psychiatry, but journalists rarely turned to religious leaders for comments.

In declining to denounce homosexual behavior, religious leaders were not signaling a tacit approval of it. For nearly two thousand years, Christian theologians had declared homosexual practices sinful. In the words of St. Augustine, "Those shameful acts against nature, such as were committed in Sodom, ought everywhere and always to be detested and punished."[49] During the Middle Ages, St. Thomas Aquinas analyzed homosexuality from the standpoint of natural law, concluding that intimate relations between two people of the same sex violated the purposes and ends of human sexuality.[50] Among all sexual sins, he claimed, only bestiality was worse. Hildegard of Bingen went beyond many medieval writers by specifically including sexual acts between women among those that God forbids.[51]

Beginning with Martin Luther in 1517, Protestants split from the Church over many points of doctrine and liturgy, but they fully agreed with Catholics on the immorality of homosexual behavior. Luther borrowed from natural law in writing, "The vice of the Sodomites . . . departs from the natural passion and desire, planted into nature by God, according to which the male has a passionate desire for the female."[52] Only the devil, Luther taught, could corrupt a man's will such that he desires another man in a sexual manner. In 1647 the Westminster Catechism, a defining statement for the Reformed tradition that developed into Presbyterianism in Scotland and England, listed "sodomy" and "unnatural lusts" among the "sins forbidden by the seventh commandment."[53] The American colonies, and later the American states, carried these sentiments into the modern era by criminalizing sodomy.

If an interviewer in the middle of the twentieth century had asked, Protestant and Catholic officials probably would have joined a long line of theologians in condemning sexual relations between two people of the same sex. So why didn't Christian leaders work harder to express their views through statements, books, articles, or denominational reports? The most likely answer is that they believed the Christian tradition was already "on the record" in calling homosexual acts sinful. Backed by public contempt of homosexuals, the psychiatric profession and the legal system had the matter under control, relieving denominations of the need to take a leadership role. With virtually everyone in America deeming homosexuality immoral, Christian leaders apparently saw no need to mount an intense campaign just to say, "Me too."

As secular society began changing in the late 1960s, the Christian leaders who were formerly quiet now began to engage the issue in a systematic manner. Leaders of the United Methodist Church (UMC) acted first through their "Resolution on Health, Welfare, and Human Development" (1968). As the document's title would suggest, it covered many topics besides sexuality, but the paragraph on homosexuality is nevertheless revealing:

> We recognize that many persons who are troubled and broken by sexual problems, such as homosexuality, suffer from discriminatory practices arising from traditional attitudes and from outmoded legal practices. We strongly recommend that wherever possible such persons be brought under the care of our health and human development services rather than under penal and correctional services. We believe that the ministry of the church extends to all human beings troubled

and broken by sexual problems and they should find forgiveness and redemption within its fellowship.[54]

In a 1972 resolution called "Social Principles," the UMC took the opportunity to extend its position:

Homosexuals no less than heterosexuals are persons of sacred worth, who need the ministry and guidance of the church in their struggles for human fulfillment, as well as the spiritual and emotional care of a fellowship which enables reconciling relationships with God, with others, and with self. Further we insist that all persons are entitled to have their human and civil rights ensured, though we do not condone the practice of homosexuality and consider the practice incompatible with Christian teaching."[55]

Taken together, the two statements reject a black-and-white position on the issue. On the one hand, the resolutions declare that homosexuality is "incompatible with Christian teaching" and that homosexuals have "sexual problems" and should seek "forgiveness" in the church. Because a person only seeks forgiveness for sinful actions, not those pleasing to God, the resolutions unambiguously pass moral judgment on homosexual behavior. On the other hand, the resolutions urge compassion and civil rights for gays and lesbians, "persons of sacred worth." Demonstrating the urgency of the UMC's message, only one state had repealed its antisodomy laws when the denomination made its pronouncements. The group's leaders wanted other states to follow suit, allowing homosexuals to receive treatment rather than punishment.

Through these statements, United Methodists began applying an old Christian saying—"Hate the sin, love the sinner"—to homosexuality. Given the popularity of the saying today, we often fail to recognize how revolutionary it was to feel and show love for homosexuals in the 1960s. At no point earlier in the twentieth century did any prominent secular or Christian organization in America call for compassion toward those with strong sexual attractions to members of the same sex. Instead the cultural consensus held that homosexuals were perverts and deviants, people who must be derided and arrested, denied employment in government and service in the military, and shunned by family and friends.

It is no coincidence that the UMC formed and announced its new position in the late 1960s and early 1970s instead of previous decades. The years immediately preceding the UMC's statements witnessed an ever so slight dampening of public hostility toward homosexuals, and some members of the denomination surely softened their attitudes too. How could they not? Methodists read newspapers, participated in everyday conversations, and absorbed ideas from their cultural surroundings. A noticeable minority of the American population, as measured in the Louis Harris and Associates poll, now viewed homosexuals as "neither helpful nor harmful" to American society, and that minority probably included some Methodists.[56] The new climate of public opinion empowered Methodist leaders to make statements far more favorable to homosexuals than had earlier Christians such as Augustine, Aquinas, and Luther.

The UMC also advocated protecting homosexuals' civil rights. The freedom to engage in consensual sexual relations within the privacy of one's own home, which not a single state granted before 1961, stood among the most important of those rights. Homosexuals also had no protection from discrimination in the employment or housing markets, and they lacked the right to serve in government or the military. By raising the subject of civil rights in 1968 and 1972, the UMC thus made a bold and innovative move. In earlier decades any Methodist leader who advocated removing the criminal sanctions against sodomy would have offended rank-and-file Christians who, like other Americans, believed that the legal system should reflect and enforce traditional morality.

Through a statement in 1969, the Council for Christian Social Action (CCSA), a body within the United Church of Christ, went even further than the UMC in its tolerance. In fact, the CCSA did not call homosexual behavior sinful, claiming that the Bible's words on the subject had been "exaggerated by wrenching scriptural verses out of context." The statement declared that the Christian ideal of heterosexual marriage "should not blind us to variations and limitations which may preclude that ideal for many," and the CCSA pledged its full support for the civil rights of gays and lesbians.[57] Although the United Church of Christ as a denomination neither endorsed nor rejected the document, within a few years some UCC congregations put the sentiments into practice by performing commitment ceremonies for gay couples.[58]

Other mainline denominations in the early 1970s took positions much closer to that of the United Methodists than the United Church of Christ. The United Presbyterian Church in the United States of America (UPCUSA), the largest branch of Presbyterianism in the country at that time, asserted in 1970 that Christians routinely mischaracterized Paul's teachings. Within Paul's writings, the statement observed, homosexual conduct "is not singled out as more heinous than other sins." The UPCUSA also proclaimed, "There is a difference between homosexuality as a condition of personal existence and homosexualism as explicit homosexual behavior." Applying its principles to the political realm, the statement affirmed that "laws which make a felony of homosexual acts committed by consenting adults are morally unsupportable, contribute nothing to the public welfare, and inhibit rather than permit changes in behavior by homosexual persons."[59]

In its 1970 statement "Sex, Marriage, and Family," the Lutheran Church in America made a similar argument. This denomination was the largest among the Lutheran bodies that would merge in 1988 to form the Evangelical Lutheran Church in America. The statement held that "homosexuality is viewed biblically as a departure from the heterosexual structure of God's creation. Persons who engage in homosexual behavior are sinners only as are all other persons—alienated from God and neighbor. However, they are often the special and undeserving victims of prejudice and discrimination in law, law enforcement, cultural mores, and congregational life. In relation to this area of concern, the sexual behavior of freely consenting adults in private is not an appropriate subject for legislation or police action. It is essential to see such persons as entitled to understanding and justice in church and community."[60]

Evangelical denominations took somewhat different approaches to the subject. In its first statement on homosexuality in 1976, the Southern Baptist Convention (SBC) echoed some of the themes of the United Methodist Church, though with two important differences. Whereas the UMC declared homosexual behavior "incompatible with Christian teaching," the evangelical leaders of the SBC wrote about "the biblical truth regarding the practice of homosexuality and sin."[61] In theory, Christian teaching could change from one period to the next, whereas biblical truth (leaving aside questions of interpretation) is understood to be fixed and certain for all time. In a second key difference, whereas the UMC had called for repealing laws criminalizing homosexual relations, the SBC made no mention of the matter one way or the other. The SBC has passed many resolutions on various aspects of homosexuality, but to this day, the group has never taken a formal stand on whether sodomy should be forbidden by law.[62]

Reliant on tradition, stability, and continuity, Roman Catholics in the 1970s faced different constraints than did the UMC and SBC. In a 1973 statement, the National Conference of Catholic Bishops (later renamed the US Conference of Catholic Bishops) related homosexuality to Church tradition and took, broadly speaking, a "Hate the sin, love the sinner" approach. The statement summarized the classic argument from natural law that homosexual sex, which occurs outside of marriage and cannot lead to procreation, violates God's plan for human sexuality. The US bishops placed sexual orientation on a continuum and contended that people vary in the degree to which they can control their desires. Some people can overcome attractions to members of the same sex through "psychological and spiritual counsel." Others invariably fail to change their sexual orientations despite intense efforts, and Catholic priests must encourage them to commit to a chaste life. Under no circumstances, the bishops stressed, should priests allow people to continue engaging in sinful homosexual conduct.[63]

## Changes in Christian Opinions about Homosexuality

Catholic and Protestant statements in the 1970s did not represent the last word for Christians. Even as denominational leaders took their stands, the ground continued to shift underneath them. Public opinion changed little on a year-to-year basis, but over the span of decades, the accumulated shifts were dramatic.

In a visual depiction of these changes, figure 4.3 plots for the general public and four Christian groups—Catholics, mainline Protestants, evangelical Protestants, and black Protestants—the percentage of people saying same-sex relations are "not wrong at all."[64] The data for this question, used earlier in the chapter in figure 4.1, come from the General Social Survey. Figure 4.3 allows us to compare the trends within Christian groups and the public at large across the life of the survey, 1973–2012. As it turns out, Catholics and mainline Protestants track the American

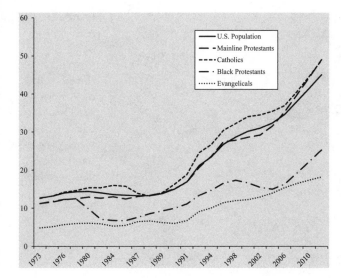

**Figure 4.3.**
Percentage saying homosexual relations are "not wrong at all," by religious tradition
*Source:* General Social Survey. Data smoothed with LOESS.

people as a whole, moving step-by-step toward greater acceptance of homosexuality after 1990.

The picture is somewhat different for evangelicals and black Protestants, two groups expressing levels of support ten to twenty points lower than the US population over the last four decades. Yet the *trends* among evangelicals and black Protestants, just like other Christians, are upward. In 2012, 17 percent of evangelicals and 25 percent of black Protestants believed sexual relations between people of the same sex were "not wrong at all" — figures more than twice the levels each group registered between 1973 and 1990. Indeed, these figures were actually higher than those of the broader US population two decades earlier. New values had diffused through the population, as evidenced by evangelicals and black Protestants in 2012 holding more tolerant beliefs about homosexuality than the country as a whole expressed in 1990. In other words, these two groups gradually shifted their views in the same direction as everyone else; they just started from a lower level and increased at a slower rate.

A similar picture emerges when we focus on civil liberties rather than morality. Figure 4.4 summarizes opinions on whether homosexuals should be allowed to give a speech in one's community, teach at a college or university, and have their books available at the local library. The

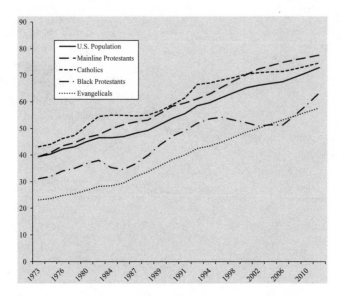

**Figure 4.4.** Percentage wanting to protect homosexuals' civil liberties, by religious tradition *Source:* General Social Survey. Data smoothed with LOESS.

graph shows that Catholics and mainline Protestants resembled the general public from the 1970s forward. The other two major Christian groups, evangelical Protestants and black Protestants, started ten to fifteen points lower than the US population but nevertheless moved upward in tandem. As of 2012, 56 percent of evangelicals and 66 percent of black Protestants would grant to homosexuals the three liberties analyzed here, levels of support higher than the US population expressed in 1990 (54 percent). Once again, evangelicals and black Protestants moved in the same direction as everyone else.

## Homosexuality in the Church and among the Clergy

How have Christian leaders responded to the evolving beliefs in American society and among their own members? Many of the crucial questions involve what happens within the church community itself. Can homosexuals be members in good standing who show their commitment to a church by attending potluck dinners, participating in prayer services, and joining Bible study groups? Can they be ordained as pastors, priests, and bishops? When forming their doctrines and writing official policies, how do Christian groups characterize the causes and consequences of same-sex relationships?

The official Catholic position in 2010 reiterated central themes from the Catholic statement in 1970 by forbidding homosexual behavior while preaching tolerance for people holding same-sex attractions. The Catholic Church states that people sin through their actions, not their desires. A person who cannot overcome a homosexual orientation through prayer, counseling, and intense effort must live a chaste lifestyle—a point that applies to both priests and the laity. Men who formerly felt same-sex attractions can join the priesthood only if they commit to celibacy and do not hold what the Church calls "deep-seated homosexual tendencies."[65]

Most mainline Protestant denominations have done more than the Catholic Church to welcome homosexuals into the church community—in some cases as ordained clergy. The United Methodist Church has considered the ordination question for decades but still does not allow what it calls "self-avowed practicing homosexuals" into the ministry.[66] In theory, United Methodists allow celibate homosexuals to become members of the clergy, but few such individuals have undergone the process of ordination. The Episcopal Church created controversy in 2003 when it ordained an openly gay bishop. In 2009 Episcopalians went even further when their General Convention established a formal policy to allow homosexuals to become priests, deacons, and bishops.[67] In 2011 the Presbyterian Church (USA) also began allowing homosexuals to serve in leadership positions, and in 2013 the Evangelical Lutheran Church in America appointed its first gay bishop.[68] These policies, unthinkable a few decades earlier, demonstrate the extent to which mainline denominations have moved with American society in accepting homosexuality.

By contrast, evangelical and Pentecostal denominations such as the Southern Baptist Convention, the Christian Reformed Church, and the Assemblies of God have made no overtures toward ordaining homosexuals and appear unlikely to do so in the near future.[69] Until recently, historically black denominations such as the African Methodist Episcopal Church, the National Baptist Convention, and the Church of God in Christ also rejected calls to consider the question of ordaining gay pastors. After President Obama and the National Association for the Advancement of Colored People (NAACP) endorsed same-sex marriage in 2012, the questions surrounding homosexuality posed a new challenge for black churches.[70]

How does the growing support among the largest Christian groups for homosexuals' civil liberties, as depicted in figure 4.4, square with the resistance in theologically conservative denominations to ordaining homosexuals? As we saw in figure 4.4, by 2012, 56 percent of evangelicals—a clear majority—would allow homosexuals to give a speech in their community, teach at a college or university, and have their books available at a local library. Could we infer similar pressure from rank-and-file evangelicals for allowing gays and lesbians to become pastors? The answer is no, because people in general, and evangelicals in particular, demand far more stringent requirements for ordination than for secular rights and liberties. In a 2006 poll a majority of the American population opposed allowing gay and lesbian pastors and bishops; among self-identified evangelicals, the margin of opposition was overwhelming—80 percent to 15 percent.[71] A majority of evangelicals will probably continue to oppose opening the ministry to homosexuals well into the future.

### Homosexuality and Christianity in the World of Books

These disputes over ordination practices have occurred within a broader Christian engagement on the subject of homosexuality. Figure 4.5 quantifies this attention, plotting by decade the number of new books released in the United States on homosexuality in Christian thought, practice, and tradition.[72] The graph indicates that publishers did not

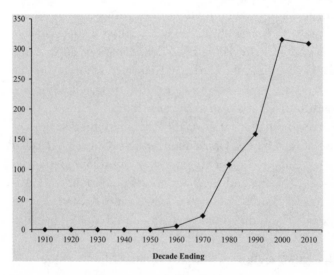

**Figure 4.5.**
Number of
new books on
homosexuality
and Christianity
*Source:* Compiled
by the author

release a single book on these questions in the first half of the twentieth century, a surprising finding from the vantage point of today. Suppose a group of American students in 1950 wanted to read a comprehensive study of how Christianity, the nation's dominant religion, treated the issues involving homosexual identities and behaviors. Some of the students might have been struggling with their own sexual orientations; others might have been curious because of the federal campaign to expel gays and lesbians from the military and other governmental posts. Regardless of how long they searched, these students would have discovered that neither public nor university libraries in the United States contained any books that focused directly on their topics.

Why were the shelves empty in 1950 and earlier in the twentieth century? Part of the answer is that no aspects of homosexuality—whether historical, biological, psychological, literary, or political—received more than passing attention in the world of books and ideas. Our hypothetical students would be just as disappointed, for example, if they searched for scholarly analyses of homosexual references in English literature. Gay and lesbian issues were simply not considered appropriate for study or deserving of careful investigation. For the specific question of the Bible and homosexuality, the fact that everybody knew (or thought they knew) what the Bible said also helps explain why no one devoted a book to the subject. Writers seldom undertake a project when both they and their prospective readers know, before any research actually begins, what the investigation will show.

The comfortable assumptions of 1950 soon unraveled as writers increasingly researched and debated all aspects of homosexuality, including the religious dimension. A handful of books—6, to be precise—addressed homosexuality and Christianity during the decade ending in 1960. The next ten years brought 23 more titles, and then the volume of literary output expanded beyond what anyone could have expected. Publishers released 108 books in the ten years concluding in 1980, and the upward trend continued thereafter. As seen in figure 4.5, a total of 159, 316, and 309 books appeared in the decades ending in 1990, 2000, and 2010, respectively. From 1950 to 2010 the available literature included 921 new books, the vast majority published in the latter part of that period.

The books address a wide range of questions, such as ministering to gays and lesbians in the congregation, how Christian parents should respond when one of their children comes out of the closet, the history of Christian responses to homosexuality, how scientific findings should inform Christian views, and whether homosexuals should be ordained as pastors. In most of these books, the authors refer to biblical material without making it their exclusive focus. Other books, of special interest here, devote their full attention to the biblical passages relating to homosexuality. Indeed, competing books on the subject proliferated in recent decades, offering readers many opportunities to engage the material.

## The Bible and Homosexuality

Thanks to a vast amount of research and writing, the debate over what the Bible says about homosexuality has matured. Each side advances a standard set of arguments and offers honed rebuttals to their opponents' arguments. The claims and counterclaims are interesting in their own right, but they also speak to the connections between the secular culture and biblical interpretations that I analyzed in my previous chapters on slavery and divorce. The contours of the debate are therefore worth examining in some detail to uncover the important lessons.

One group of writers, whom I will call "traditionalist," argues that the Bible prohibits all forms of same-sex intimacy. To some people, the label "traditionalist" connotes backward and reactionary views, but I use the term in a neutral sense to describe people who share the traditional Christian outlook on the subject. According to traditionalists, "The biblical understanding of homosexual behavior is univocal. . . . Homosexual activity is not consistent with the will of God."[73] On the other side of the debate, a group I will call "revisionist" argues that the biblical authors disparage only the forms and practices of homosexuality prominent in their own era, meaning that the Bible contains no blanket statements applicable to modern times. Calling a person a "revisionist" is sometimes meant as an insult, but I intend only the term's literal meaning as someone who revises a previous view. In the revisionist account each of the biblical passages "is so tied to a specific cultural situation that its relevance in condemning same-sex love today is in serious doubt."[74]

The exegetical controversy begins with Genesis 2, which details the origins of the first human beings. The verses describe how God created Eve to complement Adam, and traditionalists hold that God wants one man to come together with one woman in marriage. The saying "God created Adam and Eve, not Adam and Steve" thus captures a crucial theological truth: homosexual acts defy the wisdom and purpose of God's creation.[75] To revisionists, however, Genesis 2 does not teach sexual ethics in sufficient detail to yield any implications for homosexual practices.[76] Revisionists also reject the traditionalist claim that God destroyed Sodom and its neighboring city of Gomorrah because of rampant homosexuality. In the revisionists' account, the men of Sodom sinned through their inhospitality and their attempt to gang-rape Lot's visitors. No one today, whether gay or straight, approves of gang-raping a neighbor's houseguests, and so revisionists argue that the story of Sodom contains no universal prescriptions against consensual homosexuality.[77]

Traditionalists counter that the later book of Jude mentions Sodom's "sexual immorality" and "unnatural lust" which, in their view, refer to homosexuality in general rather than male-to-male gang rape.[78] Traditionalists also point to Leviticus 18:22 and 20:13, which prohibit men lying with men and require the death penalty for violators.[79] Revisionists often respond by noting that Leviticus forbids many behaviors Christians now deem unproblematic, including shaving, eating rare meat, wearing clothes made from two different fabrics, planting fields with two different kinds of crops, and men having sex with menstruating women. In this line of reasoning, it is hypocritical to retain the ban on homosexual acts while discarding many of the other rules.[80]

Traditionalists counter that the New Testament reinforces the Old Testament's prohibitions on male-to-male intercourse. Among those who will not "inherit the kingdom of God," 1 Corinthians 6:9 includes (in the original Greek) *malakos* and *arsenokoitês*. The question is, who are the *malakos* and *arsenokoitês* to whom the apostle Paul referred? Traditionalists hold that the two original Greek words, either separately or in combination, describe homosexual activity.[81] Joe Dallas, a prominent evangelical writer and speaker, contends that Paul constructed the word *arsenokoitês* "directly from the Levitical passages in the Greek translation. . . . Though the term is unique to Paul, it refers specifically to homosexual behavior."[82] Revisionists have used a contextual knowledge of the Greco-Roman world to challenge this inference. The pairing of *malakos* with *arsenokoitês* could refer specifically to male prostitution, with the former being the prostitutes and the latter their clients. The frequency of these practices in pagan temples, the argument goes, made them even more infuriating to Paul.[83] Alternatively, Paul could have been denouncing pederasty, an exploitative arrangement through which an adult male engaged in sexual relations with an adolescent boy.[84]

Traditionalists dispute these points.[85] With neither side convinced by its opponents' interpretations of 1 Corinthians 6:9 and the related verse in 1 Timothy 1:10, the controversy invariably turns to Romans 1:26–27, which reads: "For this reason God gave them up to degrading passions. Their women exchanged natural intercourse for unnatural, and in the same way also the men, giving up natural intercourse with women, were consumed with passion for one another. Men committed shameless acts with men and received in their own persons the due penalty for their error." To traditionalists, these verses demonstrate that "Paul views homosexuality as a symptom of fallen humanity, describing it as unnatural and unseemly."[86] As evidence for this interpretation, Paul mentions both women and men, and he describes the behaviors in question rather than using words like *malakos* and *arsenokoitês* that modern readers can translate in different ways.[87]

Yet revisionists remain unconvinced, observing that in the verses immediately preceding 26 and 27, Paul refers to pagans' practices during their worship of false gods. Thus many of the same issues relevant to the verses in 1 Corinthians and 1 Timothy also arise here, such as the possibility that male prostitution within pagan temples was the true problem.[88] Further debate centers on what "natural" meant to first-century readers and what happened when people "exchanged natural intercourse for unnatural." In the words of historian John Boswell, "The persons Paul condemns are manifestly not homosexual: what he derogates are homosexual acts committed by apparently heterosexual persons."[89] Departing from their natural inclinations and attractions, then, heterosexuals sinned by participating in same-sex rituals in pagan temples.

Revisionists in recent years have also studied two relationships in the Bible: Ruth and Naomi in the book of Ruth, and Jonathan and David in 1 Samuel and 2 Samuel. The latter relationship, in particular, may have homoerotic overtones. Scholars all agree that the texts do not explicitly mention any sexual intimacy between Jonathan and David, and so the dispute revolves around whether or not the biblical books imply such relations. Traditionalists insist that the relationship was platonic, an example of close bonding between two friends. "Whatever feelings David and Jonathan had for each other," one traditionalist writes, "both were definitely heterosexual in behavior, for both were married and fathered children."[90] Some revisionists, though, read more into what happened between Jonathan and David than the written account describes. The narrative implies, in their view, an actual love affair complete with longing, jealousy, and sorrow.[91]

In marshaling evidence that the Bible does not prohibit homosexual relations between consenting adults, many revisionists go beyond the account of Jonathan and David and the texts in Genesis, Leviticus, 1 Corinthians, 1 Timothy, and Romans, instead appealing to the Bible's broad themes. For instance, through commands, parables, and his personal example, Jesus taught that you must love your neighbor as yourself. He never condemned same-sex relations and often associated with social outcasts like lepers, prostitutes, tax collectors, and the downtrodden. Who are the outcasts of today needing a welcoming message and an open heart? To many revisionists, Jesus's message of inclusion and equality speaks to the slights, insults, and discrimination homosexuals have historically faced and continue to endure today. Enacting Jesus's message therefore requires accepting gays and lesbians as they are and appreciating their struggles in society.[92]

Revisionists also point to Paul's message to the Gentiles as a model for how Christians can include homosexuals among the people of God. Some members of the early Church insisted that Gentiles could not become Christians without first becoming Jewish, which meant circumcising the men. Paul rejected that requirement, declaring that all people — Jewish or Gentile — were justified by faith in Christ rather than adherence to Jewish law. In a like manner, revisionists reason, homosexuals should be welcomed into the Christian community through their faith in Christ without needing to become either straight or celibate.[93]

Traditionalists dismiss these claims. True, Jesus said nothing about homosexuality, but — as some writers observe — he also said nothing about incest. Should we then conclude that incest is morally acceptable if our society starts to embrace it? Traditionalists also note that Paul's statement on Jews and Gentiles addresses a specific theological issue — namely, the means of salvation. Everyone achieves salvation through Christ, but that does not mean that society should tolerate any and all behaviors. To learn what Paul thinks about homosexuality, traditionalists insist, Christians must rely on his passages that explicitly reference it.[94]

And so it goes, back and forth between traditionalists and revisionists, with no end in sight. Interestingly, the debate over the Bible and homosexuality parallels the biblical debates over slavery and divorce in earlier eras. Depending on their methods of interpretation, Christians can read their scriptures in divergent ways on all three issues. On a straightforward, literal reading, the Bible seems to allow slavery, forbid homosexual behavior, and forbid divorce (except possibly because of a spouse's adultery). Christians can find proof texts that support all those positions.

Yet Christians can and do adopt alternative ways of reading the Bible that yield the opposite conclusions. The most common alternatives appeal to either ancient context or the spirit and principles of the Bible. Since human bondage operated differently in ancient times, for example, one could conclude that the Bible's endorsement of ancient slavery did not legitimize American slavery. Similarly, Jesus's restrictive rules against divorce protected Hebrew women during an era when divorce would leave them destitute. Within a contextual interpretation, these rules may be modified because our economic system offers much better opportunities to women. Finally, many scholars contend that the Bible disparaged only the ancient forms of homosexuality, especially pederasty, male prostitution, and sexual rituals in pagan temples. By appealing to this context, Christians can support consensual relationships between same-sex partners today.

To the same end, many Christians also invoke the Bible's spirit and principles, especially the Golden Rule. In the eyes of modern Christians trying to follow the Bible, treating our neighbors as ourselves eliminates even the possibility of slavery. To some adherents of the Golden Rule, the same reasoning applies to divorce; since no one would want to be forced to remain in a dysfunctional marriage, we should not restrict other people's rights to obtain a divorce. In a like manner, the Bible's emphasis on compassion for all of God's children convinces some Christians to allow people holding same-sex attractions to act on their desires within a stable relationship.

In chapters 2 and 3, we learned that over time Christians moved away from literal interpretations of the Bible that once justified slavery and condemned divorce. Enlightenment ideals of personal freedom and individual autonomy eventually reshaped the Western worldview, leading Christians to oppose laws permitting slavery and forbidding divorce. In the current chapter, we see how societal values and beliefs influence Christian perceptions about homosexuality. Back when the general public overwhelmingly viewed homosexuals either as criminals needing punishment or deviants needing treatment, Christians assumed that the Bible denounced homosexuality. Authors did not analyze the biblical record in any detail until gays and lesbians formed a movement and achieved greater acceptance. Several decades later many Christians see nothing inherently objectionable about a same-sex relationship, and they interpret the Bible accordingly.

Personal experience invariably plays a role in the shifting perspectives, for the revisionist literature includes works by authors who are themselves homosexuals. Telltale signs in the books include thanking a same-sex spouse in the acknowledgments and using the pronouns *we* and *us* when referring to gays and lesbians.[95] Other revisionist authors state that they have worked with or ministered to gay and lesbian Christians, finding them just as capable of spiritual growth, service to their communities, and commitment to Christ as heterosexual Christians.[96] One such author recounts his "change in mind and heart" that occurred after he came "to know a great many people who are homosexual that I am now grateful to call my friends."[97] On the other side of the debate, traditionalists bring experiences and predispositions of their own. Many traditionalists, especially the older ones, absorbed from their upbringing beliefs about the evils of homosexual acts. To someone who has always disparaged homosexual behavior, revisionist interpretations grounded in the context of ancient times or the Bible's general principles sound unconvincing.

As this debate has unfolded in recent decades, rank-and-file Catholics, mainline Protestants, evangelical Protestants, and black Protestants have changed their opinions about homosexuals' morality and civil liberties (see figures 4.3 and 4.4). Do those changes mean that ordinary Christians have read and evaluated the literature on the Bible and homosexuality, agreeing in increasing numbers with the revisionist arguments? No, in most cases the processes of change are probably more diffuse than this simple explanation would imply. The exegetical debate occurs primarily in specialized tracts that most Christians do not actually read. Furthermore, the debate sometimes hinges on arcane points of scholarship, such as contending translations of *malakos* and *arsenokoitês* and the disputes over how to understand the homosexual practices Paul described. Revisionist arguments may exert some persuasive influence, but the shift in Christian opinion primarily reflects the tenor of the times. On homosexuality as on other issues, religious believers usually follow the same trends as the rest of society.

## *The Softening Political Rhetoric of Christian Conservatives*

Reflecting the values of a changing society, Christian leaders—including conservative evangelicals—have called for compassion and accepted certain aspects of gay rights. Even as they opposed one important right, same-sex marriage, evangelical leaders softened their political rhetoric. To understand this change, we can examine one of the earliest electoral battles over homosexuality, which occurred in Florida in Dade County (later renamed Miami-Dade County). In 1977 the county passed an ordinance prohibiting discrimination in employment or housing based on a person's sexual orientation. Dade County contained the city of Miami, home to a sizeable gay population, and supporters of gay rights viewed the ordinance as model legislation that other counties and cities might adopt.

What happened next dashed those lofty hopes. The Dade County ordinance provoked a countermovement led by Anita Bryant, a popular singer with four Top 40 singles to her name. Focused initially on a referendum to repeal the Dade County ordinance, Bryant's campaign soon galvanized nationwide resistance to gay rights. Explaining that she entered the political arena after prayer and conversations with her husband and her pastor, Bryant sprinkled her speeches and writings with references to God, Jesus, the Bible, and Christian morality. Christian conservatives rallied to her side, making her one of the first leaders of the movement subsequently labeled as the Christian right.[98] Bryant's denomination, the Southern Baptist Convention, praised her "courageous stand" in a resolution, and the group commended her yet again the following year.[99]

To coordinate her campaign, Bryant formed an organization called Save Our Children. The title was revealing, for it prompted those hearing it to ask: "From what, exactly?" Bryant explained her answer: "Homosexuals cannot reproduce—and so they must recruit. And to freshen their ranks, they must recruit the youth of America."[100] By endorsing a degenerate lifestyle, the Dade County ordinance therefore offered "an open door to homosexual recruitment." Children who resisted the siren's call of temptation could still suffer because, in Bryant's mind, homosexuals commonly engaged in pedophilia. The threat was especially intense in schools, where "a particularly deviant-minded teacher could sexually molest children."[101] To Bryant, this was no idle threat; she believed that homosexuals molested children all across America. People began sending her stories of sexual abuse that gays allegedly committed, and she told a reporter that these accounts "would turn your stomach."[102] In her view, and that of her supporters, Save Our Children captured in its title the reason why the gay rights movement must be stopped.

Within a couple of years, Bryant faded from the national scene after encountering personal and financial difficulties. With Bryant largely on the sidelines, others stepped forward to build the Christian right into a powerful movement. Rev. Jerry Falwell, cofounder of the Moral Majority in 1979, was arguably the most influential such leader among Christian conservatives in the 1980s. Throughout his long career in the public eye, Falwell attacked homosexuality and repudiated the LGBT movement's political agenda, famously blaming 9/11 partly on God's angry response to America's acceptance of the gay lifestyle.[103] Other leaders in the 1980s and 1990s, such as the Christian broadcaster and presidential candidate Pat Robertson, echoed Falwell in denouncing anything and everything associated with homosexuality.

By the second decade of the twenty-first century, however, leaders of the Christian right were using less divisive language on gay rights issues. For example, in 2010 the Family Research Council made an illuminating set of arguments in opposing the repeal of "Don't Ask, Don't Tell." In press releases and e-mail alerts to members, the FRC asserted that overturning the Clinton-era policy would undermine military effectiveness.[104] Among its other arguments, the FRC stated that Congress should focus instead on the economy and that top military officials opposed the new initiative.[105] But the FRC declined to follow in Anita Bryant's footsteps by demonizing homosexuals. The FRC's press releases and e-mail alerts never asserted or even implied that repealing "Don't Ask, Don't Tell" would allow homosexuals throughout society to recruit and sexually molest children. Whether intentionally or not, the FRC treated gays and lesbians with much more respect than Bryant did.

Christian conservatives have also softened their rhetoric on the most visible and controversial gay rights issue of the twenty-first century: marriage. In 2007 prominent Christian intellectuals and organizers formed the National Organization for Marriage (NOM), which counted fighting same-sex marriage among its primary goals. Coordinating with supporters at the state and local levels, NOM distributed information and developed strategies, giving its allies guidance, among other things, on the most effective means of political persuasion. In the section of its website called "Marriage Talking Points," which focused exclusively on same-sex marriage, NOM stated, "Extensive and repeated polling agrees that the single most effective message is: 'Gays and lesbians have a right to live as they choose, they don't have the right to redefine marriage for all of us.' This allows people to express support for tolerance while opposing gay marriage."[106]

For many years opponents of same-sex marriage used this kind of language to explain their positions. While running for vice president on the Republican ticket in 2008, for example, Sarah Palin gave a revealing answer to a question about civil unions and gay marriage. She explained that she opposed extending civil unions beyond Alaska and into the rest of the nation

> if it goes closer and closer towards redefining the traditional definition of marriage between one man and one woman. And unfortunately that's sometimes where those steps lead. But I also want to clarify, if there's any kind of suggestion at all from my answer that I would be anything but tolerant of adults in America choosing their partners, choosing relationships that they deem best for themselves, you know, I am tolerant and I have a very diverse family and group of friends and even within that group you would see some who may not agree with me on this issue, some very dear friends who don't agree with me on this issue.[107]

In her answer Palin followed both elements of NOM's messaging strategy—opposition to "redefining marriage" paired with support for "tolerance"—while avoiding once-common talking points involving deviant behavior, child molestation, and recruitment into the homosexual ranks.

Whether Palin's appeal for tolerance reflected her genuine sentiments or mere expediency, she used language undeniably more favorable to gays and lesbians than Anita Bryant and Jerry Falwell did in earlier decades. With certain exceptions, such as the campaign in 2008 to repeal a court decision for same-sex marriage in California, prominent Christian conservatives now steer clear of describing homosexuals as likely pedophiles. In short, Christian conservatives, through their public discourse, have accommodated modern attitudes about homosexuality. The need to develop and deploy political messages that resonate with Americans has encouraged Christian organizations like NOM and political figures like Sarah Palin to incorporate a central element of the contemporary culture—tolerance—into their rhetoric even as they opposed extending tolerance into support for same-sex marriage.

As of 2013 Christian conservatives had succeeded in preventing same-sex marriage from spreading to the entire country. Over a longer period, however, NOM's poll-tested strategy of political messaging may confront its natural limit. If homosexuals are perverts who deserve criminal punishment or psychiatric treatment, as Americans assumed for much of the twentieth century, then it is obvious why marriage laws should treat such people differently. If, on the other hand, homosexuals are "choosing their partners, choosing relationships that they deem best for themselves," as Sarah Palin explained, it becomes harder to claim that they should not have the right to marry the person of their choice. By showing respect and promoting tolerance, evangelical leaders and their political allies may have helped undermine the policy goals they seek to achieve.

Catholic leaders face a similar dilemma. Responding in 2013 to a question about homosexuality, Pope Francis famously answered, "If a person is gay and seeks the Lord and has good will, who am I to judge that person?"[108] According to commentators around the world, the pope had moved the Catholic Church toward greater acceptance of gays and lesbians.[109] His full statements on this and other occasions, however, contain considerable nuance. Official Catholic teachings, which he explicitly affirmed, have long distinguished between sexual orientation and sexual behavior. While Pope Francis refused to condemn people with same-sex attractions, he embraced the doctrine holding that they sin if they act upon their desires.[110] As we saw in figure 4.3, many ordinary Catholics in America reject this distinction, believing that homosexual relations are "not wrong at all." By advocating tolerance for people with the orientation, the pope ended up promoting tolerance for those who engage in the associated behaviors.

Popes rarely change the Church's official positions, but—as this episode shows—they can accommodate the modern world through the ways they explain those positions. On another occasion in 2013, Pope Francis referred to homosexuality and related issues in saying, "It is not necessary to talk about these issues all the time."[111] Whereas some Protestant groups have actually revised their teachings about the morality of homosexual relationships, such a move is unlikely in the Catholic Church. Institutionally committed to tradition and authority, the Catholic Church pays a great price when it openly overturns a long-standing doctrine. Church leaders can nevertheless adapt to cultural trends by reformulating their rhetoric. Future popes and bishops will likely follow in Pope Francis's footsteps by talking less about homosexuality and by taking a softer tone on the issue.

### The Future of Gay Rights in America

What does contemporary politics portend for homosexuality as a political issue? Polling data confirms that young people are far more liberal than their elders on this subject. In the General Social Survey I use throughout this chapter, young adults (defined to include ages eighteen to twenty-nine) were more liberal on homosexuality than the rest of the population in each year from 1973 to 2012. Given these generational differences, the natural cycles of birth, maturation, and death create steady changes in the views of the overall public. Every year a small percentage of middle-aged and elderly people die, and they are replaced in the voting population by new eighteen-year-olds. This turnover in the population ensures that the liberalizing trends in public opinion continue.

These trends cannot be stabilized or reversed unless people become more conservative on homosexuality as they age. As twentysomethings mature, start careers, get married, raise children, and eventually welcome grandchildren into the world, perhaps they will come to reject the views about homosexuality that characterized their younger years. An age gap would still remain, with young people holding more favorable attitudes than their elders, but the aging process would dampen the liberalizing momentum within the general population.

It turns out, however, that on this issue, Americans actually tend to become more liberal, not more conservative, as they age. This effect appeared with the first cohort of young adults in the GSS surveys, those aged eighteen to twenty-nine in 1973. Using subsequent GSS data through 2012, we can track their attitudes as they reached their thirties, forties, fifties, and sixties. On questions of civil liberties for homosexuals, the cohort of young adults in 1973 held steady in their levels of support until 1988, when they started becoming more liberal. In 2012, now aged fifty-seven to sixty-eight, the cohort supported civil liberties for homosexuals at a rate of 67 percent, higher than the 59 percent they expressed four decades earlier as eighteen- to twenty-nine-year-olds. On the related question of morality, this cohort became more conservative in the 1980s before turning far more liberal in the 1990s and the first decade of the twenty-first century. In 2012, 35 percent of people aged fifty-seven to sixty-eight said homosexual relations were "not wrong at all," whereas only 20 percent of the cohort took that view back in 1973. Incidentally, this finding generalizes well beyond the people who were young adults in 1973. The GSS data show that in 2012 every age cohort (those in their thirties, forties, etc.) held more liberal attitudes about homosexuality (for both civil liberties and morality) than those same cohorts did in their younger years.

Of course, the tendency for Americans to become more liberal on homosexuality with age does not change the fact that at any single point in time, younger people are much more liberal than older people. In addition, the younger Americans entering the adult population increasingly take a live-and-let-live attitude on homosexuality. Each year's set of eighteen- to twenty-nine-year-olds from 1993 to 2012 held more liberal attitudes (again, on both civil liberties and morality) than earlier groups did at the same age. As a result, the last group of young adults in 2012 was the most supportive on record.

Reflecting the changes in public opinion, the GSS eventually expanded its range of questions. For the first time in 1988 and then regularly since 2004, the GSS solicited Americans' views about same-sex marriage. Inter-

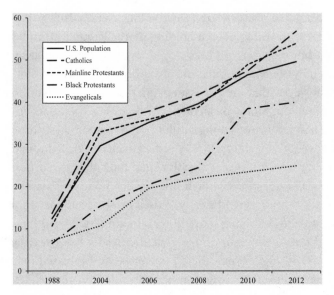

**Figure 4.6.**
Percentage supporting same-sex marriage
*Source:* General Social Survey

viewers asked respondents whether "homosexual couples should have the right to marry one another." Figure 4.6 plots the percentage of the general public, as well as four Christian subgroups, who "strongly agree" or "agree" that homosexual couples should have equal marriage rights.

In 1988, as figure 4.6 indicates, only 12 percent of the American public wanted to legalize same-sex marriage. That figure rose to 30 percent in 2004 and 50 percent in 2012—a fourfold increase in about two decades, albeit from a low starting point. Among the major Christian groups, the pattern is familiar by now. In each year captured on the graph, Catholics and mainline Protestants resemble the overall US population. Evangelical Protestants and black Protestants consistently express lower levels of support, but both groups' numbers trend upward with the rest of the American population. It is noteworthy that a greater share of evangelicals (25 percent) and black Protestants (40 percent) endorsed gay marriage in 2012 than the general public did (12 percent) in 1988.

Paralleling other public opinion questions relating to homosexuality, the American public divides by age. In 1988 only 14 percent of people aged eighteen to twenty-nine wanted to legalize same-sex marriage. Twenty-four years later in 2012, when those same people were now aged forty-two to fifty-three, their level of support had risen to 52 percent.

Meanwhile, the new group of young adults in 2012 approved of gay marriage at an even higher rate of 65 percent. With population replacement compounding the effects of people growing more liberal as they age, public support for same-sex marriage continued to rise in the following years.

How will Christian leaders respond as the views of their members and the broader society keep changing? Will Christian leaders coming of age in a society with much less animus toward homosexuals develop attitudes and beliefs different from their predecessors? As Yogi Berra once said, "It's tough to make predictions, especially about the future." For the case at hand, we can nevertheless use the history of similar issues, of which divorce might be the closest parallel, to guess what will happen with homosexuality. Both divorce and homosexuality relate to family values and involve personal morality. The two issues, too, have each attracted attention and lobbying from Christian groups in different periods.

Over the course of American history, the public has altered its judgments of both issues. From the founding of the American colonies through much of the twentieth century, local communities frequently regarded divorcées as moral degenerates. As marriages fractured at increasing rates in the nineteenth and especially the twentieth centuries, divorce gradually lost its social stigma. A similar pattern has happened with homosexuality. In the not-too-distant past, gays and lesbians commonly kept their sexual orientations private to avoid jeopardizing their relationships with employers, family members, and heterosexual friends. In today's dramatically different environment, growing numbers of straight people accept gays and lesbians, especially those they know personally. The norm of tolerance, in fact, has spread so widely that conservative politicians and Christian leaders tout their own tolerance.

As with divorce, Christians have modified their views of homosexuality and adjusted their political stances. On a literal reading, the Bible seems clear in forbidding both divorce (except possibly on grounds of a partner's adultery) and homosexual acts. Indeed, many Christian groups historically took a hard line on both issues and pressed their governments to protect the moral order through restrictive laws. Modern scholars and advocates, however, often interpret the Bible as more open to divorce and homosexuality than it first appears. In both cases, the reinterpretations emerged within cultural environments that increasingly rejected the stringent legal requirements and societal attitudes of earlier times.

For the most part, ordinary Christians do not form their views by engaging modern biblical interpretations at a deep level. In the more common process, Christians bring to their religious communities the norms and values they absorb from the larger society, with the new biblical interpretations following and reinforcing rather than preceding and causing the changing attitudes. Several generations ago, churches made the then-controversial decision to welcome divorced people into their congregations. In the late twentieth and early twenty-first centuries, some churches made a similar move in welcoming homosexuals as members in good standing.

In an obvious difference between the two issues, the long-term interplay between public opinion, religious accommodation, and changes in public policy is complete (more or less) for divorce. The same point could be made for slavery, an issue that Christian groups debated in the eighteenth and nineteenth centuries. On homosexuality, by contrast, the transformations are ongoing and people are still divided. Roughly half of the American public backed same-sex marriage in 2012 and believed homosexual relations were "not wrong at all"; the other half disagreed. Given the current rates at which attitudes are changing, it might take until 2020 or 2030 before an overwhelming majority (say, 75 percent) of Americans takes the progay positions. As the levels of support increase, we can expect that many more states will legalize same-sex marriage. The US Supreme Court, meanwhile, could make a decision legalizing same-sex marriage nationwide. Indeed, at the beginning of its 2014–2015 term, the Supreme Court accepted on appeal a case that could lead to a landmark change in the constitutionality of bans on same-sex marriage.

How will organizations that represent Christian conservatives react to a situation where most or all states allow gay marriage? Again, the history of divorce may provide some insights. Once divorce became common and Christians began opposing strict laws regulating it, their leaders backed away from divorce as a political issue. This outcome does not mean that Christian leaders now approve of divorce; to the contrary—as explained in the previous chapter—many of them still call it a blight on society and a threat to children's well-being. But those same leaders bowed to the reality of divorce in American society and among their members. Lacking a constituency to limit divorce, Christian leaders removed the issue from their list of political priorities. Divorce became a private issue handled by individual families and churches rather than a public issue marked by intense lobbying, voter mobilization, and political conflict.

If public opinion continues along its current trend, the issue of homosexuality will wind up in the same place. Such a result would not require all or even most Christian leaders to embrace homosexual behavior as normal and legitimate. Instead those who deem it sinful would merely need to treat the issue, like divorce, as a question for private morality rather than public policy. They would give up the fight to repeal same-sex marriage in individual states or the country at large. Christian leaders and affiliated organizations would deemphasize homosexuality as a staple of fundraising appeals, campaign alerts, mass rallies, and other forms of political engagement, and they would no longer use the issue to determine which candidates to endorse for public office.

A development of this kind may sound like mere speculation. The same would have been said of someone who in 1890 predicted that Christian leaders of future generations would downplay divorce as a political issue. In the first half of the twentieth century, no one expected that one day homosexuals would come out of the closet, engage in sexual relations without fearing arrest, see favorable portrayals of themselves in movies and television shows, and gain the right to serve in the military. Compared to the massive changes in attitudes, beliefs, institutions, and laws that have already occurred, it is not far-fetched to anticipate a future in which Christian leaders either embrace same-sex marriage outright, as some have already done, or accommodate it by redirecting their political efforts elsewhere.

# *Abortion*

5

Oh no—not a chapter on abortion! Is there anything original left to say on the subject? Doesn't everybody already understand the deep roots of religious perspectives on this issue?

Actually, most people know little about how Christian groups arrived at their current positions. During the 1800s, for example, conservative Protestants refused to join physicians in seeking to outlaw most abortions. Why? Many Protestants today believe that the Bible requires them to take a strong antiabortion stance. Why did their predecessors disagree? How have new translations of an obscure verse in Exodus made it easier for some Protestants to assert that the Bible treats abortion as murder?

Catholics, too, handled abortion differently in earlier times. Like death and taxes, the Catholic stance on abortion seems like a permanent fixture of our world. In reality, however, popes and councils have refined the Church's position over the centuries according to prevailing beliefs about when life begins. The Church's political involvement on abortion has also changed over time, which raises many interesting questions. For example, why didn't the Catholic Church in America advocate for restrictive abortion laws during the nineteenth century? Similarly, why have Catholic Bibles declined to translate the disputed verse in Exodus in a way that would give moral and political support to the pro-life cause? The answers to these questions, we will see, yield plenty of surprises.

## *Ensoulment and Quickening*

The Catholic Church considers itself a continuing institution rooted in the ministry of the apostles and lasting into the present. Throughout this long history, which included disputes between papal and secular authorities, the spread of Christianity to new lands, the turmoil of the Reformation, and the challenges of modernity, the Catholic Church has declared abortion sinful. According to the Didache, an early Christian document dating from the first or second century, "Thou shalt not procure abortion, nor commit infanticide."[1] Written about the same time, the letter of Barnabas used similar language in commanding, "Thou shalt not murder the child by abortion, nor again shalt thou kill it when it is born."[2] In the following centuries, theologians, popes, and ecumenical councils were nearly unanimous in opposing all abortions. In 1679 Pope Innocent XI condemned a theological position that had justified abortion under certain circumstances.[3]

During most of Catholic history, abortion raised difficult questions about ensoulment, the process through which—according to Church tradition—developing embryos gain human souls. The earliest Christians could learn about ensoulment from the Septuagint, the ancient translation of the Old Testament into Greek. Borrowing from Aristotle and other Greek philosophers, the Septuagint distinguished between a "formed" and an "unformed" fetus. Aristotle believed that males acquire human souls at forty days after conception, while females require ninety days.[4] Although they did not always accept Aristotle's precise dating, influential theologians such as St. Augustine, St. Jerome, and St. Thomas all agreed that ensoulment occurred sometime after conception.[5]

This understanding affected how the Church punished abortion at different stages of a pregnancy. As compiled and codified in 1140 by Gratian, an influential jurist from Bologna, canon law stated that abortions before the fetus was formed or animated were not homicide.[6] Passed down through the Middle Ages, canon law stipulated a lesser penance for early abortions than those a woman sought later in her term. Pope Sixtus V reversed course in 1588, applying the penalty of excommunication for women who obtained abortions at any time during a pregnancy. These stringent requirements lasted only three years, though, because Pope Gregory XIV in 1591 instructed Church officials to punish women more lightly if they aborted an unanimated fetus.[7]

The recurring theological discussions about ensoulment and animation hinged not on whether abortion was a sin—all Church authorities agreed on that point—but rather its severity at different points in a pregnancy. Among theologians who promoted the Aristotelian doctrine of "delayed animation" (a strong majority during most of the Church's history), early abortions were forbidden for the same reasons as contraception and masturbation.[8] Any acts that prevented an embryo from developing into a human being, or that wasted or spilled sperm, destroyed potential life and severed the connection between sex and procreation. The Church treated artificial forms of birth control, masturbation, and early abortions less harshly than many other offenses. By contrast, Church authorities consistently labeled postanimation abortion as homicide and required severe penalties through penance.[9]

The Church's long-running distinctions between early and late abortions influenced legal codes throughout Christendom, including England. For purposes of determining criminality, the secular law drew the line at quickening, the point at which a woman first feels her fetus move.[10] While varying from one woman to another, quickening usually occurs during the fourth or fifth month of gestation. Beyond its value to secular courts as a definitive date the mother could verify, quickening had some precedent in the Church as the moment of ensoulment. Early in the thirteenth century, Pope Innocent III called quickening a sign that the fetus was now animated, and he explained that abortion before that moment did not constitute homicide.[11]

As it developed during the Middle Ages, English common law made abortion a crime only when performed after quickening. Centuries of theological disputes about animation and ensoulment, which had offered many possible dates, yielded the single standard of quickening for determining when abortion was legal. With that marker in place, the common law departed from Church tradition in two key respects. First, the common law did not criminalize abortions before quickening, whereas the Church traditionally viewed them as less serious than homicide but still sinful. Second, the common law regarded postquickening abortions as a lesser offense than did the ecclesiastical authorities, who considered them homicide. The common law, then, treated abortions both before and after quickening more lightly than did the Church.[12]

As the great English jurist Sir Edward Coke stated in 1644, "If a woman be quicke with childe, and by a potion or otherwise killeth it in her wombe; or if a man beat her, whereby the childe dieth in her body, and she is delivered of a dead childe, this is a great misprision, and no murder."[13] Coke emphasized that the legal prohibition applied only to women who were "quicke with childe," meaning that the law permitted abortions before quickening. Furthermore, Coke noted that the law rejected murder charges for abortions after quickening, instead calling the offense "a great misprision," or what today we label as a serious misdemeanor. As Britain gained international power and expanded its American colonies in the next century, the common law's approach to abortion endured. Writing in 1769, the famous English judge William Blackstone reiterated Coke's summary of the common law, saying that abortions were a "heinous misdemeanor" — though again, only if a woman was "quick with child."[14]

The common law, we must remember, included precedents from judges throughout England and later Great Britain. To compile and summarize the common law, Coke and Blackstone surveyed the legal terrain and described the law as judges usually defined and practiced it. Because their writings were so influential, Coke and Blackstone helped solidify the tradition even further. But individual judges sometimes made decisions that departed from the common law, and scholars have uncovered English cases in which judges punished a woman for a prequickening abortion.[15] Additionally, abortions before quickening were not uniformly legal at all times and places in the colonies. In a notable deviation from the overall pattern, New York City in 1716 passed a statute prohibiting midwives from performing or advising on any abortions, regardless of the stage in a pregnancy.[16] As a general rule, abortion before quickening was legal in the British Empire, but exceptions existed too.

The common law continued to influence the American states long after they gained independence. In the American republic's first judicial case on abortion, the Supreme Judicial Court of Massachusetts held in 1812 that the government could not prosecute someone for administering an abortion drug or potion if the woman had not reached quickening.[17] This decision restated the centuries-old provision of the common law. The first statutory law on abortion, passed in Connecticut in 1821, also conformed to the tradition by prohibiting potions given to induce abortion after quickening.[18] Prequickening abortions remained legal, as had usually been true since the colonial period.

Abortion attracted little political attention in the following decades, and thirteen of the thirty-three states in the union in 1860 still had no laws regulating it. Most of the other twenty states followed the quickening doctrine and thereby left abortion unregulated for the first few months of a pregnancy. Because the relevant state provisions appeared in omnibus bills covering broad sections of the criminal code, legislatures rarely, if ever, voted separately on abortion. Public interest on the matter was low, the press seldom covered it, and no grassroots movements sought to influence lawmakers one way or the other.[19]

### Abortion and American Culture in the Nineteenth Century

Women during this era obtained abortions prior to quickening through the available methods of the day. Physical techniques such as horseback riding, vigorous jumping, and blows to the midsection were often tried but had a low success rate. If prepared properly, pills or potions derived from herbs such as pennyroyal, hellebore, tansy, savin, and seneca snakeroot were more effective. When they worked, the herbal remedies made a woman so sick that her body expelled the fetus.[20] The best techniques were surgical, for a trained practitioner could practically guarantee a successful abortion. As early as 1842 medical professionals began performing abortions with the help of the curette, an instrument for scraping tissue.[21] Lacking antibiotics and ignorant of modern antiseptic techniques, however, abortion providers sometimes inadvertently spread infections to the mother that subsequently killed her.[22]

Given the absence of comprehensive records, it is impossible to know with precision how many women in America obtained abortions in the 1800s. We can gain some clues by considering the demographics of abortion seekers. Writers from early in the nineteenth century noted that abortions were the common recourse of unmarried women who did not marry the fathers of their unborn children. Through rape, seduction, or consensual sex, a man could impregnate a woman and then refuse to marry her. Abortion often became her only alternative to living in poverty and incurring her community's shame as a fornicator. The doctor who discovered the abortion-inducing properties of seneca snakeroot, for example, wrote that its main users were "women who had indulged in illegitimate love."[23] One of the leading legal authorities on medical practices similarly observed: "The practice of causing abortion is resorted to by unmarried females, who, through imprudence or misfortune, have become pregnant, to avoid the disgrace which would attach to them from having a living child." The infrequent cases involving married women reflected their desires "to obviate a repetition of peculiarly severe labour-pains, which they may have previously suffered."[24]

With the exception of rape survivors, many of them slaves, it was uncommon in early America for single women to become pregnant and then not marry the father. When sex between unmarried partners led to a pregnancy, family and community pressure normally forced the couple to tie the knot. The high number of births occurring within a few months after a wedding testified to what later generations called "shotgun marriages."[25] Such marriages saved the family from disgrace and reduced the demand for abortions. With abortion restricted primarily to single women who did not marry the father, the overall abortion rate must have been low in the American republic's early decades. An extensive diary from a midwife operating in northern New England from 1785 to 1812, for example, makes no reference to abortion, which suggests it was rare or nonexistent among her clients.[26]

After 1840, amid westward migrations, urban growth, and the rise of an industrial economy, the demographics and the incidence of abortion shifted. Newspapers carried advertisements from abortion providers who used either surgical techniques or pills and potions. The prevalence of advertising pointed to an open market for the desired service, and observers noted the growth in the number of abortion providers. In 1871 the *New York Times* identified "a great number of male and female physicians" in the city who performed abortions, along with about two hundred "quacks" offering the same service.[27]

Concentrated primarily within the medical profession, opponents of abortion lamented both its rising rate and its spread to all segments of the population. One doctor informed his readers that abortion "belongs to, and is practiced by, the married and the unmarried; the rich and the poor; the learned and the unlearned."[28] Abortion, like the nation itself, was democratizing. According to "the testimony of American physicians prior to 1840," another doctor remarked in 1895, "Abortion was not practised by married women, but now the testimony is that all this changed."[29] The *Medico-Legal Journal* noted the frequency of abortions "among the very poor because of their true poverty; among the middle classes who feel they cannot afford to rear children and still maintain such a position in society as they wish; and sad though it may seem, among the wealthy and well-to-do, who will not assume the care of children, and who are able to secure reasonably safe professional ability."[30]

The best available evidence indicates that most of these abortions happened before quickening. Many of the newspaper advertisements explicitly referred to the early months of a pregnancy, presumably because women most often sought abortions during that period.[31] Confirming this inference, an article in a prominent medical journal stated that abortion "is most frequently done before the end of the third month, before marked enlargement of the abdomen has occurred. . . . Not many women will bring on an abortion after they have detected quickening."[32]

## *The Religious Response—and Nonresponse—to Abortion*

How did leaders of the nation's largest religious groups react to the rising abortion rates? Given the pro-life orientations many religious leaders have held from the 1970s to the present, one might expect their predecessors to have fought for limiting the availability of abortion. Many scholars have scoured the historical record of the 1800s to learn about all aspects of abortion, including the statements and positions of religious leaders. Documents from the period are striking for their omissions: no scholars have yet uncovered a single instance of a Protestant clergyman denouncing abortion or advocating tighter laws between 1776 and 1857.[33]

James Mohr, who wrote an influential book on the history of abortion in America, conducted a comprehensive search, examining several decades of nine religious periodicals plus the minutes of four large denominations.[34] Prior to the Civil War, the periodicals addressed the abortion issue only twice, with the articles covering the arrest and trial of someone accused of killing a woman during a botched procedure. Neither story quoted religious leaders or commented on the morality of abortion per se.[35] Other scholars since Mohr also investigated the history of abortion in America, uncovering a treasure trove of relevant material—and yet, like Mohr, they found no evidence of Protestant leaders between 1776 and 1857 denouncing abortion.[36] My own search, which included untold numbers of scanned documents available through Google Books, was also fruitless. At least one prominent minister objected to abortion in the early part of the colonial period, when abortion seekers were almost entirely unmarried women.[37] Perhaps a handful of other ministers, as yet unknown to scholars, spoke in a similar vein after America became a nation. Should such cases be discovered, my claims here would need to be modified to read: "Only a tiny minority of religious leaders denounced abortion from the nation's founding until shortly before the Civil War."

Religious leaders' silence during that period might seem perplexing when considering the rising number of abortions, their increased incidence among married women of the middle class, and the legality of abortions before quickening. In light of these realities, why didn't clergymen or denominational leaders condemn abortion and press for laws to prohibit it? To address this question, we can consider the situation among Catholics before turning to Protestants. Known for its vigorous opposition to abortion today, the Catholic Church could have been equally vocal in the nineteenth century—and yet it wasn't. Catholic authorities had always viewed abortions as sinful, albeit usually with distinctions according to the period of gestation; so why didn't the Catholic hierarchy proclaim those teachings loudly for Catholics and non-Catholics alike to hear?

The most likely answer is that Catholic authorities used homilies, confession, penance, and other means of instruction to teach the Church's position on abortion to their parishioners but not the larger society. The available evidence indicates that this private instruction did, in fact, succeed in discouraging abortions by Catholics. Close observers testified that Catholics aborted at a far lower rate than Protestants. One doctor relayed his experience that Protestant women procure abortions "without any apparent misgivings of its gross impropriety—provided the act is anterior to 'quickening,'" whereas "Catholic women—or at least, those I have attended, while threatened with abortion, have invariably been much distressed with the fear that they would abort, and have urged that nothing should be left undone to save the babe."[38] Horatio Storer, the most influential leader of the antiabortion movement of the nineteenth century, toured the country to publicize the cause and talked to many women who had obtained abortions. "Several hundreds of Protestant women have personally acknowledged to us their guilt," Storer wrote with his coauthor, "against whom only seven Catholics."[39]

Given that they apparently taught the immorality of abortion to their parishioners, why didn't Catholic leaders publicize their opposition in hopes of reforming the entire society? The silence of Catholic leaders reflected the particular challenges they faced in America and their desire to avoid provoking the Protestant majority. When Thomas Jefferson penned the Declaration of Independence, Catholics were only 0.2 percent of the American population, and their numbers had grown to only 5.3 percent by 1850.[40] Disproportionately foreign-born, Catholics endured considerable distrust and sometimes even discrimination. The anti-immigrant movement, reflected most notably in the Know-Nothing Party, stoked fears of a Catholic takeover of America. Catholic leaders responded by avoiding the divisive realm of politics, focusing instead on building churches and forming institutions to serve their own communities.[41]

The bishops in America explained their approach to politics in open letters to their parishioners. The most important of these letters, signed by multiple bishops as a collective, allowed the American arm of the Church to make something close to authoritative pronouncements. The earliest letters focused on spiritual matters and made no mention of politics. In 1837 several bishops finally addressed politics, but only to deny the charge that the Catholic Church was a foreign influence bent on infiltrating the political machinery of the United States. While affirming the "civil and political allegiance" of Catholics to the various states and the federal government, the bishops denied any political ambitions: "We do not aspire to power, we do not calculate by what process we should be able, at some future day, to control the councils of the republic."[42] After describing a few years later the "virulence," "ruin," "passions," "bribery," "infamy," and "recklessness" endemic to electoral campaigns, the bishops implored their followers: "Beloved brethren, flee this contamination."[43] In refraining from advocating restrictive laws on abortion, Catholic bishops followed their general stance prior to the Civil War of bypassing politics in favor of providing instruction to parishioners at an individual level. Fearing the backlash that might result, they were careful to avoid any stance that might suggest political aims.

## Protestants and Abortion in the 1800s

With their deep roots from colonial America, Protestant churches felt no such fear. The inattention of Protestant leaders to abortion there-

fore appears at first difficult to explain. Unlike their Catholic counterparts, Protestant leaders regularly engaged political issues such as divorce, slavery, Sunday closing laws, blasphemy laws, women's rights,
and temperance and Prohibition. The absence of a Protestant antiabortion movement is therefore a puzzle needing an explanation.

Centuries of Christian tradition had declared abortions sinful while
distinguishing the severity of those performed before and after animation. Although they could have embraced this tradition and applied it to
the contemporary American context, Protestant leaders were limited by
their theological orientation. The Reformation revolved in part around
whether tradition possessed any independent authority for Christians,
with Catholics answering yes and Protestants no. Christian tradition
should be affirmed, Protestants believed, only if it flowed from the
Bible — a principle captured in the phrase *sola scriptura*. In the Protestant view, historical doctrines on subjects such as indulgences, purga-
tory, the Eucharist, and the means of salvation deviated from the one and
only source of authority, the Bible.

Interestingly, the two leading figures of the Reformation — Martin
Luther and John Calvin — agreed with the Christian tradition in regarding abortion a serious sin, but neither man gave sustained attention to
the topic. In their collected writings, which span many volumes, abortion receives only a handful of lines.[44] Operating three centuries after the
split from Catholicism, Protestant leaders in America probably had not
read or had not remembered what the two great Reformation leaders said
about abortion. Still, these American Protestants followed in the footsteps of Luther and Calvin by reading the Bible and basing their doctrines on it. The principle of *sola scriptura* persisted, even though many
of Luther's and Calvin's specific statements about topics such as abortion had been forgotten.

Given that they believed in scriptural authority, why didn't Protestant leaders simply open the Bible and see that it informs and sustains
the Christian tradition by forbidding abortion? The answer, which may
sound shocking to some readers, is that those leaders could read the
Bible cover to cover without encountering any mentions of abortion. Not
a single verse explicitly covers the subject, nor do any verses describe the
act of abortion while giving it another name.[45] But the absence of explicit
references did not leave Protestants bereft of biblical resources that could

be marshaled to address the topic. In the 1970s and thereafter, conservative Protestants read a range of biblical passages to indicate that personhood begins once a sperm fertilizes an egg, thereby indicating that abortion is wrong.

Surely their predecessors in the early decades of the American republic made and publicized such a claim, right? Actually, until shortly before the Civil War, Protestant leaders in America did not speak out against abortion, let alone cite their scriptures as support. It is possible that some Protestant leaders privately interpreted the Bible to affirm the existence of human life at conception, and yet they never said so publicly. Such a scenario seems unlikely, however, because it would require that those leaders remained quiet as abortion rates increased. American women received abortions within the framework of permissive norms and laws that either regulated abortion lightly or, in about one-third of the states before 1860, placed no statutory limits at all. With their religious leaders declining to address the subject, the women who procured early-term abortions could have believed they were doing nothing wrong.

Physicians opposed to abortion often suspected that women failed to understand the moral gravity of the situation. Reporting in 1869 on women who came to him for abortions, a medical school professor with extensive clinical experience explained their beliefs "that the foetus is not alive, but only has, as one might say, a capacity for living, and hence that, to destroy it was not homicide, and hardly more criminal than to prevent conception." Another doctor and former professor gave a similar lament: "I have been often called upon by ladies of the most undoubted character, who very innocently suppose that it cannot be wrong to produce an abortion, so long as there is no quickening."[46] Protestant leaders of the nineteenth century would not have left that perception unchallenged if they believed that the Bible considered a fertilized egg to be a human being. Like most Americans, Protestant leaders accepted abortions prior to quickening without examining the matter in a careful and detailed way.

## *The Physicians' Campaign against Abortion*

Historians have shown that when abortion laws finally aroused major controversy, the driving pressure came from physicians, not religious leaders.[47] Physicians had two reasons for attempting to forbid abortion. First, they were familiar with the growing body of scientific knowledge about pregnancy. In 1827 Karl Ernst von Baer showed that mammals develop from a fertilized egg.[48] Informed by this and other findings, authoritative books and articles soon portrayed embryonic development as a continuous process rather than one with a clear divide at the point of quickening. To learned doctors, outlawing abortion was therefore a moral imperative because human life existed throughout a pregnancy. Physicians knew that they faced an uphill battle to convince ordinary Americans of this scientific understanding. According to one group of physicians, "The majority of people, erroneously believing there is no life previous to the fourth month of pregnancy, believe there is no crime committed in the practice before that period."[49]

Physicians also pushed for tighter controls on abortion to advance their economic interests in forming and consolidating the medical profession. In the 1800s many providers of health services lacked the education, training, and credentials that medical schools offered. The "regular" physicians, as they were called, wanted to strengthen the system of medical schools, create and disseminate scientific knowledge through medical journals, and improve standards by imposing licensing requirements on practitioners. These moves would professionalize the practice of medicine, improve its stature in the public eye, and eliminate competition from the "irregulars." Because abortions were disproportionately performed by midwives, distributors of folk remedies, and people without formal training, prohibiting abortion would advance the larger goal of professionalizing the practice of medicine.[50] Physicians sought to limit the availability of abortion as early as the 1830s, and they redoubled their efforts after 1859, when the American Medical Association called on doctors "publicly to enter an earnest and solemn protest against such unwarrantable destruction of human life" and to work with legislatures and governors to revise the laws on abortion.[51]

Physicians needed coalition partners to achieve their aims, and they viewed religious leaders as their natural allies. If the clergy of major denominations embraced the cause, the moral force of the pulpit could instruct women about the evils of abortion and thereby reduce the demand for it. The chairman of a physicians' committee on abortion explained this reasoning: "We are also convinced that a wide-spread diffusion of the necessary information among women, by those in whom they have confidence as moral and religious instructors, will in a very brief cycle very perceptibly diminish, and finally almost entirely prevent, the commission of the crime of abortion."[52] Physicians also hoped religious leaders would join the campaign to influence lawmakers. Recognizing these possibilities, the American Medical Association urged "each medical society" to appoint a delegation "to visit every clergyman within their respective districts."[53] In the words of one such appeal, "Let the Medical Society of Pennsylvania, then, in the name of religion, purity, and woman's elevation, beg, nay implore, all Christian ministers to organize and make systematic preparations for a well-concerted attack upon . . . the great vice of our day, the murder of unborn babies."[54]

These physicians achieved modest victories when two Catholic bishops and several Congregationalist leaders in New England and the Great Lakes states publicly denounced abortion.[55] The Presbyterian Church in the United States of America, a group known informally as Old School Presbyterians, made arguably the most important statement in 1869: "This Assembly regards the destruction by parents of their own offspring, before birth, with abhorrence, as a crime against God and against nature; and as the frequency of such murders can no longer be concealed, we hereby warn those that are guilty of this crime that, except they repent, they cannot inherit eternal life."[56]

Despite this full-throated endorsement from Old School Presbyterians, physicians failed to win the backing of other Christian groups. One leading doctor expressed his amazement "that Christian communities should especially be found to tolerate and to practice" abortion. Another physician observed, "Our clergy, with some very few exceptions, have thus far hesitated to enter upon an open crusade against it."[57] After thanking the Catholic bishop of Baltimore and the Old School Presbyterians for their firm positions, a writer on health and social reform chastised the Christian groups who had not condemned abortion, including New School Presbyterians, Baptists, Methodists, Episcopalians, Unitarians, and others.[58] The Old School Presbyterians pleaded for assistance: "We also exhort those who have been called to preach the gospel, and all who love purity and the truth, and who would avert the just judgments of Almighty God from the nation, that they be no longer silent."[59]

This call for their Christian brethren to "be no longer silent" failed to inspire an outpouring of support. Acting within a cultural milieu that influenced their beliefs, opinions, and actions, most Protestant leaders said nothing one way or the other. A clergyman testifying before a hearing in Michigan downplayed the importance of abortion, explaining, "I hardly think we can say that this is the great crime of the nineteenth century."[60] In the eyes of a leading physician, this lack of concern reflected the fact that clergymen, lawyers, and members of other professions did not understand a crucial finding of modern science: "Physiology teaches us that life is manifest as soon as the ovum is impregnated."[61] School curricula placed little emphasis on science, and in any case, most Americans of that era received few if any years of formal education.[62] Scientifically oriented doctors who read medical journals rejected the doctrine of quickening, but ordinary people and their clergy were not ready to abandon it.

The religious dynamics of abortion took a new twist in 1869, when Pope Pius IX issued a statement eliminating the concept of animation from Catholic doctrine once and for all. Whereas the Catholic Church used to punish late-term abortions more severely than those early in a pregnancy, the pope now declared all abortions to be equally sinful, all demanding the punishment of excommunication. Conversations within the Catholic Church continued over therapeutic abortions to protect the life of the mother, but after 1869 no one could justify a lesser penalty on grounds that the fetus was not yet animated. Interestingly, the pope's statement received only scattered coverage in Catholic publications and periodicals in America.[63] Although some individual bishops (notably in Baltimore) denounced abortion, Catholic authorities in America did not unite to push for legal restrictions.

### The Era of Tight Controls on Abortion

Having failed to build a broad coalition with Christian leaders, physicians sustained the political campaign against abortion almost single-handedly. Over the course of several decades, these efforts led to major legislative changes throughout the country. After 1860 many states passed laws removing the traditional distinction between abortions performed before and after quickening, and some laws subjected both women and abortion providers to criminal punishment. Many states banned advertising for abortion services, and in 1873 Congress outlawed any such advertising nationwide. By the end of the nineteenth century, prosecutors and courts worked to enforce the antiabortion statutes on the books.[64] Within a few decades abortion went from being mostly legal to mostly illegal, the exception in most states being abortions to save the mother's life.

Possessing remarkable staying power, the laws enacted in the second half of the nineteenth century faced no serious challenges from an organized, grassroots movement until the 1960s. The actual practice of abortion, however, departed from the letter of the law. Legal prohibitions did not eliminate abortion but rather drove it underground. Some women, especially the poorer and less educated ones, continued to obtain abortions from "irregular" medical practitioners. When performed by untrained or unscrupulous providers, these abortions were sometimes deadly and came to be known as "back-alley" abortions.[65] The better-off women in society often persuaded their doctors to perform abortions in a clinical setting with higher standards for competence and cleanliness. Individual doctors enjoyed considerable autonomy, and some of them justified abortions by expansively interpreting the "health of the mother" exceptions.[66]

Several factors combined to finally bring abortion back to the nation's political agenda in the 1960s. As a journalist reported in *Life* at the end of the decade, "Abortion laws are under concerted attack by doctors, clergy, social workers, and, perhaps most effectively, by increasing numbers of women."[67] The first inkling of reform occurred in 1959 when the American Law Institute, an organization founded "to clarify, modernize, and otherwise improve the law," recommended changing state laws to allow abortions for cases of rape or incest, fetal deformities, and threats to the health of the mother.[68] In 1965 the American Medical Association's board of trustees endorsed these proposed reforms.[69] Given the respect Americans accorded the medical profession, the AMA's endorsement brought new attention to the reform cause.

Prompted by the prospect of looser abortion laws, Catholic leaders responded differently than their predecessors did in the 1800s. Catholic leaders during that earlier era, aware of the tenuous status of Catholicism as a small, immigrant-based religion, directed their antiabortion teachings almost exclusively to their own parishioners. From the mid-1800s to the mid-1900s, Catholics had quadrupled as a share of the population, had entered the mainstream of American life, and had attained some of the highest-ranking positions in business, law, academia, medicine, and government. Representing an institution now strong enough to participate actively in American politics, Catholic leaders voiced their stance both inside and outside the Church. In 1969 the National Conference of Catholic Bishops stated "with strong conviction and growing concern our opposition to abortion." After repudiating the reforms the American Medical Association recommended, the bishops continued: "We strongly urge a renewed positive attitude toward life and a new commitment to its protection and support."[70]

As the reform movement grew increasingly vocal in the late 1960s and early 1970s, Protestant groups also entered the fray. In the nineteenth century the Presbyterian Church in the United States of America was the only Protestant denomination to issue a statement opposing abortion.[71] The group no longer existed as a separate entity after 1958, when it merged with the United Presbyterian Church of North America to form a new denomination called the United Presbyterian Church in the United States of America (UPCUSA). In a 1970 booklet, the UPCUSA stated that "abortion should be taken out of the realm of the law altogether and be made a matter of the careful ethical decision of a woman, her physician and her pastor or other counselor."[72] To implement this recommendation, states would need to repeal their laws and leave abortion unregulated from a legal standpoint. The next year the United Church of Christ took a similar position in its resolution "Freedom of Choice concerning Abortion."[73]

Three other denominations—the Episcopal Church, the United Methodist Church, and the Southern Baptist Convention—all took a more measured position. Although individuals and local bodies within the three groups had already engaged the subject of abortion, none of these denominations had ever taken an official stand. The General Convention of the Episcopal Church in 1967 endorsed reforming state laws "to permit the termination of pregnancy, where the decision to terminate has been arrived at with proper safeguards against abuse, and where it has been clearly established that the physical health of the mother is threatened seriously, or where there is substantial reason to believe that the child would be born badly deformed in mind or body, or where pregnancy has resulted from forcible rape or incest."[74] The Episcopal Church thus allied itself with the reform movement, for these were the same conditions for permissible abortions that the American Law Institute and the American Medical Association had proposed. The next year the United Methodist Church released a statement supporting the right to an abortion under the same circumstances.[75] In 1971 the Southern Baptist Convention added its voice to the growing chorus among Protestant denominations: "We call upon Southern Baptists to work for legislation that will allow the possibility of abortion under such conditions as rape, incest, clear evidence of severe fetal deformity, and carefully ascertained evidence of the likelihood of damage to the emotional, mental, and physical health of the mother."[76]

The doctors, women, and Protestant groups wanting to reform state laws soon achieved a measure of success. By the end of 1972, fourteen states had reformed their laws according to the recommendations of the American Law Institute, American Medical Association, and the Episcopalian, United Methodist, and Southern Baptist denominations. Four states went well beyond those recommendations by repealing all limits on abortion, bringing their policies into alignment with the desires of the United Presbyterian Church in the United States of America and the United Church of Christ. The remaining thirty-two states kept their legal codes in place, typically allowing abortion only to protect the mother's life.[77]

## Roe v. Wade *and the Religious Reaction*

The legal status of abortion across the United States soon changed dramatically. In its landmark *Roe v. Wade* decision in 1973, the Supreme Court overturned the existing laws in forty-six states and offered a trimester-based system through which states could regulate abortion. During the first trimester, the court ruled, states could not abridge a woman's constitutional right to privacy by outlawing or even regulating abortion. The court held further that as a pregnancy proceeds, the right to an abortion must be balanced against competing state interests. A state's interest in protecting the health of the mother justified safety regulations during the second trimester. From the point of viability, roughly the beginning of the third trimester, a state's interest in preserving fetal life allowed it to ban abortion entirely so long as it granted exceptions for protecting the mother's health.[78]

Catholic leaders immediately denounced *Roe v. Wade*. Cardinal Krol of Philadelphia, president of the National Conference of Catholic Bishops (NCCB), called the decision "an unspeakable tragedy for this nation."[79] Other bishops made similar statements, and in 1975 the NCCB described for parishioners the proper political response to abortion. In their "Pastoral Plan for Pro-Life Activities," the bishops described the Church's fourfold political program, including "passage of a constitutional amendment providing protection for the unborn child to the maximum degree possible," "passage of federal and state laws and adoption of administrative policies that will restrict the practice of abortion as much as possible," "continual research into and refinement and precise interpretation of *Roe* and *Doe* and subsequent court decisions," and "support for legislation that provides alternatives to abortion."[80]

Some Protestant officials also reflected on the wisdom and morality of *Roe v. Wade* in its immediate aftermath, with the reactions including both support and opposition.[81] A more comprehensive response from Protestants, however, did not emerge for several years. Today, evangelical leaders take strong antiabortion stances, but those positions did not become common until a few years after *Roe v. Wade*. In 1974, for example, the Southern Baptist Convention (SBC) simply reaffirmed its 1971 resolution that listed several conditions under which abortion was justified. The SBC in 1974 explained that its position "reflected a middle ground between the extreme of abortion on demand and the opposite extreme of all abortion as murder."[82] Abandoning this "middle ground" in the abortion controversy, the SBC in 1980 announced its support for "appropriate legislation and/or a constitutional amendment which will prohibit abortions except to save the life of the mother."[83]

Other evangelical leaders and organizations paralleled the SBC in shifting toward pro-life positions. In the mid to late 1970s, sociologist Kristin Luker has shown, Catholics predominated among the activists who devoted many hours per week to the pro-life movement.[84] Within a few years evangelicals surpassed Catholics in giving significant amounts of time, money, and energy to the cause. When Rev. Jerry Falwell cofounded the Moral Majority in 1979, he made winning strict legal limits on abortion one of the group's central goals. Organizations with evangelicals as their primary constituency, such as the Family Research Council and the National Association of Evangelicals, continue to emphasize abortion as one of their core issues.

Amid this loud and persistent opposition to abortion, one might mistakenly assume that evangelicals have always expressed pro-life positions in the political arena. In fact, for the first two-thirds of the nineteenth century, few evangelical clergymen or denominational officials attacked the practice of abortion or sought to enact tighter legal controls. Evangelical leaders in that era, like the general public, still accepted the doctrine of quickening. By the end of the twentieth century, though, knowledge about embryonic development had sufficiently diffused through society that no reasonable person could believe that a fetus came alive when the mother first felt it move. The morality of abortion now had to be decided without reference to an archaic dividing line between inanimate matter and human life.

With the moral and political debate resting on other grounds, Americans split into competing camps. Showing abortion's symbolic importance, various activists, journalists, scholars, and legislators connected it to a cluster of family-related issues. Reflecting on these understandings, political scientist Amy Fried calls abortion a "condensational symbol" with consequences that reach far beyond the question of whether a woman should be allowed to terminate a pregnancy.[85] Abortion became and remains a proxy for a range of questions involving sexuality, the family, traditional values, and women's roles in the workplace and society.[86] People's beliefs and opinions about these other issues affect how they view abortion.

By the 1980s abortion formed a central element of larger worldviews, and religious groups divided on whether it should be generally legal or generally illegal. The SBC took a firmly pro-life position for the first time in 1980 and has not wavered since then.[87] The Assemblies of God described several steps for concerned Christians to take, including praying for divine intervention, counseling mothers with unwanted pregnancies to consider adoption, and supporting pro-life candidates and legislation.[88] Other Protestant denominations with a conservative theological orientation voiced similar sentiments. Whereas the Old School Presbyterians stood virtually alone among Protestants in opposing abortion in the nineteenth century, almost the entire evangelical wing of Protestantism now sought tight legislative or judicial controls on the practice. The Catholic Church, meanwhile, continued its struggle against legalized abortion.

On the other side of the debate, mainline Protestant denominations such as the United Methodist Church, Episcopal Church, and Presbyterian Church (USA) typically defended the legal right to abortion.[89] In every case the official denominational statements recognized the moral dilemmas surrounding abortion and recommended better education and more widespread use of birth control to eliminate the need for abortions. The United Church of Christ, for example, paired its support for "legal abortions as one option" with calls for adoptions, family planning services, and responsible sexual behavior to reduce the number of unwanted pregnancies.[90] Many Protestant denominations cooperated with various Jewish groups and representatives of other religions in forming the Religious Coalition for Reproductive Choice, an interest group that uses publicity, lawsuits, and lobbying to promote its cause.

## The Bible and Abortion

Attempting to build a persuasive case for their members and the broader public, the competing religious groups soon appealed to the Bible for support. The Bible could not, by itself, determine someone's position because it says nothing directly about abortion. Had it spoken clearly, Protestants of the nineteenth century would have used it when forming their beliefs on whether and when abortion was permissible. Once abortion gained public visibility in the 1970s, however, the contending sides found biblical material to justify their views.

In summarizing these views, I borrow from conventional usage by designating those supporting and opposing a legal right to abortion as "pro-choice" and "pro-life," respectively. Theoretically, someone who is pro-choice might conclude that the Bible forbids abortion, and a pro-lifer might interpret the Bible as allowing it. It will surprise no one to learn that those cases are rare. In the far more common pattern, the inferences people draw from the Bible match the positions on abortion they already hold. No matter what expectations they bring to the task, advocates on both sides must address the Bible's silence on abortion. Pro-life writers sometimes assert that abortion rarely if ever occurred in the ancient religious communities of the Bible, alleviating the need for any formal prohibitions.[91] In the pro-choice view, by contrast, "it is much more probable that abortion was not mentioned because it was not specifically prohibited."[92]

Because the absence of direct references can be interpreted both ways, the debate turns to passages and verses that might be relevant. Randy Alcorn, a prominent evangelical writer, establishes a principle to resolve the question: "All that is necessary to prove a biblical prohibition of abortion is to demonstrate that the Bible considers the unborn to be human beings."[93] If someone can show that the Bible regards an embryo as a person from the moment of conception, Alcorn argues, it follows that any abortion kills a human being. Alcorn and his allies offer several such possibilities. In the Gospel of Luke, for example, Mary traveled to the hill country and entered the home of her cousin Elizabeth, who was six months pregnant. Luke 1:42 records a crucial element of the story: "When Elizabeth heard Mary's greeting, the infant leaped in her womb."[94] The reader later learns that the infant was none other than John the Baptist, and his "leaping for joy" in the womb, the argument goes, shows that the unborn are human beings from the moment of conception.[95]

Similarly, the prophet Isaiah proclaimed, "The LORD called me from birth. . . . For now the LORD has spoken who formed me as his servant from the womb" (Isaiah 49:1, 5). If Isaiah was God's servant even in the womb, then an abortion necessarily kills innocent life.[96] Pro-life advocates reinforce this inference with verses from Jeremiah and Job as well as Psalms 139:13, where the Psalmist cries out to God, "You formed my inmost being; you knit me in my mother's womb."[97] On the other side of the debate, Christians who support abortion rights read the same verses to indicate that the developing fetus reaches personhood sometime after conception. If God "formed" Isaiah and "knit" the Psalmist in the womb, there must be a discrete time during which the fetus becomes a human being. Before that point, known historically in the Church as "animation," abortion would therefore be permissible.[98]

Abortion's opponents counter by pointing to biblical passages suggesting God's foreknowledge of each person's destiny. The bioethicist John Ling emphasizes the story in Genesis 25 where God knows everything about Esau and Jacob from the dawn of time.[99] "Since God has a plan for all human lives," another writer claims, any and all abortions must be forbidden.[100] The pro-choice side replies that the prevalence of miscarriages should make people skeptical that divine foreknowledge leads ineluctably to a policy of prohibiting abortion. Scientific research indicates that, among women who know they are pregnant, approximately 15 percent of all pregnancies end in a miscarriage; when including cases where a woman did not know she was pregnant, the figure rises as high as 50 percent.[101] Was it really God's plan to create all those lives at conception only to snuff them out shortly thereafter? Pro-choice Christians believe that God's plan applies only to the actual human beings he forms at some point after conception.[102]

These disagreements about the importance of conception affect interpretations of Exodus 21:22–25, which one author calls "a favorite passage used by both pro- and anti-abortion groups."[103] In the King James Version, the verses read as follows: "If men strive, and hurt a woman with child, so that her fruit depart from her, and yet no mischief follow: he shall be surely punished, according as the woman's husband will lay upon him; and he shall pay as the judges determine. And if any mischief follow, then thou shalt give life for life, eye for eye, tooth for tooth, hand for hand, foot for foot, burning for burning, wound for wound, stripe for stripe."

Examining some of the key words sheds light on what this passage means. "Strive" is an old-fashioned word for "fight" or "struggle," and a woman "with child" is pregnant, so the verses describe a situation where she is an innocent bystander during a conflict between two or more men. The men accidentally hurt the pregnant woman such that "her fruit depart from her," and the legal penalties hinge on whether any "mischief follow." In the seventeenth century, "mischief" referred to significant misfortune or hardship; translations now typically use "harm" instead of "mischief." In the absence of subsequent harm, the offending men must pay a fine that the woman's husband requests and the judges award; should harm follow, though, justice for the quarreling men requires life for life, eye for eye, tooth for tooth.

The possible harms that could trigger the most severe kind of retribution depend on what happens when "her fruit depart from her" or, in what scholars agree is a literal translation of the Hebrew words, "her children come out."[104] A blow to the pregnant woman could cause her child to come out either dead (a miscarriage) or alive (a premature birth). Note the meaning of the verses if her injury led to the first alternative, a miscarriage, and the two men must compensate the woman's husband through a fine. Any subsequent harm stemming from the initial injury can affect only the mother, for the baby is already dead. Should the mother die too, the legal code stipulates that the offending men must be put to death.

Taken together, these verses place the life of the baby on a separate plane from the life of the mother. The men must be punished through a fine should they hurt the mother in a way that kills the baby, but they receive the death penalty if the mother also dies. Losing the baby leads only to monetary compensation, whereas the mother's death demands full retribution. By implication, the author of Exodus did not consider the fetus a person from the moment of conception; otherwise, the penalty of life for life would apply to anyone causing it to die. Without even mentioning abortion, the passage allows a pro-choice interpretation.

Now consider the upshot if, instead, the phrase "her children come out" describes a premature birth. The men pay a fine for injuring the woman and forcing her to give birth before she had planned. The possible harms afterward could affect either the mother *or* the baby, both of whom are still alive. All parties on the scene presumably hope for a full recovery for the woman and her child, but the legal code can handle the worst outcomes, too. If the mother or the baby subsequently dies from any lingering injuries stemming from the fight, the quarreling men face the death penalty. Such a punishment treats the lives of the baby and mother equally, with a judgment of life for life applying to someone who accidentally kills either one of them. It follows that killing the unborn through an abortion must be forbidden in the same way as killing any other human being.

Given the importance of this passage to today's abortion debate, let us persist a little longer in drawing out its implications. We want to know whether the author of Exodus portrays the triggering event as a miscarriage or a premature birth.[105] Suppose an accident caused a pregnant woman in ancient Israel to begin labor. Would the baby be more likely to be born dead or alive? In developed countries today, advances in medical technology have lowered the age of viability, the point at which a baby can survive outside the womb. Assuming that the mother and child receive high-quality health care, the age of viability in the West currently stands at about twenty-two weeks. For most of the twentieth century, researchers gave higher estimates of twenty-eight weeks.[106] Needless to say, a newborn in ancient Israel had no access to the neonatal care available in the twentieth century, let alone the twenty-first. One can therefore assume that age of viability was at least twenty-eight weeks and possibly twenty-nine or thirty.

What would happen if an Israelite woman sustained an injury making "her children come out" during the third, fourth, fifth, sixth, or seventh months of her pregnancy? Clearly, the woman miscarried in those instances. She could give birth prematurely only during the limited window of the last two months of her term. Additionally, a premature birth would normally require summoning a midwife to the site of the accident to ensure that the baby faced the right direction in the birth canal, the umbilical cord didn't wrap around its head, and other potential problems were averted. If the midwife arrived too late, the woman could lose the baby due to any number of possible complications. Finally, the accidental blow to the woman would need to be sufficiently intense to induce labor but not strong enough to kill the baby, a description that fits only a narrow range of injuries.

Putting these considerations together, hurting the pregnant woman would have a far greater chance of causing a miscarriage than a premature birth. Yes, the stars could align to allow the baby to be born alive rather than dead, but readers of Exodus — especially those knowledgeable about pregnancy and childbirth — would naturally assume the more likely outcome of a miscarriage or stillbirth. In fact, a long Christian tradition removes any ambiguity in the passage by translating the crucial clause as "has a miscarriage." Completed in the year 405, the Vulgate translation of the Hebrew into Latin used the word *abortivum*, meaning (in this context) "miscarriage." Because the Church in the West for over a millennium relied on the Vulgate for theological and devotional purposes, readers and listeners could not help but understand that the passage in Exodus referred to a miscarriage.

Monks and theologians in England eventually translated parts of the Bible into Old English or Middle English. John Wycliffe and his collaborators translated the entire Bible from the Vulgate, and the historical evidence suggests they finished the first copy of their work in approximately 1384.[107] Posthumously declared a heretic by the Council of Constance, Wycliffe followed convention in translating Exodus 21:22-25 to indicate a miscarriage. Wycliffe's Bible rendered the relevant phrase as "makith the child deed boren"—or in awkward but modern English, "makes the child dead born."[108] In the aftermath of the Reformation, the Douay-Rheims Bible (1609) also used the Vulgate as its source text and recorded the central phrase as "she miscarry indeed." The Douay-Rheims Bible served as the dominant English translation for Catholics until well into the 1900s.

New Catholic Bibles appeared after 1943, when Pope Pius XII encouraged scholars working in vernacular languages to translate from the original Hebrew and Greek rather than Latin. Catholic scholars subsequently published English translations in the Jerusalem Bible (1966), New American Bible (1970), New Jerusalem Bible (1985), and New American Bible Revised Edition (2011), all of which include the terms *miscarry* or *miscarriage* in the verse in question. For example, Exodus 21:22-25 in the New American Bible Revised Edition reads as follows: "When men have a fight and hurt a pregnant woman, so that she suffers a miscarriage, but no further injury, the guilty one shall be fined as much as the woman's husband demands of him, and he shall pay in the presence of the judges. But if injury ensues, you shall give life for life, eye for eye, tooth for tooth, hand for hand, foot for foot, burn for burn, wound for wound, stripe for stripe." Among Protestant Bibles, similar formulations of "miscarriage," "miscarry," or "loses her child" appear in the Moffatt New Translation (1922), Revised Standard Version (1952), Berkeley Version (1959), Amplified Bible (1964), Living Bible (1971), New American Standard Bible (1971), Good News Bible (1976), New Revised Standard Version (1989), Contemporary English Version (1995), The Message (2001), and Common English Bible (2011).[109] These versions differ from each other in the philosophies and principles guiding their translation methods, and yet all of them parallel Catholic Bibles in describing a miscarriage in Exodus 21:22-25.

Not all English versions produced over the centuries explicitly refer to a miscarriage. Through a competing tradition, scholars give readers a more literal translation of the Hebrew words. In trying to duplicate the phrasing of the original text ("her children come out"), such an approach requires the discerning reader to infer that the accident caused a miscarriage. As mentioned earlier, the King James Version (1611) took this approach in saying that "her fruit depart from her." Christians today often assume that King James instructed his translators to work from scratch in developing the elegant style they employ throughout the Old and New Testaments, but they actually copied most of their verses verbatim from previous translations, most notably the Bishops' Bible (1568).[110] The Bishops' Bible, favored by authorities in the Church of England, included the identical words "her fruit depart from her."[111]

Within a few decades after its publication, the King James Version (KJV) captured the imagination of Protestants in the English-speaking world and remained their Bible of choice until the twentieth century. Some Protestants still prefer the KJV, but growing numbers of individuals and churches eventually began using newer translations. Some of these Bibles follow the KJV's lead through phrases such as "her fruit depart from her" or "her children come out," including Young's Literal Translation (1862), Revised Version (1885), American Standard Version (1901), 21st Century King James Version (1994), and English Standard Version (2001).[112]

Two approaches thus characterized all English translations beginning with the Wycliffe Bible (1384) and lasting through most of the twentieth century. These Bibles either called the crucial event a miscarriage or else led readers to infer a miscarriage from the context. Then, in 1978, the New International Version (NIV) quietly broke with six centuries of tradition in English Bibles. According to the 1978 edition of the NIV, the proper translation of Exodus 21:22–25 is the following: "If men who are fighting hit a pregnant woman and she gives birth prematurely but there is no serious injury, the offender must be fined whatever the woman's husband demands and the court allows. But if there is serious injury, you are to take life for life, eye for eye, tooth for tooth, hand for hand, foot for foot, burn for burn, wound for wound, bruise for bruise."[113]

What seems at first a minor change ("she gives birth prematurely") profoundly affects the situation at hand: namely, the baby is born alive. The possible "serious injury" thereafter could occur to the baby, who might die in the subsequent hours or days, or the mother. Published in the United States by Zondervan, one of the founding members of the Evangelical Christian Publishers Association, the NIV gained a large following among evangelicals. Several later translations made the same choice as the NIV for the passage in question, including the New King James Version (1982), God's Word Translation (1995), New Living Translation (1996), Holman Christian Standard Bible (2004), New English Translation (2005), and Today's New International Version (2005).

It is worth pausing to consider how much had happened between the time of the Wycliffe Bible (1384) and the New International Version (1978). In the economic sphere, the industrial revolution and its continuing legacy shifted workers from farming to manufacturing to services, and the corresponding growth in productivity multiplied the standard of living many times over. In the religious realm, the Reformation divided Christendom and secular influences challenged the authority of all religions. In the world of politics, new countries formed, empires emerged and split apart, democracy arose as an ideal, individuals acquired basic rights, and governments expanded their powers. In society at large, literacy spread to the common people, women redefined traditional gender roles, and antibiotics, vaccines, and public health measures lengthened the average lifespan. Throughout these six centuries of remarkable transformations, stability could be found in an unusual place: no English translation ever used a phrase like "she gives birth prematurely" in Exodus 21:22–25.

Why would such a translation first appear in 1978? The year is no accident. By that point, each Anglo country had just completed a centuries-long cycle where abortion went from being usually legal to usually illegal and then back to usually legal. In the United States, evangelical leaders mounted resistance to *Roe v. Wade* and made abortion one of their central political issues. By translating the key words in Exodus 21:22–25 as "she gives birth prematurely," the NIV aided the pro-life cause. With this translation in place, readers could believe that the Bible treats the lives of the baby and mother equally, with the same judgment brought to someone who harms or kills either one. A short chain of reasoning then leads to affirming that personhood begins at conception and abortion is a heinous crime. The NIV's bold and innovative translation also served a defensive purpose in countering the Protestant Bibles that yielded pro-choice implications through their use of the term *miscarriage*.

This explanation for why the new translation first appeared in 1978 answers one question but raises another: Why didn't the Catholic scholars who produced English versions of the Bible give the same translation as the evangelicals who released the NIV? Over the years, the Catholic Church has faced many accusations; leniency on abortion is not among them. Given that Catholic translators held positions of authority within the teaching and ministerial institutions of the Church, the puzzle becomes even more interesting.[114] It thus seems odd that every Catholic Bible has declined the opportunity to introduce language favorable to a pro-life interpretation. By using the word *miscarriage* in Exodus 21:22–25, Catholic Bibles actually seem to undermine the Church's position.

The differing theological orientations of evangelicals and Catholics make this puzzle easier to understand. Upholding the Protestant principle of *sola scriptura*, evangelicals seek to ground all of their religious beliefs and practices in the Bible alone. According to the doctrines of Luther, Calvin, and their followers, mere tradition cannot lay claim to the Christian conscience. Yet the Bible never mentions abortion, which presents a challenge for people wanting to derive a pro-life stance from their scriptures. Nor does the Bible ever say that an embryo should be considered a person, which would indirectly show that abortion is immoral. People who want to oppose abortion and yet adhere to *sola scriptura* can square the circle by working a pro-life position into their translation of Exodus 21:22–25.

The New American Standard Bible (NASB) offers an illuminating capstone to the forces at work in the evangelical community. (The NASB bears no relationship to the New American Bible; owing to the limited number of obvious ways to name a Bible, some of the titles invariably sound alike.) In its 1971 translation, released in slightly modified editions during the 1970s, the NASB used the term *miscarriage*. A popular Bible among evangelicals, the NASB nevertheless endured persistent criticism for its translation of Exodus 21:22–25. For example, one author called the NASB "normally a good version, but not here."[115] Stung by dissent from its core constituency, the NASB in its 1995 edition switched the operative clause from "she has a miscarriage" to "she gives birth prematurely."[116] By changing just a few words, the NASB cast aside the pro-choice implications of its previous version and gave the pro-life position powerful support from scripture.

The connections between theological doctrines and Bible translations differ in the Catholic Church. Lacking a commitment to *sola scriptura*, Catholics do not need to justify a pro-life stance with citations to specific verses. Sure, it would be helpful to Catholics for the Bible to condemn abortion, but Catholics can appeal to another source of authority: Church tradition and the logic of natural law that undergirds it. Against a backdrop of two thousand years of writings from theologians, popes, and ecumenical councils, the translation of a few words in Exodus makes little difference one way or the other. Catholic scholars are therefore free to make what they deem the most accurate translation, even one that seems to advantage supporters of abortion rights.

Incidentally, translations of Jewish Bibles (what Christians call the Old Testament) also differ from those favored by evangelical Protestants. Jews historically read and studied the Bible in the original Hebrew, but scholars began making translations into vernacular languages in the twentieth century. Given rabbis' deep knowledge of the Hebrew language, the Jewish translations start with a base level of credibility. Among the prominent English translations, the Jewish Publication Society version (1917) and the Koren Jerusalem Bible (2008) both resemble the King James Version in saying that "her fruit depart" from the pregnant woman. The Complete Jewish Bible (1998) gives a translation of "her unborn child dies." Living Torah (1981), Jewish Publication Society TANAKH (1985), and Complete Tanach with Rashi (2007) use the phrases "causing her to miscarry," "a miscarriage results," and "she miscarries," respectively. The pattern is clear: not a single Jewish translation describes a premature birth in the verse in question.

In defending their preferred translation of Exodus 21:22–25, evangelical scholars have failed to convince a majority of other Protestants, let alone Catholics and Jews. Most Protestant Bibles, along with all Catholic and Jewish ones, reject the translation of a premature birth. Nevertheless, there is little reason to doubt the sincerity and integrity of the translators who produced the NIV and its successors. Surely something more complicated happened than a clandestine group attempting to fool everyone through a literary sleight of hand. Evangelical scholars have written many essays, articles, and pages in books explaining why they believe "gives birth prematurely" is the correct translation.[117] Their case hinges on Hebrew style and syntax, parallels from other law codes, word usages elsewhere in the Bible, and the context of Exodus. For the purposes of this book, the important question is: Why do some evangelical scholars find those arguments convincing even though Jewish, Catholic, and other Protestant scholars do not? The best answer, again, is that for theological reasons, evangelicals need to appeal to the Bible to justify an anti-abortion stance. Evangelicals' desire for what the text in Exodus *should* say has influenced their beliefs about what the text actually *does* say.

### Linking Abortion to Other Issues

Of course, abortion is not the only issue on which contending sides have appealed to the Bible for support. Compared with slavery, divorce, and homosexuality, abortion contains both similarities and differences in the history of its religious politics. On all these issues cultural assumptions and mentalities influenced both Christians and non-Christians. During the early decades of the American republic, ordinary citizens adhered to a long-standing consensus emerging from medieval England: abortion was morally acceptable when performed before but not after quickening. State laws and judicial decisions reinforced these shared norms, and religious groups did not demand stricter policies. When physicians of the nineteenth century wanted to criminalize abortion throughout a pregnancy, they criticized Protestant leaders for declining to support the campaign. Physicians received only limited help from Christian denominations, most notably the Old School Presbyterians, in persuading state legislatures to outlaw most abortions.

Enacted throughout the country after 1860, restrictive abortion laws lasted for an entire century. Several years after the *Roe v. Wade* decision of 1973, the issue of abortion created the religious and political alignments that persist into the present day. In many respects abortion in recent decades posed political difficulties for Christian leaders similar to those of slavery from 1830 to 1860. When abortion, like slavery, began to arouse intense controversy, Christian leaders could not easily withdraw from the conflict and maintain a neutral posture. Unfortunately for Christian leaders, their members—like Americans more generally—disagreed on whether and when abortion should be legal. In a replay of the politics of slavery, any positions Christian leaders announced on abortion would alienate part of their constituencies.

As happened with slavery, along with divorce and homosexuality, the Bible became a touchstone for the controversy over abortion. But unlike the other issues covered in this book, abortion is never actually mentioned in the Bible. Advocates thus fought over how to interpret passages that could indirectly offer guidance, and these exegetical disputes differed from those on slavery, divorce, and homosexuality. Whereas partisans often reinterpreted biblical passages to support their views on the other issues, on abortion one group actually retranslated a crucial verse. On all these issues, people used their scriptures to justify the positions they formed for other reasons, but on abortion it took a new translation to demonstrate the Bible's malleability.

These issues also differed on whether and how the laity's changing opinions encouraged their leaders to adopt new positions and political strategies. Throughout much of American history, Christian leaders fought rearguard battles against the spread of divorce and the loosening of state regulations. As divorce gained acceptability in American society, including among Christians, the issue lost its political edge. Christian leaders responded by deemphasizing divorce within their political priorities, thereby making the goal of preventing marital breakups a matter of private morality rather than public policy. On homosexuality, too, Christian leaders had to acknowledge sweeping changes in public opinion that engulfed their own members. Leaders accommodated these changes by declining to push for recriminalizing sodomy, by calling for tolerance and mutual respect, and, in some cases, by embracing marriage and other rights for gays and lesbians.

On abortion, by contrast, public opinion has changed very little in recent decades. Polls have surveyed Americans' views on the issue hundreds, possibly thousands, of times since the early 1970s. The General Social Survey (GSS), which I used in the two previous chapters, includes some of the most informative questions. Unlike many other surveys that cast their questions at an abstract level, the GSS inquires about the actual conditions under which a person would—or would not—permit an abortion. The GSS has asked the same questions in identical form for four decades, allowing us to track changes and trends.

The GSS gives respondents an opening prompt followed by six qualifiers: "Please tell me whether or not you think it should be possible for a pregnant woman to obtain a legal abortion . . . if there is a strong chance of serious defect in the baby," "if she is married and does not want any more children," "if the woman's own health is seriously endangered by the pregnancy," "if the family has a very low income and cannot afford

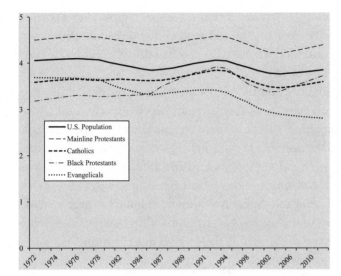

**Figure 5.1.**
Number of conditions for which abortion should be allowed
*Source:* General Social Survey. Data smoothed with LOESS.

any more children," "if she became pregnant as a result of rape," and "if she is not married and does not want to marry the man."[118] Someone on the far end of the pro-choice spectrum would answer yes to each question, while the pure pro-life position would require a person to say no each time. As it turns out, a strong majority of Americans (71 percent) lie somewhere in the middle, allowing abortion for at least one but fewer than six of the conditions.[119]

Figure 5.1 summarizes responses to these questions from 1972 to 2012. The graph indicates, for the American public as well as four Christian groups, the average number of conditions under which a person would allow a legal abortion.[120] One can observe from figure 5.1 the stability in abortion attitudes over four decades. In 1972—right before *Roe v. Wade*—Americans would allow a legal abortion for, on average, slightly more than four of the six conditions. With only minor year-by-year fluctuations, Americans expressed approximately the same level of support in 2012. Incidentally, other public opinion questions asked in an identical form over a long period show a similar stability in abortion attitudes.[121]

Among Christian groups, evangelical Protestants and mainline Protestants have the most and least restrictive attitudes, respectively, with Catholics and black Protestants usually falling in between. Over time Catholics and mainline Protestants hardly changed their opinions at all.

Evangelical Protestants decreased their levels of support for abortion rights, while black Protestants moved in the other direction. Within the American population as a whole, these trends offset each other, leading to the overall picture of stability.

We can now identify one of the distinctive features of the abortion issue. Unlike divorce and homosexuality, in which attitudes and norms trended in one direction, public opinion on abortion barely budged from the early 1970s to the present. The line in the sand many Christian leaders once drew on divorce and homosexuality kept shifting because their own members followed the same trends — albeit sometimes with a lag — as the rest of society. On abortion, by contrast, public opinion has been remarkably stable for over four decades. Given this stability, religious and political strife on the issue will probably persist well into the future.

# Women's Rights

Unlike today, few lawyers of the nineteenth century attended a law school. They often held other careers before practicing law and learned about the profession through a combination of self-study and apprenticeships.[1] One aspiring lawyer of that era, Myra Bradwell, had taught in a private school, participated in philanthropic causes, and founded a legal newspaper. She gained her legal knowledge by reading every relevant book she could locate and serving an apprenticeship at a law office. On August 2, 1869, she passed with high honors the bar exam a judge administered in Illinois. After years of planning and preparation, Bradwell neared the point at which she could add "Attorney at Law" after her name.[2]

To enter the legal profession in Bradwell's home state, candidates had to pass the bar exam and then petition for approval from the Illinois Supreme Court. The high court declined her petition by highlighting the one quality distinguishing her from other candidates—her sex. The court held that she could not practice law effectively because, as a married woman, she was legally prohibited from signing contracts without the consent of her husband. Illinois also forbade single women from practicing law, but the court did not address that exclusion in its ruling. After she submitted a forceful rebuttal, the Illinois Supreme Court declared itself powerless to admit a woman to the bar.[3] The statute establishing the process for licensing lawyers, the court explained, took "as an almost axiomatic truth" the principle that "God designed the sexes to occupy different spheres of action."[4] The court asserted that God, not the state of Illinois, created the rules excluding women from the professions.

Bradwell appealed this ruling to the United States 171

Supreme Court. She built her case around the recently ratified Fourteenth Amendment, which declared, "No State shall make or enforce any law which shall abridge the privileges or immunities of citizens of the United States." The Supreme Court denied her claim by holding that the right to practice law was not included among those privileges and immunities. Justice Joseph Bradley's concurring opinion grounded this ruling in God's eternal decrees: "The constitution of the family organization, which is founded in the divine ordinance as well as the nature of things, indicates the domestic sphere as that which properly belongs to the domain and functions of womanhood. . . . The paramount destiny and mission of woman are to fulfill the noble and benign offices of wife and mother. This is the law of the Creator."[5]

This decision sounds jarring to us today. At most cocktail parties, announcing that you think women should be forbidden from entering the professions would earn you about as much respect as confessing your lifelong pedophilia. To be sure, Americans still vigorously debate certain aspects of women's rights. In 2014, for example, many liberals were outraged when the Supreme Court ruled that closely held private corporations could claim a religious exemption to a government mandate for contraceptive coverage in employer health insurance plans. But note how this conflict differed from those of the nineteenth century. Back then the questions involved whether women should be legally entitled to vote, hold property, seek an education, and earn a living. The 2014 controversy revolved around whether a small minority of women—those working for companies that request the religious exemption—might have to pay out of pocket for contraceptives.

Why has the debate over women's rights changed so dramatically? How did the Bible's teachings undergird the traditional system of gender relations? How have secular ideas about the equality of women and men spread through the entire population, thereby influencing both Christians and non-Christians? How have modern conceptions of women's rights encouraged Christians to reinterpret the Bible? This chapter seeks to answer these questions. We can begin by taking an intellectual journey back to earlier centuries to understand the biblical thinking that distinguished the respective temperaments, responsibilities, talents, duties, and rights of women and men.

## Women and the Bible

In earlier centuries these discussions often began by considering the Fall of Adam and Eve in the Garden of Eden. In the famous account of Genesis 3, Eve succumbed to the serpent's temptation and ate from the forbidden tree of knowledge of good and evil. She then gave some of the fruit to Adam, who also ate. God punished Eve in Genesis 3:16, promising: "I will greatly multiply your sorrow and your conception; In pain you shall bring forth children; Your desire shall be for your husband, And he shall rule over you."[6] God also punished Adam by cursing the ground, encouraging thorns and thistles to grow, and forcing him to labor assiduously to cultivate crops.

The New Testament spoke in greater detail about the relationship between husbands and wives. In Ephesians 5:22–25, the apostle Paul instructed: "Wives, submit to your own husbands, as to the Lord. For the husband is head of the wife, as also Christ is head of the church; and He is the Savior of the body. Therefore, just as the church is subject to Christ, so let the wives be to their own husbands in everything. Husbands, love your wives, just as Christ also loved the church and gave Himself for her." Paul gave the same commands in Colossians 3:18–19: "Wives, submit to your own husbands, as is fitting in the Lord. Husbands, love your wives and do not be bitter toward them." The language of 1 Peter 3:1–7 was similar, adding that the wife was the "weaker vessel." In 1 Corinthians 11:8–9, Paul explained why women must submit by reminding his readers and listeners of God's order of creation in Genesis 2: "For man is not from woman, but woman from man. Nor was man created for the woman, but woman for the man."

Expanding the focus from the family to the church, Paul gave additional instructions in several of his letters. He declared in 1 Corinthians 14:34–35: "Let your women keep silent in the churches, for they are not permitted to speak; but they are to be submissive, as the law also says. And if they want to learn something, let them ask their own husbands at home; for it is shameful for women to speak in church." In 1 Timothy 2:11–15, traditionally ascribed to Paul, readers encountered similar words: "Let a woman learn in silence with all submission. And I do not permit a woman to teach or to have authority over a man, but to be in silence. For Adam was formed first, then Eve. And Adam was not deceived, but the woman being deceived, fell into transgression. Nevertheless she will be saved in childbearing if they continue in faith, love, and holiness, with self-control."

What do all these passages mean? How did Christians historically use them to define women's roles and responsibilities in the home, workplace, and society? Leading Christian writers from the seventeenth to the nineteenth centuries thought the Bible's meaning was simple and straightforward: a woman must direct her talents and energies to the home, and even there she must submit to her husband's authority. Influential analyses of the Bible, such as the *Commentary on the Whole Bible* by Matthew Henry (1662–1714), codified these understandings and passed them to succeeding generations. Like others before him, Henry explained that God responded to the Fall by putting each wife "under the dominion of her husband." The Presbyterian theologian continued: "We have here the sentence passed upon the woman for her sin," with God condemning her to "a state of sorrow, and a state of subjection, proper punishments of a sin in which she had gratified her pleasure and her pride."[7]

In Henry's view, many New Testament passages elaborated on God's plan for female subordination. Commenting on Paul's words in Colossians 3:18–19 and Ephesians 5:22–25, Henry observed that submission "is the same word which is used to express our duty to magistrates." By obeying their husbands, wives comply "with God's authority, who has commanded it." Henry quoted Paul in saying that "the husband is the head of the wife," with God giving "the man the pre-eminence and a right to direct and govern by creation." Paul's analogy between the "superiority and headship" of Christ over the church and man over the woman led Henry to state that "Christ's authority is exercised over the church for the saving of her from evil, and the supplying of her with every thing good for her. In like manner should the husband be employed for the protection and comfort of his spouse; and therefore she should the more cheerfully submit herself unto him."[8]

Henry made similar points when analyzing 1 Timothy 2:11–15, where Paul discussed God's creation of Adam and Eve and their subsequent fall from grace. God subjected women to men's authority, Henry stated, because "woman was last in the creation" and "first in the transgression."

God initially formed Adam and then created Eve from Adam's rib "to denote her subordination to him and dependence upon him." To demonstrate his purpose through this order of creation, God ensured that "she was created for the man, and not the man for the woman." Eve later took the first bite from the fruit "and brought the man into the transgression," causing God to reaffirm his plan for male authority as "part of the sentence" for her sin.[9]

Paralleling this hierarchy in marriage, women in church "must be silent, submissive, and subject, and not usurp authority. . . . According to Paul, women must be learners, and are not allowed to be public teachers in the church; for teaching is an office of authority, and the woman must not usurp authority over the man, but is to be in silence. But, notwithstanding this prohibition, good women may and ought to teach their children at home the principles of religion." The apostles thus offer a "word of comfort" for women, who can "be saved in child-bearing." Giving birth and raising children allows a woman to find her calling, which involves supporting her family and instilling morality in her children. To fulfill God's plan, a woman "shall bring forth, and be a living mother of living children."[10]

Through these interpretations, Matthew Henry gave the standard Christian perspective on gender relations. Henry's admirers included one of the leaders of the Great Awakening, George Whitefield, who wrote in his journal, "How sweetly did my hours in private glide away in reading and praying over Mr. Henry's *Comment upon the Scriptures!*"[11] Calvinist theologian Charles Hodge later echoed Henry in holding that "the doctrine that women should be in subjection is clearly revealed" in the Old and New Testaments.[12] Albert Taylor Bledsoe, an influential clergyman, lawyer, and author of the nineteenth century, asserted that "there is no deformity of human character from which we turn with deeper loathing than from a woman forgetful of her nature, and clamorous for the vocation and rights of man."[13] These perspectives on the duties of women shaped not only the pronouncements of church officials but also legislative and judicial decisions, as Myra Bradwell learned to her dismay.

### Women Leaders Respond

The movement for women's rights in America, which historians generally date from the Seneca Falls Convention of 1848, had to confront this received wisdom about what the Bible said. Given that most Americans of that era were Protestants who trusted the Bible as the word of God, prevailing understandings of its content put advocates of women's rights on the defensive. To achieve their goals, advocates needed to challenge a cultural and religious environment where separate spheres for women and men were not only axiomatic but ordained by God. Finding an effective response, however, was not so easy. Illustrating this uncertainty in the best path forward, three prominent leaders — Susan B. Anthony, Elizabeth Cady Stanton, and Lucretia Mott — differed in how they handled the Bible and Christianity.

Scholars count Anthony, Stanton, and Mott among the most influential leaders of the nineteenth-century women's movement. After meeting through their abolitionist work, Stanton and Mott worked with three other women to organize the landmark Seneca Falls Convention.[14] Anthony soon joined the movement, and over the next half century she organized meetings and conventions, delivered speeches, communicated with other leaders, and drew publicity through her arrest and trial for voting in the 1872 presidential election. With Stanton she founded a women's suffrage organization in 1869, and both women served terms as the group's president.[15] Mott, meanwhile, rallied other activists, defended the cause, and served as an officer in key organizations.[16] Honoring their place in history, a marble sculpture of Anthony, Stanton, and Mott adorns the Rotunda of the US Capitol building.

Despite their friendship and cooperation over several decades, the three women employed different strategies to address the Bible and Christianity. Raised by Quakers, Anthony attended a Unitarian church in her thirties and forties before becoming an agnostic later in life.[17] She mostly kept her religious views private and adopted a stance of studied neutrality toward Christianity in her public appearances. Anthony advised the next generation of leaders: "These are the principles I want you to maintain, that our platform may be kept as broad as the universe, that upon it may stand the representatives of all creeds and no creeds — Jew or Christian, Protestant or Catholic, Gentile or Mormon, pagan or atheist."[18] Anthony believed that the movement's success hinged on uniting adherents of different religions and no religion at all. Sustained attacks on Christianity would splinter that coalition.

Differing from Anthony on this point, Stanton in her later years increasingly believed that women's rights would not advance until supporters overcame what she regarded as their greatest obstacle. In her essay "Has Christianity Benefitted Woman?" Stanton answered no and asserted that "the moral degradation of women is due more to theological superstitions than to all other influences together."[19] Stanton had attended an Episcopal church during her upbringing, but lost her faith while studying at a women's boarding school. "The memory of my own suffering," Stanton wrote, "has prevented me from ever shadowing one young soul with any of the superstitions of the Christian religion."[20] She described religions as "human inventions" and said that "bibles, prayer-books, catechisms, and encyclical letters are all emanations from the brains of man."[21]

Stanton's religious skepticism led her to mount a systematic attack on Christianity for impeding women's progress. Her most important work on this subject was *The Woman's Bible*, a two-volume commentary on all biblical passages relating to women that she wrote, edited, and compiled with the assistance of twenty-five women scholars and activists. "From the inauguration of the movement for woman's emancipation," Stanton lamented in her introduction, "the Bible has been used to hold her in the 'divinely ordained sphere,' prescribed in the Old and New Testaments." She believed that the "unvarnished texts speak for themselves," with many passages ruling out a "liberal interpretation" favorable to women. Noting that she long ago denied the "divine authority" of the Christian scriptures, she sought to retain respect for certain parts of the Bible while jettisoning the rest.[22]

Early in *The Woman's Bible*, Stanton tried to undermine the doctrine, grounded in the story of Adam and Eve, "that woman was made after man, of man, and for man, an inferior being, subject to man." That doctrine arose from the second creation story in Genesis 2:7-25, in which God created Adam first and later created Eve as a helper by taking a rib from Adam's body. Stanton instead emphasized the first creation account in Genesis 1:26-28 that described God creating man and woman simultaneously. In that passage each partner shares "equal dominion" over

God's creation, and "not one word is said giving man dominion over woman." Stanton denounced the second creation story as a fraud, stating that it appeared in the Bible because "some wily writer, seeing the perfect equality of man and woman in the first chapter, felt it important for the dignity and dominion of man to effect woman's subordination in some way."[23]

In commenting on the New Testament, Stanton sought to counter the common notion that it brought "promises of new dignity and of larger liberties for woman." Through their "specific directions for woman's subordination," the apostles actually reached beyond the prophets and patriarchs of the Old Testament by "more clearly and emphatically" degrading the female sex. Stanton cited as evidence the standard verses commanding women to submit to their husbands, stay silent in church, and find solace only through childbearing. Since the raw texts could not be salvaged, Stanton urged women "to demand that the Canon law, the Mosaic code, the Scriptures, prayer-books and liturgies be purged of all invidious distinctions of sex, of all false teaching as to woman's origin, character and destiny."[24] Excising the offensive parts of Christian teachings and texts would allow the remainder to exalt rather than denigrate women.

*The Woman's Bible* became a best seller, suggesting that Stanton's approach to Christianity resonated with many readers.[25] Other Americans, however, were aghast at how she treated what they considered the word of God. Referring to writers like Stanton, one critic proclaimed that "one reason why so many of the modern agitators for Woman's Rights, so called, are in the ranks of infidelity and free-thought, is this: that they know, and all the world knows, that the Church and the Bible are, and must always be, dead against them."[26] Aware of this perceived link between women's rights and religious skepticism, many Christian women who supported Stanton's political agenda nevertheless distanced themselves from her later writings. Stanton's position as the former president of the National American Woman Suffrage Association did not prevent the group from passing a resolution declaring "that it has no official connection with the so-called 'Woman's Bible,' or any theological publication."[27] A majority of the voting members resisted the implication of *The Woman's Bible* that they must choose between endorsing women's rights and recognizing the divine inspiration of every book, chapter, and verse in the Bible.

### Reinterpreting the Bible

For women unwilling to deny the Bible's authority, reinterpreting the problematic passages was a far better option. Writers and scholars of the nineteenth century began arguing that the Bible, when properly translated and interpreted, actually promoted the cause of women's rights. Lucretia Mott, a devout Quaker throughout her life, read some of this literature and incorporated it into her speeches and sermons. She advised Christians to study the scriptures "rationally for yourselves, and not follow the teaching which interprets them in support of the wrong, instead of the right."[28] With the correct understanding in hand, believers learn that "it is not Christianity but priestcraft that has subjected woman as we find her."[29]

Writing a decade before the Seneca Falls Convention, Mott's fellow Quaker Sarah Grimké had pioneered this approach to understanding the Bible. Through a series of letters published in 1837 in Massachusetts newspapers, Grimké offered the first serious attempt to reinterpret the passages involving women. Despite their small numbers, Quakers were uniquely situated to produce the first person who would challenge the traditional understandings. For Quakers, the correct biblical interpretation did not emerge through the writings and teachings of theologians and ministers. Bypassing the need for any centralized authority, Quakers did not even have ministers and instead allowed the Holy Spirit to lead each believer to God's truth. By privileging the "inward light" over tradition or a church hierarchy, Quakers found it easier than other Christians to read the Bible in a new way.

Grimké arrived at her new reading by focusing on God's initial creation, where man and woman "were both made in the image of God; dominion was given to both over every other creature, but not over each other." Grimké handled the Fall by observing that "there was as much weakness exhibited by Adam as by Eve. They both fell from innocence, and consequently from happiness, *but not from equality*." As for Adam ruling over Eve after the Fall, Grimké argued that people have mistranslated the relevant Hebrew word, from which the English equivalent should be "will" rather than "shall." The passage thus predicted Eve's subjection (Adam "will" rule over Eve) but did not ordain it (Adam "shall" rule over Eve) as her punishment. In fact, Grimké noted, the apostle Paul in Romans 5:12 actually blamed Adam rather than Eve for the entry of sin into the world.[30] To Grimké, God's original plan for equality between the sexes continued even after the Fall.

Shifting her attention to the New Testament, Grimké held that Jesus and Paul placed men and women "on the same ground" by overturning the Mosaic law allowing husbands but not wives to obtain a divorce. She repeatedly referred to Paul's statement in Galatians 3:28 that in Christ "there is neither male nor female," with salvation available to everyone. Grimké pointed to "the Scripture doctrine of the perfect equality of man and woman," and she tried to counter Paul's statements that suggest otherwise. To address Paul's commands that wives must submit to their husbands and women must be silent in church, Grimké claimed that "his mind was under the influence of Jewish prejudices respecting women." She argued that the verses must be interpreted in the context in which they were written: the "directions given to women, not to speak, or to teach in the congregations, had reference to some local and peculiar customs, which were then common in religious assemblies."[31] Those verses did not establish a requirement for all people to follow throughout history.

Other writers developed and expanded Grimké's themes. In her 1849 book *A Scriptural View of Women's Rights and Duties*, Elizabeth Wilson — the daughter of a Presbyterian minister — highlighted the women in the Bible who served as political, social, and religious leaders. Deborah, for example, was one of Israel's judges (divinely ordained leaders) for over forty years and thereby stood "above her husband." In the New Testament, Paul praised the women who preached and prophesied in the early Christian communities. Wilson accused the translators of the King James Version of writing their biases into Romans 16:1 by calling Phoebe "a servant of the church." Using her knowledge of Greek, Wilson revealed that "the word here translated servant is, in the original, the same that is translated minister when applied to Tychicus" — a man — in Ephesians 6:21. The King James Version thus called Phoebe a servant of the church but Tychicus a minister, leading Wilson to ask, "Why not be *honest* and give the *literal translation* and let people judge for themselves?"[32]

Wilson believed that acknowledging the roles of Phoebe and other women would allow people to interpret accurately the verses where Paul forbade women from serving as ministers. In Wilson's mind, Paul imposed those restrictions "only to correct some local improprieties" where a group of married women had created a ruckus at church. Had Paul intended his command to apply to all women for all time, she asserted, he would not have mentioned it while describing how a wife could wait until later to ask her husband about something that happened at church. To support her claims further, Wilson pointed out that in 1 Corinthians 11:3–16, Paul required head coverings for women who pray or prophesy, thus recognizing that certain women will, in fact, take the ministerial actions of praying and prophesying.[33] Since Paul would not contradict himself, his comments in other verses that exclude women from ministerial positions must have a local rather than universal application.

Wilson also attempted to overturn common understandings of Paul's command for wives to submit to their husbands. God made husbands the titular heads of their families but, Wilson claimed, this title did not give husbands the authority to rule over their wives. She canvassed the entire Bible and discovered "not one approved scripture example, of husbands commanding or giving a law" to their wives. Paul's statement, then, carried no probative weight within the context of the scriptures as a whole. Instead biblical stories supported an equal partnership in marriage, whereby the husband and the wife have the "duty to rebuke each other" when necessary. The Old Testament marriages of Hannah, Hagar, and Rebekah demonstrated to Wilson that wives possessed the same parental rights as husbands. Showing a wife's authority over marital property, Abigail actually violated her husband's wishes by giving gifts to King David. For Wilson, "an approved scripture example is equivalent to a precept."[34]

Although they seemed revolutionary to some people, Wilson's biblical claims were based on methods of interpretation that Christian abolitionists had already embraced. The overlapping memberships of the movements for abolition and women's rights made it easier for interpretive approaches to spread from one group to the other. Many leaders of the women's rights movement, such as Susan B. Anthony, Antoinette Brown Blackwell, Frederick Douglass, Matilda Joslyn Gage, Sarah Grimké, Lucretia Mott, Elizabeth Cady Stanton, Lucy Stone, and Sojourner Truth, honed their skills in persuasion by first participating in antislavery meetings and organizations.[35] Having constructed, read, or heard abolitionist interpretations of the Bible, promoters of women's rights could apply those same approaches to the passages involving women.

Members of the two movements began at a disadvantage, for the Bible appeared both to authorize chattel slavery and to subordinate women to men. Leviticus 25:44–46 allowed the permanent enslavement of heathens and foreigners, and the apostles instructed slaves to obey their masters. The apostles also told wives to submit to their husbands, stay silent in church, and not usurp authority over a man. The plain language of these verses, however, did not keep abolitionists or defenders of women's rights from engaging in public debate. Advocates could and did interpret the Bible by considering its context, such as how ancient cultures practiced slavery and how married women caused commotion in one of the churches Paul founded. Understanding these contexts would confirm that the associated commands applied only to the specific circumstances the verses addressed.

Writers and speakers also appealed to biblical passages more favorable to their causes, such as verses condemning "manstealing" and describing women in leadership positions. Advocates argued that those verses undermined the competing ones that seemed to authorize slavery and subordinate women. Sometimes advocates appealed to the spirit of the scriptures by holding that "the Bible is a book of principles, and not a book of disjoined aphorisms."[36] To some readers the principles Jesus offered through the Golden Rule, the Sermon on the Mount, and his other teachings required Christians to outlaw slavery and extend rights to women. Believers in both causes often cited Galatians 3:28: "There is neither Jew nor Greek, there is neither slave nor free, there is neither male nor female; for you are all one in Christ Jesus." If all people are united through faith in Christ, the reasoning went, then we should no longer enforce a societal distinction between slave and free or male and female.

These new interpretations failed to change traditionalists' minds. Just as people could mount a biblical defense of slavery, so too could they appeal to scripture to justify male authority. Amid the growing threat the women's movement posed, traditionalists redoubled their efforts to establish that the Bible supported them. One author summarized his case by simply noting that "the scriptural position of woman is of subjection to man."[37] Horace Bushnell, a Congregational minister and theologian, wrote that assertions of the social and political equality of the sexes "would have shocked any apostle, or other scripture writer."[38] Traditionalists disputed the lessons drawn from the presence of female leaders in the Bible: "Deborah, though she was a wise woman and judged Israel, did not go at the head of the army. Huldah was endowed with the prophetic gift; but she does not stand forth prominent in the civil and religious history of the Jews. Anna, though she devoted herself to the service of God in the temple, did not at all go beyond the bounds of female modesty and propriety."[39]

Many traditionalists emphasized the one area where a woman could legitimately exert influence: the home. In their view God ordained a separate sphere for the woman and made her "the lawful queen of the little world of home."[40] Traditionalists stressed that women's roles, though distinct from men's, were just as important to a well-functioning society. The domestic realm of women was "second to no other secular sphere for honor or importance" because mothers cultivated morals and shaped a child's lifelong character.[41] "By holding in her plastic hand the minds and hearts of those who are to mould the coming age," another writer observed, the wife and mother "presides at the very fountain head of power."[42] Seeking entry into politics and the professions would force the woman "to descend from her throne" and "lay her honour in the dust."[43]

## Progress on the Women's Rights Agenda

This opposition did not dissuade advocates from continuing to press for women's rights, but they recognized the difficulty of their undertaking. "In entering the great work before us," Stanton wrote, "we anticipate no small amount of misconception, misrepresentation, and ridicule." Stanton sketched six broad areas for the movement to address: voting rights, property rights, divorce, and opportunities for women through education, gainful employment, and ordination as ministers.[44] This was an ambitious agenda, for the nation's laws and practices deviated markedly from what Stanton wanted. To what extent did the movement win reforms on Stanton's six issues during her lifetime?

The movement's greatest successes occurred on married women's property rights. American states in the early decades of the republic practiced coverture, a system whereby a husband's legal identity subsumed (or covered) his wife's. Married women could not own property, collect rents, sign contracts, or control any wages they earned. Besides ensuring that husbands made the family's economic decisions, these restrictions limited the ability of married women to start a business or enter the professions. Pressure from the women's movement led almost all states to enact major reforms during the second half of the nineteenth century. By the time Stanton died in 1902, states had eliminated almost all distinctions between the property rights of wives and husbands.[45]

In the other five areas, however, activists won only limited victories. Just a handful of states allowed women's suffrage in general elections by 1902, and women did not gain the right to vote nationwide until 1920. Divorces were somewhat easier to obtain and judges no longer automatically awarded custody of children to the father.[46] Norms, customs, and legal barriers still prevented more than a token number of women from entering the nation's most prestigious professions, and the outcomes in educational institutions were only slightly better. Despite constituting 37 percent of all college students at the turn of the twentieth century, most women either failed to graduate or else enrolled in degree programs such as home economics that did not boost their employment prospects.[47] On the final piece of Stanton's original agenda, several smaller denominations — including Unitarians, Universalists, and the Disciples of Christ — opened the ministry to women, but none of the nation's largest denominations did so.[48]

Around the time of Stanton's death, the push for ordaining women into the ministry gained momentum. The Pentecostal movement, which began on the eve of the twentieth century, welcomed women in leadership roles. Pentecostals believed that both women and men could receive gifts of the Holy Spirit, including prophesy, singing, prayer, speaking in tongues, and — most important here — teaching and preaching. Florence L. Crawford, Ida Robinson, and Aimee Semple McPherson established missions, churches, and denominations in the Pentecostal tradition. Another Pentecostal denomination, the Assemblies of God, began ordaining women as pastors in 1935.[49]

Other Protestant groups took similar actions in the succeeding decades. In 1956 the Presbyterian Church in the United States of America, the largest Presbyterian denomination, began opening the full slate of ministerial offices to women. That same year the largest branch of Methodists began ordaining women as pastors, a practice that continued when a merger created the United Methodist Church in 1968. The biggest Lutheran body took similar actions in 1970, with Episcopalians following in 1976.[50] Some Protestants resisted this trend, including the largest denomination in the country—the Southern Baptist Convention—and conservative groups such as the Lutheran Church-Missouri Synod. The Catholic Church also continued its tradition of excluding women from the priesthood.

In his 1994 encyclical *Ordinatio Sacerdotalis*, Pope John Paul II reaffirmed this Catholic practice. The priestly office, John Paul II noted, "has in the Catholic Church from the beginning always been reserved to men alone." He quoted his predecessor Pope Paul VI, who described the reasons for excluding women: "the example recorded in the Sacred Scriptures of Christ choosing his Apostles only from among men; the constant practice of the Church, which has imitated Christ in choosing only men; and her living teaching authority which has consistently held that the exclusion of women from the priesthood is in accordance with God's plan for his Church." John Paul II concluded by declaring "that the Church has no authority whatsoever to confer priestly ordination on women and that this judgment is to be definitively held by all the Church's faithful."[51]

To understand how Protestants differ from Catholics in explaining and justifying their stances on women's ordination, we can compare and contrast statements of the Southern Baptist Convention (SBC) and the Assemblies of God (AG). Conservative in their theological orientations, the two denominations share similar positions on faith, salvation, sin, redemption, and the Trinity. In its "Resolution on Ordination and the Role of Women in Ministry," the SBC declares—as Protestants have done for centuries—"the final authority of Scripture in all matters of faith and practice."[52] The AG's statement, "The Role of Women in Ministry as Described in Holy Scripture," includes almost identical wording: "The Bible is our final authority in all matters of faith and practice."[53] With both denominations pledging to follow the Bible, their differences on women's ordination are all the more striking.

According to the SBC, the Bible resolves the matter with certainty: "The Scriptures teach that women are not in public worship to assume a role of authority over men lest confusion reign in the local church (1 Cor. 14:33–36)." The statement adds: "While Paul commends women and men alike in other roles of ministry and service (Titus 2:1–10), he excludes women from pastoral leadership (1 Tim. 2:12) to preserve a submission God requires because the man was first in creation and the woman was first in the Edenic fall (1 Tim. 2:13ff)." In a not-so-subtle criticism of denominations that open the ministry to women, the SBC resolution rejects any attempt to determine Christian "doctrine and practice by modern cultural, sociological, and ecclesiastical trends or by emotional factors," and the resolution demands "that we remind ourselves of the dearly bought Baptist principle of the final authority of Scripture in matters of faith and conduct; and that we encourage the service of women in all aspects of church life and work other than pastoral functions and leadership roles entailing ordination."[54]

The AG infers a different message from the Bible. The group's statement notes that "Old Testament history includes accounts of strong female leadership in many roles," and the "New Testament also shows that women filled important ministry roles in the Early Church." Furthermore, "there are only two passages in the entire New Testament that might seem to contain a prohibition against the ministry of women (1 Corinthians 14:34 and 1 Timothy 2:12). Since these must be placed alongside Paul's other statements and practices, they can hardly be absolute, unequivocal prohibitions of the ministry of women. Instead, they seem to be dealing with specific, local problems that needed correction. Therefore, Paul's consistent affirmation of ministering women among his churches must be seen as his true perspective, rather than the apparent prohibitions of these two passages, themselves subject to conflicting interpretation."[55]

Throughout its statement, the AG relies on similar methods of interpretation as nineteenth-century writers like Sarah Grimké and Elizabeth Wilson. To understand the apparent prohibitions on female pastors in

1 Corinthians 14:34 and 1 Timothy 2:12, the AG interprets the verses within the context of the entire Bible. Using biblical examples where women did hold authority as leaders and pastors, the AG concludes that Paul directed his restrictions in 1 Corinthians and 1 Timothy to specific churches rather than the Christian community as a whole. Demonstrating that society's changing values and practices inspire new biblical interpretations, these kinds of claims were nonexistent until women began asserting their rights in the 1800s. Before then the meaning of the Bible seemed obvious: people could read the passages for themselves and see that God set aside the ministry for men alone. Without necessarily realizing it, the Assemblies of God and other Protestant groups who embrace women's ordination live in the shadow of the first women's rights movement.

### Second-Wave Feminism

The Assemblies of God began ordaining women in 1935, and the issue resurfaced during what scholars and activists call second-wave feminism. Initiating this wave with her book *The Feminine Mystique* (1963), Betty Friedan captured the frustration many middle-class women felt toward the lifestyle American society prescribed for them.[56] Friedan subsequently put her ideas into action by helping found the National Organization for Women (NOW) in 1966. In 1968 NOW offered a "Bill of Rights," including an Equal Rights Amendment to the Constitution, maternity leave, enforcement of bans on sex discrimination, tax deductions for home and child care expenses for working parents, publicly funded day care centers, equal treatment in job training and other antipoverty programs, and rights to birth control and abortion.[57] The employment and educational focus of several items in NOW's Bill of Rights revived core concerns of the nineteenth-century women's movement. NOW expanded this agenda by pushing to protect reproductive rights and change several tax, child care, and welfare policies.

Over the next few decades, the women's movement continued to push for women's rights in the workplace — an agenda including protections from sexual harassment, opportunities in the professions, equal pay for equal work, and family and medical leave. Feminists also addressed the entertainment media's depiction of women, norms and practices surrounding equality in the home, and violence against women. New groups and leaders demanded that society address domestic violence through education, law enforcement, and services for battered women. Advocates established rape crisis centers and sought to reform how the criminal justice system handled investigations, prosecutions, and trials for rape.[58] The women's movement overlapped with the LGBT movement in challenging discrimination based on a person's sexual orientation. Third-wave feminists in the 1990s and beyond brought greater attention to issues of race, diversity, and social class.[59]

In recent decades feminists have also examined how language both reflects and codifies society's expectations for women. In *The Handbook of Nonsexist Writing* (1980), Casey Miller and Kate Swift observed that "conventional English usage, including the generic use of masculine-gender words, often obscures the actions, the contributions, and sometimes the very presence of women."[60] The works of C. Wright Mills, one of the most famous sociologists of the 1950s, offer an illustrative example. Mills's opening sentence in his influential book *The Sociological Imagination* put "men" as its subject: "Nowadays men often feel that their private lives are a series of traps." In light of the rest of the paragraph, Mills probably intended for "men" to denote "adult males and females," but his word choice left some doubt as to whether women were included. Two pages later Mills said the first fruit of the sociological imagination was "the idea that the individual can understand his own experience and gauge his own fate only by locating himself within his period."[61] Again, the unspecified "individual" in the sentence probably could be female, though the references to "his own experience," "his own fate," "himself," and "his period" might prompt the reader to think primarily about males.

To overcome these biases in language, many writers in the 1970s began making their prose more inclusive. Miller and Swift, among others, encouraged teachers, journalists, and other writers to adopt the new practices.[62] For example, *person* or another word could replace *man*, descriptions of occupations could include both genders, and writers could construct their sentences in plural forms to avoid having to specify the gender of a subject. Documents began referring to *police officers* instead of *policemen*, *flight attendants* instead of *stewardesses*, and *the average person* instead of *the man on the street*. To refer back to subjects with an unspecified gender such as *anyone, no one,* or *everyone,* many grammarians eventually deemed it acceptable to use *their* rather than *his.*[63]

## Feminism and Christianity in the 1960s and Beyond

Like their predecessors a century earlier, second-wave feminists differed in how they addressed and engaged the nation's largest religion. Following the path Susan B. Anthony had blazed, Betty Friedan neither attacked Christianity nor invoked its history, practices, theologians, and scriptures for support. By the time she wrote *The Feminine Mystique,* Friedan was a nonobservant Jew who framed her arguments entirely in secular terms, drawing from and analyzing social science research, the experiences of the women she interviewed, her own career path, the expectations of society, and the messages advertisers conveyed to women about housework, employment, and the requirements of domestic tranquility. *The Feminine Mystique* made scattered references to religion in general but none specifically to Christianity.[64]

One of Friedan's contemporaries, Mary Daly, took a different course. Raised in a working-class Catholic community, Daly attended Catholic educational institutions from grade school through college and graduate school. In 1968 she published her first book, *The Church and the Second Sex,* which confronted what she considered the patriarchal foundations and history of Catholicism while rediscovering its principles, doctrines, and images that could contribute to feminism.[65] Daly channeled Elizabeth Cady Stanton by subsequently renouncing the faith of her youth and envisioning a "post-Christian" world.[66] Daly's later books analyzed patriarchal language, the ontological status of the women's movement, and women's connection to nature.[67] She occasionally attacked Christian ideas and apostles directly, as when she dismissed Paul as "one more very macho asshole described as a saint and as enlightened."[68] On another occasion, she proclaimed that "a woman's asking for equality in the Church would be comparable to a black person's demanding equality in the Ku Klux Klan."[69]

Aided by her provocative ideas and colorful writing style, Daly gained a wide readership within and beyond the academy. She also provoked strong opposition from critics, who said her later books "spun off into the ether" in pursing "eco-feminist witchcraft."[70] Summing up her life's work, one writer identified her as "an example of someone whose rejection of the authority of Scripture has led also to a radical recasting of morality."[71] Needless to say, Daly's work did not appeal to these critics or to other Americans who considered themselves Christians. Although many people who identify as Christians do not pray, attend church, or seek guidance from tradition or scriptures, others enthusiastically participate in these religious practices. Mainstream Christians could never embrace Daly's ideas.

In contrast to Daly's approach, Letha Scanzoni and Nancy Hardesty gave these Christians the opportunity to reconcile feminism and Christianity through a 1974 book, *All We're Meant to Be: A Biblical Approach to Women's Liberation*.[72] Following in the footsteps of Lucretia Mott and many other women from the 1800s, Scanzoni and Hardesty championed women's rights from inside rather than outside Christianity, and their book contributed to a movement that came to be called "evangelical feminism." Seemingly an oxymoron in 1974, evangelical feminism gained new waves of adherents in the subsequent decades. In typical fashion for writers who cherished their identity as evangelicals, Scanzoni and Hardesty fully accepted biblical authority; they also insisted that the correct interpretation revealed how the Bible sustained the case for women's rights.

In their methods of interpretation and their conclusions, Scanzoni and Hardesty owed a debt to Sarah Grimké, Elizabeth Wilson, and other first-wave feminists. Like their counterparts from the nineteenth century, Scanzoni and Hardesty emphasized the first creation account in which God made both males and females in his own image. *All We're Meant to Be* cited Galatians 3:28 to encourage the church to erase "social distinctions between men and women." Borrowing from earlier works, the book interpreted Paul's statements in 1 Corinthians 14:34 and 1 Timothy 2:12 contextually in holding that "the verses do not prohibit a ministry for women in the church but simply assert that Christian meetings should be orderly." After completing their analysis of Paul's letters, Scanzoni and Hardesty devoted a chapter to the ways in which Jesus—whom they dubbed a "woman's best friend"—advanced the status and conditions of women.[73]

Working with others to found the Evangelical Women's Caucus (EWC) in 1974, Hardesty reinforced her writing through her activism. Originally a subgroup within a larger organization called Evangelicals for Social Action, the EWC called for ordaining women, enacting the Equal Rights Amendment, and ending sexist language in Bible translations and Christian publications. In the following years the group publicized evangelical feminism through conferences that included workshops, lectures, music, prayer, and worship. Its members split in 1986 when the EWC adopted a resolution demanding civil rights for homosexuals. Already operating at the edge of evangelical acceptability, the more conservative members of the group proved unwilling to accept homosexuality as compatible with biblical teachings.[74]

In 1987 these dissenters joined other evangelical feminists in a new organization, Christians for Biblical Equality (CBE). Describing the Bible as "the inspired word of God" and "the final authority for faith and practice," the CBE's "Statement of Faith" reiterated the doctrines Protestants had stressed for centuries: the unity of God through three coequal persons, the full deity and full humanity of Jesus Christ, the debilitating effects of sin, and the power of the Holy Spirit to reshape believers' lives.[75] An evangelical reading these claims would not notice anything out of the ordinary.

The CBE's innovation occurred through its accompanying statement, "Men, Women and Biblical Equality." The statement cited verses from throughout the Old and New Testaments to build a case for men's and women's equality in creation, the Fall, and redemption. The CBE rejected the traditional understanding of a wife's submission in favor of a different model: "The Bible teaches that husbands and wives are heirs together of the grace of life and that they are bound together in a relationship of mutual submission and responsibility (1 Cor 7:3-5; Eph 5:21; 1 Peter 3:1-7; Gen 21:12). The husband's function as 'head' (*kephale*) is to be understood as self-giving love and service within this relationship of mutual submission (Eph 5:21-33; Col 3:19; 1 Peter 3:7)." The CBE also referenced a slew of verses to dispute old beliefs about biblical restrictions on ordaining women: "The Bible teaches that both women and men are called to develop their spiritual gifts and to use them as stewards of the grace of God (1 Peter 4:10-11). Both men and women are divinely gifted and empowered to minister to the whole Body of Christ, under His authority."[76]

The CBE's perspective on gender relations soon attracted a following but also created controversy within the evangelical community. Shortly after the CBE began its work, a different group of evangelical leaders founded the Council on Biblical Manhood and Womanhood (CBMW) to, in their words, "help the church defend against the accommodation of secular feminism." The CBMW explained its mission "to set forth the teachings of the Bible about the complementary differences between men and women, created equally in the image of God, because these teachings are essential for obedience to Scripture and for the health of the family and the church."[77] The principles at stake, the group claimed, affect everything important to Christians — worship practices, Bible translations, the authority of the Bible, the family and home, the life of the church, and the advance of the gospel.

The CBMW opposed the CBE in holding that the Bible affirms "the principle of male headship in the family and in the covenant community (Gen 2:18; Eph 5:21-33; Col 3:18-19; 1 Tim 2:11-15)." Both men and women must fulfill their God-given roles: "In the family, husbands should forsake harsh or selfish leadership and grow in love and care for their wives; wives should forsake resistance to their husbands' authority and grow in willing, joyful submission to their husbands' leadership (Eph 5:21-33; Col 3:18-19; Tit 2:3-5; 1 Pet 3:1-7)." God's plan for the family resembles his plan for the church: "In the church, redemption in Christ gives men and women an equal share in the blessings of salvation; nevertheless, some governing and teaching roles within the church are restricted to men (Gal 3:28; 1 Cor 11:2-16; 1 Tim 2:11-15)."[78]

Allies of the CBE battled defenders of the CBMW in sermons, newsletters, books, articles, journals, conferences, and denominational meetings. The mere existence of this debate demonstrates how far feminism had penetrated the worldviews of evangelicals. The few voices professing a biblically based equality a century earlier won virtually no support within mainstream Protestantism. Their successors at the end of the twentieth century could at least gain a respectful hearing. The CBMW's steadfast opposition shows that evangelicals did not universally embrace new ideas about gender equality, but the secular culture nevertheless left a mark. That influence led the CBMW to condemn what it called the growing "accommodation" in the church to secular beliefs.

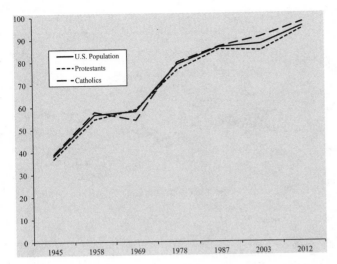

**Figure 6.1.**
Percentage who would vote for a woman for president
*Source:* Gallup surveys

## Americans' Attitudes toward Women's Rights

Just how much have secular beliefs about women influenced the consciousness of Christians and the nation at large? We can gain some insights by examining public opinion polls about women's roles in politics, the family, and the workplace. In 2012 the Gallup organization asked a random sample of Americans: "If your party nominated a generally well-qualified person for president who happened to be a woman, would you vote for that person?" Gallup has been asking similar questions for several decades. Using the accumulated data, we can document the shifts in American attitudes.

In 1937, the first year Gallup asked the question, 33 percent of Americans said they would vote for a well-qualified woman for president. Gallup's survey that year did not ask people about their religion, so there is no way to determine the extent to which Americans differed according to their religious backgrounds. Starting in 1945 and lasting through most of the subsequent surveys, Gallup did ask about the respondent's religion. Gallup placed people into a few broad categories, allowing us to compare the two largest groups of Christians in America—Protestants and Catholics—to each other and to the general population.[79]

Figure 6.1 shows these comparisons from 1945 through 2012, and the results are revealing. Only 39 percent of Americans in 1945 expressed a

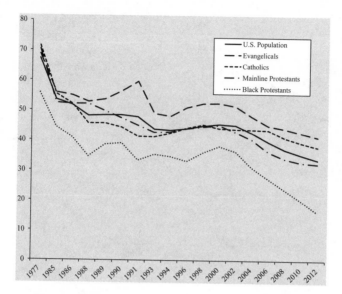

**Figure 6.2.** Percentage agreeing that a preschool child suffers if mother works
*Source:* General Social Survey. Data smoothed with LOESS.

Legend:
—— U.S. Population
— — Evangelicals
---- Catholics
— · Mainline Protestants
······ Black Protestants

willingness to vote for a woman for president. Protestants (37 percent) were slightly less likely than other Americans to take that stance, while the Catholic figure (39 percent) equaled the national average. In the following decades more people said they would elect a woman as president, with Protestants and Catholics shifting their views nearly in lockstep with everyone else. By 2012 the willingness to vote for a woman for president was almost universal among Protestants (95 percent), Catholics (98 percent), and the US population as a whole (96 percent).

We gain additional insights into how Americans think about gender roles from the General Social Survey (GSS), which I used in earlier chapters.[80] One such question, graphed in figure 6.2, asks people to agree or disagree that "a preschool child is likely to suffer if his or her mother works." In 1977, the first year the GSS included the question, 67 percent of Americans agreed.[81] That figure declined significantly in later decades, falling to 34 percent in 2012.

The GSS asks people detailed questions about their religious affiliations, allowing us to track the trends among four major Christian groups: evangelical Protestants, black Protestants, mainline Protestants, and Catholics. Evangelical Protestants were consistently the most likely to say that preschool children suffer if their mothers work. Black Protes-

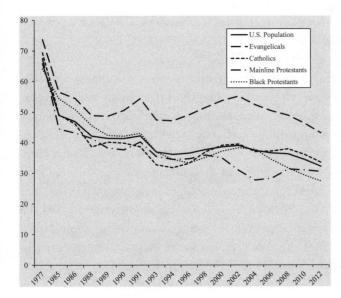

**Figure 6.3.**
Percentage
saying it's
better with wife
at home and
husband at work
*Source:* General
Social Survey.
Data smoothed
with LOESS.

tants were the least likely to take that position, with mainline Protestants and Catholics in between. All four groups, however, modified their views in a similar way as the broader population. The magnitude of these changes would probably be larger had the GSS started conducting its surveys in the early 1960s. By 1977, when the GSS first asked the question at hand, some of the attitudinal changes resulting from second-wave feminism had already occurred. Thus figure 6.2 probably understates the extent to which attitudes shifted.

In another GSS question, presented in figure 6.3, respondents must agree or disagree that "it is much better for everyone involved if the man is the achiever outside the home and the woman takes care of the home and family."[82] Paralleling the results from the two previous questions, Americans increasingly resisted the traditional view of a sexual division of labor. Whereas 66 percent of Americans took the traditionalist position in 1977, the first year the GSS included this question, only 31 percent agreed by 2012. Over that period evangelical Protestants, black Protestants, mainline Protestants, and Catholics all decreased their levels of agreement by more than thirty points. Evangelicals continually expressed the most traditional views of the four Christian groups, but they changed their attitudes in the same direction and by roughly the same amount as everyone else. Moving from attitudes to behaviors, scholars have shown that evangelical women in recent decades worked outside the home at nearly the same rates as other women.[83]

These data stand in some tension with what we might expect considering the messages conveyed at many evangelical churches. Evangelical pastors often instruct their members to adopt a traditional family structure with a wife who submits to the authority of her husband. Some denominations in the evangelical tradition, such as the Southern Baptist Convention, include this exhortation in their official documents.[84] How do ordinary evangelicals reconcile these messages with their own beliefs and practices? To find out, sociologist Sally Gallagher analyzed the data she collected from a systematic survey of evangelical attitudes about family and marriage. Gallagher's data revealed strong support among evangelicals for a traditional conception of the family, with 90 percent agreeing that the "husband should be the head of the family." At the same time, 87 percent of evangelicals endorsed the seemingly antithetical statement that "marriage should be an equal partnership." To top it off, 78 percent of evangelicals agreed with both statements![85]

How can these apparently contradictory attitudes be harmonized? Through in-depth interviews, Gallagher, Cristel Manning, and other scholars have documented the complex world of evangelical women.[86] Embracing both traditional and modern values, evangelical women affirm the *symbol* of the husband's headship and the wife's submission, even while striving for equality in their own marriages. Evangelicals expect fathers to be active participants in the lives and activities of their children, not distant authority figures.[87] Wives, meanwhile, should work with their husbands to make important decisions about finances, child rearing, and household maintenance. As one of Manning's interviewees explained, "Submission does not mean you become a floor mat to your husband. . . . It's just that somebody has to be in charge. Now, if the submission thing is working right, you're both in charge really."[88] This woman is typical of evangelicals who "mix and match the language of hierarchy and egalitarianism in describing contemporary marriage."[89]

Manning quoted one woman who clarified that "submission doesn't mean what most people think," because a wife must submit only to her husband's "prayerful, God-fearing, *wife-considering* decisions." If the two partners differ on an important decision, the wife should ask her husband to "go pray some more" so that they can reach an agreement. When asked whether she submitted to her husband, another woman stated, "Yes, I submit to my husband, but not with big decisions. . . . I want my say! Plus I feel like if it's the Lord's will, you're both going to hear the same answer anyway." In this way, evangelical women uphold the symbol of male headship while engaging in the give-and-take of any modern marriage. In the workplace it is even easier for evangelical women to accommodate contemporary attitudes. As one remarked, "I think it's OK for a woman to be the boss. I mean, if God's given her the ability."[90]

With few exceptions, evangelical women do not consider themselves feminists; as Manning puts it, they say "yes to feminist values" but "no to the feminist movement." This discrepancy exists because of how evangelical women define and understand feminism. Evangelicals believe that feminists want to emasculate men, devalue mothers, break up families, deprive women of their femininity, and promote abortion on demand—a set of beliefs that evangelicals reject. Evangelicals often fail to realize, however, how many feminist ideas they accept. Through interviews and other research methods, scholars have shown that evangelicals—along with other Americans—support equal pay for equal work, oppose discrimination in hiring and promotion, endorse the political equality of men and women, and demand that violence against women be taken seriously.[91] Evangelicals resist the feminist label even as they embrace many feminist principles.

### Gender-Neutral Bible Translations

Evangelicals also resemble other Americans in the way they make masculine and feminine references in everyday language. As norms changed in the 1970s and 1980s around gender inclusiveness in language, many members of translation committees desired a Bible whose words, forms, and constructions kept pace with the emerging patterns in English. The New Revised Standard Version (NRSV, 1989), one of the first English Bibles to strive for gender-neutral language, defended its approach in a prefatory note: "During the almost half a century since the publication of the RSV, many in the churches have become sensitive to the danger of linguistic sexism arising from the inherent bias of the English language towards the masculine gender." To achieve an accurate translation, "masculine-oriented language should be eliminated as far as this can be done without altering passages that reflect the historical situation of ancient patriarchal culture."[92]

The NRSV typically implemented this principle "by simple rephrasing or by introducing plural forms when this does not distort the meaning of the passage." For example, Jesus's aphorism in Matthew 4:4, rendered in the King James Version as "man shall not live by bread alone," became in the NSRV "one does not live by bread alone." In other instances the NRSV introduced plural forms to translate Hebrew and Greek originals that used a masculine word to refer to a generic person. Whereas the King James Version recorded Jesus in John 14:23 as saying, "If a man love me, he will keep my words: and my Father will love him," the NRSV rendered the sentence as, "Those who love me will keep my word, and my Father will love them." The NRSV translators believed that these changes gave readers deeper insights into the Bible, for the older translations "often restricted or obscured the meaning of the original text."[93]

Other Christians disagreed, especially when the New International Version (NIV) moved toward a gender-neutral revision. The earlier Bibles such as the NRSV that took this approach held a small share of the US market. The NIV, however, was both the best-selling Bible in the country and the most popular Bible among evangelicals.[94] In 1996 the NIV Inclusive Language Edition appeared in the UK, and its US publisher, Zondervan, worked with the copyright holder, the International Bible Society (IBS), on a plan to publish it stateside the following year. Public controversy erupted when Susan Olasky conveyed these intentions in the Christian magazine *World*, where she published her article "The Stealth Bible: The Popular New International Version Is Quietly Going 'Gender-Neutral.'"[95]

After learning of this plan, James Dobson and Charles Jarvis organized a meeting attended primarily by evangelical leaders opposing gender-neutral language in Bibles. Dobson, a clinical psychologist by training and a specialist in child development, founded Focus on the Family and headed it for twenty-six years; Jarvis was the organization's executive vice president. Two hours before the meeting began, the IBS announced that it would not release the gender-neutral update of the NIV in the United States. Notably, the IBS conceded no ground on the accuracy of gender-neutral translations and defended its decision by noting the public's attachment to the current NIV. Dobson's group proceeded to issue a set of guidelines calling for translators to use the English words *he, him, his, man, mankind, father, son,* and, *brother* to translate their equivalents from the Hebrew and Greek originals.[96]

Dobson's side in this dispute won a temporary victory when the IBS and Zondervan dropped their plans for the new translation, but the issue did not lie dormant for long. In 2005 Zondervan published Today's New International Version (TNIV), which included, among other changes, gender-neutral language. For the moment, readers could continue buying the NIV, which Zondervan preserved without any modifications. In 2011, however, Zondervan overcame pressure from traditionalists and issued a revised version of the NIV. After 2011 anyone who bought and read a copy of the NIV encountered far fewer masculine references than appeared in older Bibles. The Southern Baptist Convention soon condemned this decision in a resolution and pressed LifeWay, a Christian bookseller, to refuse to stock the NIV on its shelves. After careful deliberations, LifeWay's governing board decided to continue selling the NIV.[97]

In 1997 Susan Olasky had described the movement toward gender-neutral Bibles as "the feminist seduction of the evangelical church."[98] More seduction of evangelicals occurred a decade and a half later when Zondervan released its revised NIV. According to the Christian Booksellers Association (CBA), the NIV's revision did not cause a steep drop in sales; the NIV in 2012 once again outsold all other Bibles in America. According to the CBA's data from bookstores, five of the ten most popular Bibles that year used gender-neutral language, and the equivalent number at Amazon.com was also five of ten.[99] Showing a growing adherence to the new norms about gender usage in English, none of the top-selling Bibles was gender neutral just three decades earlier.

Mainline Protestants are even more likely than their evangelical counterparts to adopt a gender-neutral Bible for worship services, study groups, and official communications. For example, a poll conducted by the Presbyterian Church (USA) found that a majority of its pastors preferred the gender-neutral NRSV.[100] The Evangelical Lutheran Church in America—which, despite its name, exists within the mainline tradition—uses the same NRSV for the Bible verses it posts on its website.[101] The largest mainline denomination, the United Methodist Church, has a publishing arm that produces teaching resources drawing from two

Bibles, both of them gender neutral.[102] The two most prominent Catholic Bibles in English, the New American Bible and the New Jerusalem Bible, are also gender neutral.

## Gender-Neutral Language in Everyday Use

Extending well beyond Bible translations, Christians use more inclusive language in their writings and ordinary speech than earlier generations did. Consider the case of Wayne Grudem, arguably the intellectual leader of the opposition to gender-neutral Bibles. Grudem is a seminary professor, cofounder of the Council on Biblical Manhood and Womanhood, and author of *Systematic Theology*, which has sold over 450,000 copies and is required reading at seminaries around the world.[103] He has also written or cowritten several books and reports on the controversies surrounding gender-neutral Bibles.[104] As a believer in biblical inerrancy, Grudem holds that the original biblical texts contained no errors about faith, morals, history, or science. If the surviving Hebrew or Greek copies used a masculine reference, then the English translation must follow suit; doing otherwise tampers with the word of God. Grudem also argues that gender-neutral translations can distort the meaning of the Bible. Changing singular masculine words to inclusive plural words, for example, directs the reader's attention away from the one-to-one relationship between God and each believer.[105]

Yet Grudem's own writings are remarkably modern in their use of language. By employing phrases like *he or she* and *his or her*, Grudem's book *Politics According to the Bible* shows obvious signs of an author striving for inclusive language.[106] Like any competent writer, he avoids overusing those inelegant constructions and employs them only nine and sixteen times, respectively.[107] More often he uses plural pronouns and gender-inclusive referents such as *individual, person,* or *people*. In fact, Grudem offers a masculine word to indicate a generic person only when he quotes or refers back to earlier documents, most often the Bible. Grudem maintains that translations must preserve the masculine language of the Bible, but he crafts his own sentences to be inclusive. When even religious and political conservatives take this approach in their articles and books, we know that feminism has transformed the English language.

Feminist influences also appear, to many people's surprise, in the ideas and beliefs of James Dobson. One of the most prominent evangelicals in the country, Dobson has reached millions through his books and radio shows on child rearing, marriage, and other family-related matters. Perhaps the best indicator of Dobson's clout is the outrage his proclamations receive from his secular and religious competitors on the Left.[108] If you had to name the religious leaders least likely to uphold feminist values, James Dobson would rank near the top of the list.

It is thus noteworthy that James Dobson endorses much of the agenda that the women's movement has historically promoted. From his writings, we can infer that Dobson supports women's suffrage, married women's property rights, and employment and educational opportunities for women.[109] That's not to say that Dobson opposes traditional gender roles; for example, he advises married women with young children to avoid working outside the home. Dobson has never expressed any support, however, for the nineteenth-century legal codes and social norms that prevented single or married women, with or without young children, from having even the chance to enter many professions. For financial reasons, many mothers in the twenty-first century must seek paid employment, and Dobson has no interest in seeing them form tight bonds with their children on the way to the poorhouse. "All things being equal," he writes, "I recommend that mothers *who do have an option* consider the welfare of their children first, especially when they are young."[110]

In the political realm, Dobson thinks women should not only vote but also attain the highest offices in the land. In 2008 Dobson initially refused to endorse John McCain's presidential candidacy after McCain won the Republican nomination. Overjoyed when McCain picked Sarah Palin as his running mate, Dobson reversed himself and threw his weight behind the Republican ticket.[111] During an interview with Palin on his radio show, Dobson talked with her about stem cell research, gay marriage, abortion, the Republican platform, her children, and how the campaign affected her personal life. He concluded the interview by assuring her, "There are millions of people praying for you and Senator McCain."[112] Clearly, Dobson thinks women can exercise political leadership and would enthusiastically vote for a woman whose political stances agree with his own.

We thus reach a surprising conclusion: James Dobson embraces much of the content of the F-word. I refer, of course, to feminism. Dobson supports many of the goals that first-wave and second-wave feminists advanced, such as equality in the political realm and opportunities in the workplace. During his career Dobson has articulated conservative views on gender-related issues, but the society around him has moved steadily toward feminism. The spectrum of mainstream views has changed so much, in fact, that someone with his beliefs would have been considered liberal in 1950.

Some readers may suspect that these observations merely restate the obvious; after all, doesn't everyone in America today hold dramatically different beliefs about women's rights than were common in earlier generations? Yes—and that is precisely the point. Whether they identify as evangelical Protestants, Catholics, Mormons, Jews, atheists, or something else, Americans now accept many feminist ideas that were formerly controversial.

Columnist E. J. Dionne makes a similar observation: "Every father of a daughter, no matter his politics, is a feminist when it comes to her education and her ambitions."[113] According to third-wave feminists Jennifer Baumgardner and Amy Richards, "The presence of feminism in our lives is taken for granted. For our generation, feminism is like fluoride. We scarcely notice that we have it—it's simply in the water."[114] Even conservatives like James Dobson have filled their glasses and taken big gulps.

# Religion, Politics, and Morality

7

On January 11, 2012, Jessica Ahlquist won her lawsuit against the city of Cranston, Rhode Island. The sixteen-year-old Ahlquist wanted the school board to remove a banner containing a prayer from the wall of her high school auditorium. A committed atheist who stopped believing in God at the age of ten, Ahlquist claimed that the prayer forced religion on students who should have the freedom to decide their own beliefs. Written decades earlier by a seventh grader at the town's middle school, the prayer adorned the auditorium wall for forty-nine years until Ahlquist, having failed to convince the school board to act on its own, brought her legal challenge. Citing a string of Supreme Court precedents on the establishment clause of the First Amendment, Judge Ronald Lagueux sided with Ahlquist in ruling that posting the prayer in a public school was unconstitutional.[1]

Lagueux's decision mentioned "the hostile response she has received from her community," and that hostility intensified in the following days.[2] The area's representative in the state legislature called her "an evil little thing" on a radio talk show.[3] When the Freedom From Religion Foundation tried to send her flowers, three different local florists refused.[4] Ahlquist's opponents packed the room for the next school board meeting and sang "God Bless America" while they waited for the proceedings to begin.[5] Other people went well beyond orderly protests and threatened her well-being through Facebook, Twitter, and letters sent to her home address.[6] After suggesting that his posse might gang-rape her and toss her body from a moving car, one writer concluded his profanity-laced tirade with the words, "We will get you—look out!"[7]

Few people would actually threaten violence in this manner, but negative attitudes toward atheists are wide- 203 spread in America. According to one national survey, 48 percent of respondents said they would "disapprove if my child wanted to marry" an atheist. The same survey discovered that 40 percent of people believe that atheists do not "at all agree with my vision of American society."[8] Gallup polls have regularly found that 50 percent or more of Americans would not vote for a well-qualified nominee of their party for president if that person happened to be an atheist.[9] In all these surveys, people evaluated atheists much more harshly than other minority groups such as Muslims, Mormons, African Americans, immigrants, and homosexuals.

The negative evaluations are grounded in public perceptions that atheists flout the moral rules that religious believers take for granted. In one prominent study, research subjects making judgments of people in hypothetical situations linked atheism with dishonesty.[10] Participants in the study assumed that atheists lack the inspiration for ethical behavior that religious adherents derive from a faith commitment. In this view the fear of divine retribution keeps people from acting on their darkest impulses, leading to moral behavior in the here and now. Without the belief in an afterlife where God will reward the righteous and punish the wicked, atheists might freely lie, cheat, steal, rape, and murder if those actions would serve their interests and they could get away with it.

Suspecting atheists of immorality is nothing new. When intellectuals during the Enlightenment began to question the existence of God, Christians responded not only by defending traditional beliefs but also by imagining an atheist dystopia. If morality cannot exist without religion, atheism necessarily leads to moral degradation. Jonathan Swift made this point in one of his satirical essays, where the Christian character confronts the atheist head-on: "Why, if it be as you say, I may safely whore and drink on, and defy the parson."[11] Dostoyevsky later put similar words into the mouth of his character Ivan Karamazov. Should humanity lose its belief in God and the afterlife, Karamazov cries out, "nothing would be immoral, everything would be lawful, even cannibalism."[12]

The problems could worsen if an entire society is founded on atheist beliefs. Christian writers cite as evidence the wars and genocides of atheist regimes in the twentieth century, most notably the Soviet Union.[13] Karl Marx famously dismissed religion as the opiate of the masses, and communist ideology emphasized the need to teach people to wake up and embrace their true interests as the proletarian vanguard. Deeming religious belief and practice a threat to their authority, leaders of the Soviet Union attempted to eliminate all vestiges of religion from the population. After consolidating power and driving religion underground, Soviet leaders created the Gulag, banished dissenters to Siberia, ruled through terror, and killed millions of people. Political authorities committed similarly heinous crimes in other communist countries such as China under Mao Zedong and Cambodia under Pol Pot. Reflecting on these experiences, one Christian intellectual remarked that "all the religions of the world put together have in three thousand years not managed to kill anywhere near the number of people killed in the name of atheism in the past few decades."[14]

Besides its practical consequences, atheism also suffers in the eyes of Christian writers from its inability to ground a moral system on a sound philosophical base. If there is no God, "moral values are simply the byproduct of sociocultural evolution," and "there is no authority for rightness or wrongness of human behavior outside of human beings themselves."[15] Christianity offers a clear alternative: God—not human beings—established the moral rules by which we ought to live. C. S. Lewis contends that God implanted into people a basic moral code such that everyone understands statements such as "It's not fair!" or "That's wrong!" or "You promised!"[16] All societies therefore share a core morality while differing on many of the particulars. In *What's So Great about Christianity*, conservative intellectual Dinesh D'Souza summarizes Lewis in affirming that "conscience is nothing other than the voice of God within our souls."[17]

Christians commonly identify the Bible as the fullest expression of what one author calls God's "objective, universal, and unchanging" moral standards.[18] In part to teach us how to live, God gave humanity his scriptures and ensured that they would be translated into different languages, preached around the world, and passed from one generation to the next. With the Bible in hand, complemented in Catholicism by the continuing work of the Holy Spirit through Church tradition, we can know the moral code God wants us to follow. In these discussions about morality, Christians frequently invoke the Ten Commandments, which offer "ethics for the twenty-first century" and "a profound, enduring source of wisdom for all mankind."[19] Biblical passages covering the teachings of the prophets, the wisdom literature, the Golden Rule, and the Sermon on the Mount give people additional instruction. By denying the existence of a divine lawgiver who speaks through the scriptures, atheists cannot establish a definitive moral system.

To many Christians, atheism thus leads inevitably to moral relativism.[20] Christians know that adultery is wrong because the Bible says so; atheists cannot be sure one way or the other. The Bible commands Christians to be generous toward the poor, but atheists cannot derive such a rule from any objective and absolute source of authority. Morality becomes merely a matter of conjecture and opinion, varying radically from one person, situation, or society to another. One person says that stealing is wrong; another asserts that during wartime victorious soldiers can take whatever they want. One person says that murder is wrong; another counters that some societies permit and even encourage honor killings and blood vendettas. "Without God," the argument goes, "we are all left to figure out the meaning of good for ourselves, and the concept of objective good disappears."[21]

Learned defenders of Christianity acknowledge that atheists might happen to arrive at the same moral principles as Christians, but only because Christianity continues to influence society. Any ethical action by an atheist "is then derivative and parasitic," arising "from a culture permeated by religion; it cannot survive if the surrounding religious culture is not sustained. In short, morality as we know it cannot be maintained without Judeo-Christian religion."[22] Outside of societies grounded in Christian values, atheists could only attempt to "reason their way to kindness and ethics"—a process bound to fail.[23] Catholic intellectual Michael Novak gives his take on the problem: "If morality were left to reason alone, common agreement would never be reached, since philosophers vehemently—and endlessly—disagree."[24] To behave morally, many Christians believe, people need a faith commitment and an environment that cultivates their virtues.

Not surprisingly, atheist authors contest all these claims. Various writers cite personal anecdotes and survey evidence indicating that atheists can uphold moral standards equal to, if not higher than, those of religious adherents.[25] Atheists also dispute the conclusions Christians draw from the Marxist-Leninist countries. Best-selling author Sam Harris pins the blame for the crimes of the Soviet Union, China, and Cambodia solely on their communist ideology, claiming that it stifled the essence of atheism: a reliance on reason and evidence.[26] In this account political leaders acted on communist rather than atheist motivations. If low rates of religious observance led inexorably to immorality, then Sweden, Norway, Denmark, and Finland, which rank among the least devout countries in the world, would sink into a state of social and moral chaos. Instead, as atheists are quick to point out, the Scandinavian countries have high levels of social trust, personal happiness, and life expectancy, along with low levels of crime, depression, and infant mortality.[27]

Most provocatively, atheist intellectuals turn the philosophical question about religion and morality on its head. Rather than asking whether morality can exist without religion, they ask instead whether morality can exist *with* religion. Philosopher Bertrand Russell answered no in proclaiming that "the Christian religion, as organized in its churches, has been and still is the principal enemy of moral progress in the world."[28] Voltaire, although a deist rather than an atheist, similarly lamented, "For seventeen hundred years the Christian sect has done nothing but harm."[29] Reflecting their backgrounds as Westerners living in countries comprised primarily of Christians, Voltaire and Russell directed most of their firepower at Christianity in particular rather than at religion in general, but they minced no words in their limited observations and analyses of other religions.

Voltaire, Russell, and others often develop their case by first referencing the horrors committed in the name of Christianity, such as the Church's approach to heresy during the Middle Ages. Meeting in 1215 amid local and uncoordinated attempts to stamp out heresy, the Fourth Lateran Council used forceful language in demanding immediate action: governing authorities must "exterminate in the territories subject to their jurisdiction all heretics pointed out by the Church."[30] The various institutions that historians call the Inquisition proceeded to torture heretics and execute those who refused to recant.[31] In the early modern era the targets of Christian persecution expanded to include witches, who were punished for allegedly worshipping Satan, engaging in sorcery, and committing malevolent acts. Christians periodically conducted actual witch hunts, burning at the stake women (and some men) accused of practicing witchcraft. Historians estimate that over forty thousand people lost their lives during the witch hunts common in Europe and, to a far lesser extent, the American colonies.[32]

Atheists often save their harshest words for Christians' treatment of Jews. On the basis of Matthew 27:25, a crucial biblical verse that blames all Jews for the crucifixion of Jesus, many Christians historically considered Jews "Christ killers" and targeted them with discrimination, expulsions, pogroms, blood libels, and forced conversions under the threat of death.[33] Living in a milieu that demonized Jews, many participants in the Crusades began their journeys by massacring Jewish communities in Europe before marching to the East.[34] During the Black Death epidemics, Christians slaughtered Jews whom they accused of deliberately poisoning wells to spread the disease, and the Reformation reinforced this long-standing anti-Semitism.[35] In his book *On the Jews and Their Lies*, Martin Luther instructed "our rulers who have Jewish subjects" to act like "a good physician who, when gangrene has set proceeds without mercy to cut, saw, and burn flesh, veins, bone, and marrow." Luther demanded that rulers burn down synagogues, raze and destroy Jews' houses, confiscate prayer books and Talmudic writings, and forbid rabbis to teach "on pain of loss of life and limb."[36]

Further challenging Christians' claim to the moral high ground, atheists argue that "many moral precepts of the Bible are just plain bad, even dangerous."[37] In the *Born Again Skeptic's Guide to the Bible*, Ruth Green devotes eight pages to listing the "mass killings ordered, committed, or approved by God."[38] Most notably, God commanded his chosen people to commit genocide while seizing the Promised Land (Deuteronomy 20:16–18). As described in the book of Joshua, the Israelites obeyed God by massacring every last inhabitant of various Canaanite towns (Joshua 6:20–21, 8:22, 10:28–40, 11:8–14, 21:44). To complete the slaughter, God temporarily revoked the free will of Israel's opponents and hardened their hearts to prevent the possibility of any peace agreements (Deuteronomy 2:30–34; Joshua 11:20).[39] At other times, God acted only slightly better, telling the Israelite soldiers to kill all the men, boys, and married women among their enemies, but to "spare the lives of the young girls who have never slept with a man, and keep them for yourselves" (Numbers 31:17–18).[40] Later in Israelite history, God ordered King Saul to exterminate the Amalekites by destroying all the men, women, children, infants, and animals. Saul led his soldiers in annihilating the Amalekites but spared their king and the best of their livestock. Because Saul failed to finish the genocide, God deposed him from the throne (1 Samuel 15:1–16:1).

According to atheists, the Bible's immorality extends well beyond its genocides. Attempting to undermine the religious basis of our morals, atheists point to God's decrees and punishments in the Bible that violate contemporary principles of justice.[41] Modern legal systems use elaborate rules and procedures to ensure that judgments reflect the notion of individual accountability for one's actions.[42] Yet God in the Bible regularly ignores that principle, as when he promises to punish people for the sins committed by their grandparents and great-grandparents (Exodus 34:6–7). God orders King Saul to exterminate the Amalekites because their distant ancestors opposed the Israelites hundreds of years earlier during the escape from Egypt (1 Samuel 15:1–3). The Israelites themselves are not immune from punishment for other people's sins. When some Israelite men commit sexual immorality with the Midianites, for example, God sends a plague to kill twenty-four thousand people throughout the ranks of Israel (Numbers 25:1–9). Dating back to the Garden of Eden, God punishes all women through pain during childbirth because of Eve's transgression.

In the cases where God holds individuals responsible only for their own actions rather than someone else's, he violates another principle of justice by imposing punishments grossly disproportionate to the severity of the wrongdoing. In one noteworthy example, God strikes dead a man who had sex with his brother's widow but intentionally "spilt his seed" and refused to impregnate her (Genesis 38:9–10). During the Israelites' wandering in the wilderness, God orders Moses to execute a man who worked on the Sabbath by collecting wood (Numbers 15:32–36). Later in Israel's history, God calls forth she-bears from the woods to kill forty-two children who taunted the prophet Elisha for being bald (2 Kings 2:33–34). In the mocking words of evangelical-turned-atheist Dan Barker, who was once a preacher in Pentecostal and Charismatic churches, "True bible believers are forced to pretend that this nonsense is historical as well as moral."[43]

Upping the ante further, Barker and his allies call key elements of God's moral system in the Bible "cruel and barbaric."[44] For example, several verses explain God's command that children must be beaten with rods, with the punishment escalating to death if they disobey their parents or speak evil of them (Proverbs 13:24, 23:13-14; Deuteronomy 21:18-21; Mark 7:9-13). God also demands the death penalty for adultery (Leviticus 20:10), witchcraft (Exodus 22:18), bestiality (Leviticus 20:15-16), murder (Leviticus 24:17), kidnapping (Exodus 21:16), male homosexuality (Leviticus 20:13), false prophecy (Deuteronomy 13:5), Sabbath breaking (Exodus 31:14-15, 35:2), and perjury during judicial proceedings for murder (Deuteronomy 19:16-21). Sometimes the Bible specifies the means of execution, such as stoning to death as punishment for a blasphemer (Leviticus 24:16) or a woman discovered on her wedding night not to be a virgin (Deuteronomy 22:13-21).

Atheists also find numerous commands they deem immoral in the New Testament. The apostles Paul and Peter perpetuate the institution of slavery by telling slaves to obey their masters (Colossians 3:22; Ephesians 6:5; 1 Peter 2:18). Paul demands that people give this same allegiance to all governments, no matter how oppressive their laws or reprehensible their conduct. "Everyone is to obey the governing authorities," Paul affirms, "because there is no authority except from God and so whatever authorities exist have been appointed by God. So anyone who disobeys an authority is rebelling against God's ordinance; and rebels must expect to receive the condemnation they deserve." (Romans 13:1-2) Anyone who followed this biblical command would submit to even the most tyrannical regime and then attribute its authority to God. After quoting these sorts of passages, Sam Harris writes: "Anyone who believes that the Bible offers the best guidance we have on questions of morality has some very strange ideas about either guidance or morality."[45]

To atheists, the Bible's commands and stories demonstrate instead how *not* to live. Illustrating this lesson, a passage in Genesis praises Lot as the only righteous man in Sodom and Gomorrah. God wreaks destruction on the mass of degenerate people in those two cities, but saves his loyal servant Lot. As the narrative builds toward its conclusion, Lot demonstrates his righteousness by protecting his houseguests from an angry mob who wants to rape them. Lot steps outside his house and intervenes by offering the mob his virgin daughters to rape instead (Genesis 19:1-11). After recounting the story of Lot, comedian Bill Maher quipped, "If I ever had to swear an oath, why would I want to put my hand on the King James Bible? I think I could find more morality in the Rick James Bible."[46]

## Culture as the Key Driver of Morality

The stakes are high in this controversy. The fates of entire countries could rest on the question of whether religion sustains or undermines morality. If Christian writers are correct, a nation that loses its religious devotion would soon sink into a state of moral decay. If the atheist view holds, a shrinking faith community would instead make way for a period of moral growth.

So who is right in this debate? Would morality be better promoted by increasing or decreasing the amount of religious commitment in society? Like many debates, the contest between Christians and atheists over morality is oversimplified. The entire dispute rests on an unspoken assumption that we can compare a distinctively *Christian* morality to the alternative moral system of atheists. Within this assumption, Christians learn their morals from the teachings, traditions, and scriptures of their religion, which invariably leads to conflicts with adherents of other religions and atheists. However, we have seen in previous chapters that culture is more powerful than religion in determining a person's moral code. Culture is so powerful, in fact, that it shapes how Christians define their beliefs, interpret the Bible, and form political stances. As sociologists studying religion have long understood, religion exists within a society, not outside of it.[47] Evolving values and behaviors lead people to update their religious beliefs and identify new political implications flowing from those beliefs.

The history of Christianity demonstrates evolving rather than fixed moral and political stances—a point that becomes obvious when comparing the behavior of Christians in the Middle Ages and today. Yes, Christians once burned at the stake people accused of witchcraft, but the witch hunts ceased hundreds of years ago. Public opinion polls show that few people today, Christian or non-Christian, think that Satanic witches actually exist.[48] The small minority of Americans (for example, certain Pentecostals) who still believe in devil-worshipping witches do not treat the matter as a political question. Demonstrating that they have separated the private from the public on this issue, these believers do not ask governing authorities to find, torture, and execute the witches in our midst. Thus even the people who continue believing in witches reject the political solutions their predecessors sought in earlier centuries.

We can observe a similar transformation on questions of religious liberty. Generally speaking, Christian leaders in the Middle Ages did not recognize the freedom of religion. Heretics kept quiet to avoid persecution from local authorities and the Inquisition. After the Protestant Reformation, rulers favored one or another branch of Christianity and allowed little room for dissenters to worship and preach openly. Religious intolerance continued in the American colonies, where the Puritans in Massachusetts hanged four Quakers for violating a ban on Quaker preaching. The colonies often denied voting and property rights, and sometimes even the right to proselytize, to atheists, Jews, Unitarians, Catholics, and many Protestant sects.[49] As late as 1864, Pope Pius IX condemned religious liberty in his *Syllabus of Errors*. He denied the proposition that "every man is free to embrace and profess that religion which, guided by the light of reason, he shall consider true."[50]

Christian attitudes about religious freedom are dramatically different today. Groups as diverse as Baptists, Mormons, Methodists, and Seventh-day Adventists have endorsed each person's right to profess his or her religious convictions.[51] Baptist influence and advocacy helped shape the First Amendment to the US Constitution, which offered one of the earliest political statements of religious freedom in the modern world.[52] Other countries later established similar protections through their governing norms, precedents, and documents. Within the United States, the Constitution eventually protected citizens against violations of religious liberty not only by the federal government but also by state and local governments.[53] At the end of the Second Vatican Council in 1965, the Catholic Church, too, embraced the concept of religious freedom. In its "Declaration on Religious Freedom," the council asserted that the "right of the human person to religious freedom is to be recognized in the constitutional law whereby society is governed and thus it is to become a civil right."[54] This reversal brought all major branches of Christianity into agreement that governments cannot infringe the religious liberty of any person.

Christians have changed just as much in their views of Jews. Outside of Russia and Eastern Europe, Christian anti-Semitism had declined by the nineteenth century.[55] In the twentieth, some Christians collaborated with the Nazis but others joined the resistance movement and paid with their lives.[56] A sensitivity to the history of Christian anti-Semitism became even more common after World War II. One of the Second Vatican Council's most prominent documents denied the historical label of "Christ killers" for all Jews: "True, the Jewish authorities and those who followed their lead pressed for the death of Christ; still, what happened in His passion cannot be charged against all the Jews, without distinction, then alive, nor against the Jews of today."[57] Various ecumenical groups formed in the following decades to promote Christian-Jewish dialogue.[58] Evangelicals, for their part, gained a newfound respect for Jews because of Israel's role in the increasingly popular end-times prophesies. Among both Catholics and Protestants, relations with Jews have never been better.

Christians have also revised—and in some cases overturned—their interpretations of the Bible. While the words of the Bible are fixed within any given translation, the possibility of multiple readings of the same text allows Christian beliefs to change with the times. For example, non-Christians can easily find biblical passages that justify slavery, but Christians counter with other interpretations—based on other verses, the context of ancient slavery, or the spirit of the Bible—that yield a different conclusion. Similarly, no Christians think the genocidal decrees and actions in the Bible provide legitimate models for someone who wants to undertake a genocide today. Bill Maher's quip notwithstanding, Christians of the twenty-first century abhor the morality implied in the story of Lot (and in other verses), where a father literally owns his daughters and can sell them into slavery or offer them to be raped.

Modern Christians also reinterpret or overlook the biblical provisions requiring extensive use of the death penalty. Unlike most developed countries, America (in thirty-two states) still executes people, but only for murder. Public opinion polls show that majorities of both Christians and non-Christians in America support the death penalty for this purpose.[59] Other than fringe groups such as Christian Reconstructionists, however, no one in America presses the government to follow the Bible in requiring capital punishment for adulterers, blasphemers, homosexuals, and nonvirgin brides. Neither Christian denominations, such as the Assemblies of God, United Methodist Church, and the Catholic Church, nor lobbying organizations with religious affiliations, such as the Christian Coalition and Family Research Council, advocate bringing US laws on the death penalty into harmony with the Bible.

Because Christians often reinterpret or ignore the Bible, their moral and political positions evolve from within their own society. Wide-ranging cultural trends affect Christians and non-Christians alike, leading to changes over time in the prevailing morality. The best predictors of people's moral beliefs are not their religious convictions or lack thereof but rather when and where they were born. Christians in America today hold more in common morally and politically with their atheist neighbors than their Christian predecessors in the America of 1800. The gap grows even more apparent as we consider other times and places. Christians in twenty-first-century America repudiate much of the moral code of fifteenth-century Christians in Europe who hated Jews, burned witches, and denied religious freedoms.

Once we grasp that cultural trends sweep across the entire population, we see that the debate over the connection between religion and morality is largely theoretical. In theory, Christians and atheists could hold contrasting moral visions; in practice, they share a common morality in America today except on the scattered questions where Christians challenge the prevailing culture. Authors who debate whether religion sustains or undermines morality often use the rhetorical trick of linking their opponents to the atrocities of another time and place, and yet they fail to examine the morality those opponents profess today. If the authors on both sides paused to allow their opponents to speak for themselves, the competing camps would discover their common ground. Consider a small sampling of the moral and political stances that the vast majority of Americans now endorse:

> Child labor must be prohibited. In earlier eras parents often forced their children to work in factories, and the government did not regulate the practice until the turn of the twentieth century.
> Employers should be prohibited from discriminating in hiring, firing, and promotion decisions based on a person's race, ethnicity, or national origin. Just a few decades ago this subject split the country along racial and regional lines.

> The government should not require retailers and other businesses to close on Sundays. From colonial times through part of the twentieth century, many Christians in America appealed to the Bible to condemn commerce on Sundays. Far fewer Christians today believe that all forms of buying, selling, and working on Sundays are immoral, and the political movement to pass laws forbidding those activities has vanished.

> It is wrong for factories and other businesses to pollute the environment. Within the span of American history, environmental regulations are a recent phenomenon.

> Child abuse—including abuse by parents—must be taken seriously as a public problem and addressed through legal measures that might, in some cases, remove a child from the parents' household. Under the prevailing norm that parents enjoyed complete control over their homes and children, Americans used to tolerate levels of physical and sexual abuse that would be unacceptable today.

Pundits typically ignore areas where Americans have reached a consensus, highlighting instead the moral conflicts that currently exist and remain unresolved. It is understandable that commentators focus on the differences rather than the similarities in Americans' attitudes, beliefs, and desires. After all, no one wants to write (or read!) a book that describes how much people agree with each other. Writers instead grab the reader's attention by documenting conflicts, which are inherently more interesting and include colorful rhetoric, backroom maneuvering, and larger-than-life antagonists. While entertaining, this process creates a biased sample from the full range of actual and potential issues. Ignoring the areas where people hold common opinions and values leads us to overestimate the amount of conflict in our society.

Illustrating this phenomenon, we often hear that the country is so divided morally that Americans for decades have waged a "culture war." In his speech to the Republican National Convention in 1992, Patrick Buchanan pointed to a culture war where "the soul of America" rested in the balance. "This election is about more than who gets what," Buchanan declared, revolving instead around "what we believe and what we stand for as Americans."[60] Buchanan later described a gulf between the competing sides so wide that "we no longer inhabit the same moral universe."[61] Provocateurs like Buchanan can attract large audiences by calling attention to this divide and then taking one side or the other on the polarizing issues that define it.

Just a year before Buchanan's famous speech, sociologist James Davison Hunter popularized the term *culture war*.[62] Subsequent research by social scientists such as Alan Wolfe and Morris Fiorina, however, challenged Hunter's understanding of American culture. Surveys and interviews revealed Americans to be far less divided than the metaphor of a culture war would predict.[63] Some scholars advanced a less sweeping claim that the culture war applies to elites, especially activists and interest groups, but not the public at large.[64] If my analyses in this book are correct, we can push the critique even further. More specifically, claims of a persistent culture war are overblown even when we restrict our focus solely to elites. Yes, intense divisions often exist at a given moment on certain issues, but the nature of the conflict can change markedly from one period to the next.

The shifting moral and political attention to divorce that we examined in chapter 3 illustrates these points. Common sense suggests that the subject of divorce hypothetically could join the cluster of culture-war issues, many of which revolve around family values. If "family values" refer to morals and the resulting behaviors that affect, well, families, then divorce obviously should qualify. In fact, in earlier centuries divorce actually did lead to political strife as state lawmakers regularly debated the grounds for which divorce should be legally permissible. Through formal organizations and informal pressure, Christian groups often pushed for changes in public policy to make it consistent with the Bible's prescriptions.

During the twentieth century, leaders of those same groups backed away from vigorous political advocacy on divorce even as they mobilized around other issues tied to their religious beliefs. The frequency of divorce rose across the entire society, affecting the rank and file of different Christian groups. People increasingly concluded that government should not tightly regulate divorce because, in the modern view, the decision to end a marriage properly rests with the partners themselves. As we saw, some Christian leaders acknowledged the rising tide of marital breakups by offering biblical interpretations that loosened the New Testament's restrictions. Other leaders quietly took a more flexible stance toward divorce and remarriage within the church, redirecting their moral instruction and political advocacy to other matters.

By morphing from a political subject worthy of passionate debate into a private matter governed by personal choice, divorce illustrates how cultural changes prompt religious groups to update their moral and political positions. The same pattern happened on many other issues. In the late nineteenth and early twentieth centuries, for example, conservative Protestants deemed alcohol consumption immoral and sought to outlaw nationwide the sale and distribution of alcoholic beverages. On more than a dozen occasions, the Southern Baptist Convention pledged "opposition to the liquor traffic in any and all forms and our sympathy with every righteous measure looking to its annihilation."[65] Most Americans today remember the resulting policy of Prohibition as a failure, and few demand its reinstatement. Even further back in time, Christian leaders once denounced collecting interest on loans as immoral and demanded that authorities prohibit the practice, whereas now nearly everyone in America accepts interest as an integral part of the economy.

The evolution of Christian morality sheds new light on a prominent debate about church growth and decline. Building on the earlier research of legal scholar Dean Kelley, economist Laurence Iannaccone contributed to this debate through his influential article "Why Strict Churches Are Strong."[66] Iannaccone defined strictness broadly to cover not just morality but also theological exclusiveness and distinctive dress, diet, or lifestyle. In the blogosphere and other public outlets, commentators have commonly simplified Iannacone's ideas by focusing solely on doctrines and morality. According to one popular view, mainline churches lost members in recent decades because they abandoned the traditional tenets of the Christian faith.[67] Evangelical churches supposedly fared better because they defended biblical authority, affirmed traditional teachings, and demanded adherence to moral truths. In short, the argument goes, evangelical churches prospered by being strict.

Throughout this book we have seen how much this perspective overlooks about the Protestant experience in America. No one could deny that evangelical churches are stricter than their mainline counterparts, but the evangelical wing of Christianity is not strict in any absolute sense.

Evangelical churches are better described as selectively strict, upholding some elements of traditional morality while discarding others. Through the processes of cultural accommodation, evangelicals on many issues now hold the same moral beliefs as mainline Protestants, Catholics, members of other religions, and even atheists.

Influential evangelical leaders recognize and lament the extent to which evangelicals accommodate the culture. Francis Schaeffer, one of the most prominent evangelical theologians of the twentieth century, titled his final book *The Great Evangelical Disaster* and argued that "with exceptions, the evangelical church is worldly and not faithful to the living Christ." To confront an environment in which "the Christian influence on the whole of culture has been lost," Schaeffer observed, "we must ask where we as evangelicals have been in the battle for truth and morality." In his view, "the mentality of accommodation is indeed a disaster," arising whenever "the Bible is bent to the culture instead of the Bible judging over society and culture." Two different mechanisms produce this result: "For some the accommodation is conscious and intentional; for many more it involves their unreflective acquiescence to the prevailing spirit of the age."[68]

Schaeffer included three issues I address in this book—divorce, women's rights, and homosexuality—among those for which evangelicals accommodate the culture and reinterpret the Bible. "Under the guise of love," Schaeffer wrote, "much of the evangelical world has abandoned any concept of right or wrong on divorce and any pretext of dealing with divorce according to the boundaries established in the Scriptures." Compounding the error, certain evangelical leaders "have changed their views about [biblical] inerrancy as a direct consequence of trying to come to terms with feminism." Finally, "there are others who call themselves evangelical and then affirm the acceptability of homosexuality and even homosexual 'marriage.'"[69]

In recent decades other evangelical leaders reiterated Schaeffer's call for a "loving confrontation" with the culture—a confrontation requiring Christians to "affirm the inerrancy of Scripture and then live under it in our personal lives and society."[70] R. Albert Mohler Jr., president of the Southern Baptist Theological Seminary, wants evangelicals to challenge the culture on many of the same issues Schaeffer emphasized. Citing evangelicals' high rates of divorce and the absence of political action on the issue, for example, Mohler deems divorce "the scandal of the evangelical conscience."[71] Mohler has also repeatedly called for evangelicals to follow the Bible's teachings, declare homosexual behavior sinful, and resist its acceptance in society and the law.[72]

Despite their best efforts, leaders such as Schaeffer and Mohler cannot easily persuade evangelicals, let alone other Americans, to reject the contemporary opinions, values, and behaviors that conflict with traditional Christian doctrines. Outside of small sects who wall themselves off from society, such as the Amish, cultural transformations affect Protestants, Catholics, other Christians, adherents of other religions, and those holding no religion at all. As a result, societies—including those as large and diverse as America—often find common ground on issues that used to spark conflicts.

No society will ever achieve total consensus because new conflicts arise to replace the old ones. Religious leaders, in fact, can solidify their members' commitments to the group by taking strong stands against particular aspects of secular culture. Religion is a form of social identity that allows people to define who they are, bond with their group, and distinguish themselves from others.[73] Sociologist Christian Smith argues that maintaining some tension with the broader society actually strengthens the vitality of evangelical churches. Smith suggests that evangelical churches that became genuinely countercultural would alienate their current and prospective members, but those same churches sometimes grow their memberships by drawing contrasts with other religious traditions and society at large.[74] Non-Christian religions also contain distinctive beliefs and practices that create a sense of belonging and solidarity among their adherents.

Despite these differences between groups at any given moment, over time Americans often reach a rough consensus on a formerly contentious issue. Christians now link hands with atheists and others in affirming positions that the vast majority of people opposed in previous generations. During a moral and political transition, different segments of the population look like the ships in a convoy.[75] Some groups take positions at the front and others follow in the middle or the rear, but the groups nevertheless move together. When we examine the long sweep of history, we find that Americans commonly resolve their moral conflicts and discover the principles on which most people can agree.

The vantage point of history also allows us to see that participants in the culture war fight over a narrow set of issues. The current struggles typically involve abortion, homosexuality, religious displays on public property, teaching intelligent design in schools, and a scattering of related controversies. Earlier generations battled over different issues but commonly formed a consensus as public opinion moved either steadily or quickly in one direction. The subjects that define today's culture war are thus only a small share of all potential conflicts. To understand the culture war properly, we must remember the areas of agreement that exist alongside the areas of disagreement. In one of their fundamental mistakes, James Davison Hunter and his intellectual allies fail to consider the full range of actual and potential issues. This omission leads them to overly dramatize a handful of conflicts.

In perhaps their greatest exaggeration, Hunter and his followers assert that combatants in the culture war start from incompatible worldviews. In the words of columnist Ross Douthat, unceasing conflict is inevitable because "there's no common ground on which to call a truce."[76] Once we examine the actual beliefs of the warring activists, intellectuals, and politicians, however, we discover that their worldviews overlap. As Americans living in the twenty-first century, the culture warriors all agree on the desirability of individual rights and representative democracy. Unlike many of their predecessors, few participants in the culture war want to criminalize blasphemy, ban interracial marriage, prosecute adultery as a felony offense, or restrict entry into the professions to men. Contrary to Hunter's assertions, the two sides in the culture war share a set of starting assumptions that limit the scope of their conflicts.

Rather than a battle of incompatible worldviews, the culture war is best described as a struggle between people with overlapping worldviews who fight over their differences. The issues dividing them often do not persist. Divorce, for example, does not create political controversy in contemporary America, even though it did in earlier times. Homosexuality emerged in the 1970s as a major front of the culture war, but it is now becoming less contentious with each passing year. Moral rules can become tighter, too. In a striking change from earlier times, Americans are now nearly unified in denouncing slavery, discrimination, child abuse, and domestic violence. American history has repeatedly shown that today's moral conflict can evolve into tomorrow's moral consensus. Our country captures this enduring reality in the motto on our national seal: *E pluribus unum*—Out of many, one.

# Acknowledgments

During my six years of research and writing, many institutions and individuals gave me crucial assistance. The University of Washington provided a sabbatical leave that allowed me to refine my theoretical framework and collect evidence for several chapters. I had the opportunity to present my research at seminars at the University of California at San Diego, The Ohio State University, Columbia University, the University of Minnesota, and the University of Washington. John Evans, Isaac Martin, Jack Wright, Greg Caldeira, Mike Ting, Wendy Rahn, Joanne Miller, and Chris Federico asked tough questions and helped me articulate my claims. Chris Parker, John Gastil, and George Lovell read one or more chapters and encouraged me to rethink certain aspects of my reasoning, approach, and presentation.

I owe my biggest debts to my family. While I was working on this book, my daughters, Julie and Ali, grew from little kids into teenagers, and I have enjoyed every step along the way. My mom and dad (Diane and Lee), my brother (Brian), my mother-in-law (Jean), and my sister-in-law and brother-in-law (Karen and Bill) were inquisitive about the project but also gave me a chance to talk about something other than religion and politics. My wife, Kristen, read my first drafts of every chapter, and she was forced to identify my errors in logic and evidence (of which there were many!). My father-in-law, John, gave me detailed comments and writing assistance on multiple drafts of my chapters, and the final versions show his profound influence. The world lost one of its warmest and most compassionate people with his untimely passing, and I miss him dearly.

Students in three classes—two undergraduate honors seminars and one graduate seminar—served as test audiences for various iterations of the book. I thank them for their insights into what the book was saying and how it could be improved. I also thank Sarah Cypher and Bud Bynack, my developmental editors, who helped integrate the parts of the book into a cohesive whole and worked to make my prose more clear and concise. An earlier version of chapter 3 appeared as "Religion, Divorce, and the Missing Culture War in America" in *Political Science Quarterly* (2010), and I thank the publishers for permission to reuse the material.

At the University of Chicago Press, I had the pleasure of working again with John Tryneski. He not only guided the manuscript through its submission, reviews, and production, but he also showed me how I could streamline the introduction and clarify my arguments. The anonymous reviews he solicited encouraged me to situate the manuscript within the scholarly study of religion in political science, sociology, religious studies, and history. Kelly Finefrock-Creed, my copyeditor, caught many errors and moved the manuscript along in its journey to print.

To all these institutions and individuals, I give my sincere thanks for helping bring the book to completion.

# Notes

PREFACE

1 James Davison Hunter, *Culture Wars: The Struggle to Define America* (New York: Basic Books, 1991), 42, 44.

2 Bill O'Reilly, *Culture Warrior* (New York: Broadway Books, 2006).

3 Ross Douthat, "The Persistence of the Culture War," *New York Times*, February 7, 2012.

4 Sam Harris, *The End of Faith: Religion, Terror, and the Future of Reason* (New York: Norton, 2004); Richard Dawkins, *The God Delusion* (Boston: Houghton Mifflin, 2006); Daniel C. Dennett, *Breaking the Spell: Religion as a Natural Phenomenon* (New York: Viking, 2006); Christopher Hitchens, *God Is Not Great: How Religion Poisons Everything* (New York: Twelve Books, 2007); Victor Stenger, *God, the Failed Hypothesis: How Science Shows That God Does Not Exist* (Amherst, NY: Prometheus Books, 2007).

5 Edward Feser, *The Last Superstition: A Refutation of the New Atheism* (South Bend, IN: St. Augustine's Press, 2008); Timothy J. Keller, *The Reason for God: Belief in an Age of Skepticism* (New York: Dutton, 2008).

6 Dan Barker, *Godless: How an Evangelical Preacher Became One of America's Leading Atheists* (Berkeley, CA: Ulysses Press, 2008), Elizabeth Anderson, "If God Is Dead, Is Everything Permitted?," in *The Portable Atheist: Essential Readings for the Nonbeliever*, ed. Christopher Hitchens (Philadelphia: Da Capo Press, 2007).

7 Dinesh D'Souza, *What's So Great about Christianity* (Washington, DC: Regnery Publishing, 2007); William Lane Craig, "The Kurtz/Craig Debate: Is Goodness without God Good Enough?," in *Is Goodness without God Good Enough?*, ed. Robert K. Garcia and Nathan L. King (Lanham, MD: Rowman & Littlefield Publishers, 2009).

8 Alan Wolfe, *One Nation, After All: What Middle-Class Americans Really Think about God, Country, Family, Racism, Welfare, Immigration, Homosexuality, the Right, the Left, and Each Other* (New York: Viking, 1998); Morris P. Fiorina, with Samuel J. Abrams and Jeremy C. Pope, *Culture War? The Myth of a Polarized America* (New York: Pearson Longman, 2005); Paul DiMaggio, John Evans, and Bethany Bryson, "Have Americans' Social Attitudes Become More Polarized?" *American Journal of Sociology* 102 (November 1996): 690–755; Nancy J. Davis and Robert V. Robinson, "Are the Rumors of War Exaggerated? Religious Orthodoxy and Moral Progressivism," *American Journal of Sociology* 102

(November 1996): 756–87; and Wayne Baker, *America's Crisis of Values: Reality and Perception* (Princeton, NJ: Princeton University Press, 2005).

9 Alan I. Abramowitz, *The Disappearing Center: Engaged Citizens, Polarization, and American Democracy* (New Haven, CT: Yale University Press, 2010). See also David C. Barker and Christopher Jan Carman, *Representing Red and Blue: How the Culture Wars Change the Way Citizens Speak and Politicians Listen* (New York: Oxford University Press, 2012), and William G. Jacoby, "Is There a Culture War? Conflicting Value Structures in American Public Opinion," *American Political Science Review* 108 (November 2014):754–71.

10 James Davison Hunter, "The Enduring Culture War," in *Is There a Culture War? A Dialogue on Values and American Public Life*, by Hunter and Alan Wolfe (Washington, DC: Brookings Institution, 2006).

CHAPTER ONE

1 All biblical quotes in chapter 1 are from *The Holy Bible, English Standard Version* (Wheaton, IL: Crossway, 2001).

2 Benjamin N. Nelson, *The Idea of Usury: From Tribal Brotherhood to Universal Otherhood* (Princeton, NJ: Princeton University Press, 1949), ch. 1.

3 "Second Lateran Council 1139 A.D.," Daily Catholic, accessed October 25, 2010, http://www.dailycatholic.org/history/10ecumen.htm.

4 John T. Noonan Jr., *The Scholastic Analysis of Usury* (Cambridge, MA: Harvard University Press, 1957), 51–57.

5 Lawrin Armstrong, *Usury and Public Debt in Early Renaissance Florence: Lorenzo Ridolfi on the Monte Comune* (Toronto: Pontifical Institute of Mediaeval Studies, 2003), 53–84.

6 Nelson, *The Idea of Usury*, 17–25; Sidney Homer and Richard Sylla, *A History of Interest Rates*, 3rd ed. (New Brunswick, NJ: Rutgers University Press, 1991), 71–73.

7 Homer and Sylla, *A History of Interest Rates*, 77–78.

8 As quoted in John T. Noonan Jr., "The Amendment of Papal Teaching by Theologians," in *Contraception: Authority and Dissent*, ed. Charles E. Curran (New York: Herder and Herder, 1969), 74.

9 Noonan, *The Scholastic Analysis of Usury*, 202–29.

10 Noonan, "The Amendment of Papal Teaching by Theologians," 58–72.

11 Homer and Sylla, *A History of Interest Rates*, 79–80.

12 *Online Etymology Dictionary*, s.v. "usury," accessed October 26, 2010, http://www.etymonline.com/index.

13 The situation differs in Muslim countries, where the bans on interest in the Qur'an sometimes remain in effect and pose major challenges to banks.

14 Homer and Sylla, *A History of Interest Rates*, 70–72.

15  For a related book that views the history of American politics through struggles over morality, see James A. Morone, *Hellfire Nation: The Politics of Sin in American History* (New Haven, CT: Yale University Press, 2003).

16  Laura R. Olson and Sue E. S. Crawford, "Clergy in Politics: Political Choices and Consequences," in *Christian Clergy in American Politics*, ed. Sue E. S. Crawford and Laura R. Olson (Baltimore: Johns Hopkins University Press, 2001), 3–14.

17  Ted Jelen, *The Political World of the Clergy* (Westport, CT: Greenwood Press, 1993), 94–95.

18  Mark Driscoll, "Kingdom: God Reigns," sermon to Mars Hill Church, Seattle, Washington, June 30, 2008. Available online as an iTunes podcast.

19  Jennifer Sullivan, "Embattled Mars Hill Pastor Mark Driscoll Resigns," *Seattle Times*, October 15, 2014.

20  Ernest Q. Campbell and Thomas F. Pettigrew, *Christians in Racial Crisis: A Study of Little Rock's Ministry* (Washington, DC: Public Affairs Press, 1959); Jeffrey K. Hadden, *The Gathering Storm in the Churches* (Garden City, NY: Doubleday, 1969).

21  Robert Wuthnow and John H. Evans, eds., *The Quiet Hand of God: Faith-Based Activism and the Public Role of Mainline Protestantism* (Berkeley: University of California Press, 2002).

22  Paul A. Djupe and Christopher P. Gilbert, *The Prophetic Pulpit: Clergy, Churches, and Communities in American Politics* (Lanham, MD: Rowman & Littlefield, 2003); James L. Guth, John C. Green, Corwin E. Smidt, Lyman A. Kellstedt, and Margaret M. Poloma, *The Bully Pulpit: The Politics of Protestant Clergy* (Lawrence, KS: University Press of Kansas, 1997).

23  Daniel J. B. Hofrenning, *In Washington but Not of It: The Prophetic Politics of Religious Lobbyists* (Philadelphia: Temple University Press, 1995). According to his research, denominational leaders have more leeway when lobbying on issues of low visibility.

24  R. Albert Mohler Jr., "Against an Immoral Tide," *New York Times*, June 19, 2000.

25  See "Charter, Constitution, and Bylaws," Southern Baptist Convention, accessed August 6, 2010, http://www.sbc.net/PDF/SBC-CharterConstitutionByLaws .pdf. The relevant bylaw is no. 20.

26  Thomas J. Reese, *Inside the Vatican: The Politics and Organization of the Catholic Church* (Cambridge, MA: Harvard University Press, 1996).

27  On the number of ex-Catholics in America, see "US Religious Landscape Survey," Pew Forum on Religion and Public Life, accessed August 6, 2010, http:// religions.pewforum.org/pdf/report-religious-landscape-study-full.pdf.

28  Andrew S. McFarland, *Common Cause: Lobbying in the Public Interest*

(Chatham, NJ: Chatham House, 1984); Ronald G. Shaiko, *Voices and Echoes for the Environment: Public Interest Representation in the 1990s and Beyond* (New York: Columbia University Press, 1999).

29 Similar points emerge from the concept of "confirmation bias" in psychology and the perspectives of reader-response criticism in literary theory. For entry points into these literatures, see Raymond S. Nickerson, "Confirmation Bias: A Ubiquitous Phenomenon in Many Guises," *Review of General Psychology* 2 (1998): 175-220; Jane P. Tomkins, ed., *Reader-Response Criticism: From Formalist to Post-Structuralism* (Baltimore: Johns Hopkins University Press, 1980).

30 Rudolf Bultmann, "Is Exegesis without Presuppositions Possible?" [1957], in *New Testament and Mythology and Other Basic Writings*, trans. Schubert M. Ogden (Philadelphia: Fortress Press, 1984), 145-53.

31 Joseph J. Fahey, *War and the Christian Conscience: Where Do You Stand?* (Maryknoll, NY: Orbis Books, 2005), 43, 72-82.

32 William Safire, "On Language: Phantom of the Phrases," *New York Times*, March 13, 1988.

33 John Harwood, "Flip-Flops Are Looking Like a Hot Summer Trend," *New York Times*, June 23, 2008.

34 For similar arguments, see Alan Wolfe, *The Transformation of American Religion: How We Actually Live Our Faith* (New York: Free Press, 2003); and Liz Fawcett, *Religion, Ethnicity, and Social Change* (New York: St. Martin's Press, 2000).

35 Other small groups in America have also found it difficult to adhere in practice to strict pacifist doctrines. See Theron F. Schlabach and Richard T. Hughes, eds., *Proclaim Peace: Christian Pacifism from Unexpected Quarters* (Urbana: University of Illinois Press, 1997).

36 Cecil B. Currey, "The Devolution of Quaker Pacifism: A Kansas Case Study, 1860-1955," *Kansas History* 6 (1983): 120-33.

37 Peter Brock, *The Quaker Peace Testimony, 1660 to 1914* (Syracuse, NY: Syracuse University Press, 1990).

38 Currey, "The Devolution of Quaker Pacifism."

39 James Davison Hunter, *American Evangelicalism: Conservative Religion and the Quandary of Modernity* (New Brunswick, NJ: Rutgers University Press, 1983); Marsha G. Witten, *All Is Forgiven: The Secular Message in American Protestantism* (Princeton, NJ: Princeton University Press, 1993).

40 Kathleen A. Tobin, *The American Religious Debate over Birth Control, 1907-1937* (Jefferson, NC: McFarland, 2001).

41 Pope Benedict XVI, *Light of the World: The Pope, the Church, and the Signs of the Times*, trans. Michael J. Miller and Adrian J. Walker (San Francisco: Ignatius Press, 2010), 119.

42 The joke has been reprinted many times, including in H. Aaron Cohl and Barry Dougherty, *The Friar's Club Encyclopedia of Jokes: Over 2,000 One-Liners, Straight Lines, Stories, Gags, Roasts, Ribs, and Put-Downs* (New York: Black Dog & Leventhal, 1997), 57.

43 Walter D. Mosher and Jo Jones, *Use of Contraception in the United States: 1982–2008*, Vital and Health Statistics, series 23, no. 29 (Hyattsville, MD: US Department of Health and Human Services, Centers for Disease Control and Prevention, National Center for Health Statistics, 2010), 5. The population in question is American women aged fifteen to forty-five who have had sexual intercourse on one or more occasions.

44 John T. McGreevy, *Catholicism and American Freedom: A History* (New York: Norton, 2003), 221–49.

45 Andrea Tone, *Devices and Desires: A History of Contraceptives in America* (New York: Hill and Wang, 2001); James Hennesey, *American Catholics: A History of the Roman Catholic Community in the United States* (New York: Oxford University Press, 1981), 327–29.

46 Current statements can be found at the website of the United States Conference of Catholic Bishops (http://www.usccb.org, accessed November 23, 2014). Earlier statements are printed in Hugh J. Nolan, ed., *Pastoral Letters of the United States Catholic Bishops, 1792–1983*, 4 vols. (Washington, DC: Office of Publishing Services, National Conference of Catholic Bishops, United States Conference of Catholic Bishops, 1984).

47 Giuseppe Benagiano, Sabina Carrara, Valentina Filippi, and Ivo Brosens, "Condoms, HIV and the Roman Catholic Church," *Reproductive BioMedicine Online* 22 (2011): 701–9.

48 Anthony Gill, *Rendering unto Caeser: The Catholic Church and the State in Latin America* (Chicago: University of Chicago Press, 1998).

49 Antonio Spadaro, SJ, "A Big Heart Open to God: The Exclusive Interview with Pope Francis," *America: The National Catholic Review*, September 30, 2013, accessed November 4, 2013, http://www.americamagazine.org/pope-interview.

50 F. Donald Logan, *A History of the Church in the Middle Ages* (New York: Routledge, 2002).

51 Elizabeth L. Eisenstein, *The Printing Revolution in Early Modern Europe*, 2nd ed. (New York: Cambridge University Press, 2005).

52 David B. Barrett, George T. Kurian, and Todd M. Johnson, *World Christian Encyclopedia: A Comparative Survey of Churches and Religions in the Modern World*, 2nd ed. (New York: Oxford University Press, 2001), 16.

53 William D'Antonio, James Davidson, Dean Hoge, and Ruth Wallace, *American Catholic Laity in a Changing Church* (Kansas City, MO: Sheed and Ward, 1989).

54 Christian Smith, with Kari Christoffersen, Hilary Davidson, and Patricia Snell Herzog, *Lost in Transition: The Dark Side of Emerging Adulthood* (New York: Oxford University Press, 2011).

55 "Bishops' Program of Social Reconstruction" [1919], Hesburgh Libraries of the University of Notre Dame, accessed November 23, 2014, https://repository .library.nd.edu/view/649/000751083.pdf.

56 Franklin D. Roosevelt, "Address at Oglethorpe University, May 22, 1932," New Deal Network, accessed March 29, 2013, http://newdeal.feri.org/speeches /1932d.htm.

57 Benjamin I. Page and Robert Y. Shapiro, *The Rational Public: Fifty Years of Trends in Americans' Policy Preferences* (Chicago: University of Chicago Press, 1992), ch. 7.

58 Alan Wolfe, *The Transformation of American Religion: How We Actually Live Our Faith* (Chicago: University of Chicago Press, 2003).

59 Robert D. Putnam and David E. Campbell, *American Grace: How Religion Divides and Unites Us* (New York: Simon & Schuster, 2010).

60 In the first biblical quote from each chapter, I give the full citation for that particular translation.

## CHAPTER TWO

1 Peter Mancall, ed., *Envisioning America: English Plans for the Colonization of North America, 1580–1640* (Boston: Bedford Books of St. Martin's Press, 1995).

2 Arthur O. Lovejoy, *The Great Chain of Being: A Study of the History of an Idea* (Cambridge, MA: Harvard University Press, 1936).

3 Winthrop D. Jordan, *White over Black: American Attitudes toward the Negro, 1550–1812* (Baltimore: Penguin Books, 1968), chs. 1–2.

4 Cotton Mather, "The Negro Christianized. An Essay to Excite and Assist That Good Work, the Instruction of Negro-Servants in Christianity" [1706], Digital Commons, University of Nebraska–Lincoln, accessed December 5, 2013, http:// digitalcommons.unl.edu/cgi/viewcontent.cgi?article=1028&context=etas.

5 Betty Wood, *The Origins of American Slavery: Freedom and Bondage in the English Colonies* (New York: Hill and Wang, 1997).

6 William Sewel, *History of the Rise, Increase, and Progress of the Christian People Called Quakers*, 6th ed. (London: Darton and Harvey, 1824), 2:1–115.

7 "Memoir of the Life of George Fox," in *The Friends' Library: Comprising Journals, Doctrinal Treatises, and Other Writings of Members of the Religious Society of Friends*, ed. William Evans and Thomas Evans (Philadelphia: Joseph Rakestraw, 1837), 1:33.

8 Thomas D. Hamm, *The Quakers in America* (New York: Columbia University Press, 2003).

9 Jean R. Soderlund, *Quakers and Slavery: A Divided Spirit* (Princeton, NJ: Princeton University Press, 1985).

10 Stephen Prothero, *Religious Literacy: What Every American Needs to Know—and Doesn't* (San Francisco: HarperCollins, 2007).

11 All Bible references in this chapter are from *The Holy Bible, Authorized King James Version* (Nashville, TN: World Publishing, 2004). Following standard practice in quoting the KJV, I do not include the italics that the translators applied to certain words.

12 David M. Goldenberg, *The Curse of Ham: Race and Slavery in Early Judaism, Christianity, and Islam* (Princeton, NJ: Princeton University Press, 2003).

13 Mather, "The Negro Christianized."

14 George Bourne, *A Condensed Anti-slavery Bible Argument* (New York: S. W. Benedict, 1845), 24–26; Theodore Dwight Weld, *The Bible against Slavery; or, An Inquiry into the Genius of the Mosaic System, and the Teachings of the Old Testament on the Subject of Human Rights* [1864] (Detroit: Negro History Press, 1970), 95–98.

15 Stephen R. Haynes, *Noah's Curse: The Biblical Justification of American Slavery* (Oxford: Oxford University Press, 2002).

16 Weld, *The Bible against Slavery*, 86–92; Albert Barnes, *An Inquiry into the Scriptural Views of Slavery* (Philadelphia: Perkins & Purves, 1846), 83–104; John G. Fee, *The Sinfulness of Slaveholding, Shown by Appeals to Reason and Scripture* (New York: John A. Gray, 1851), 10–11.

17 Thornton Stringfellow, "A Scriptural View of Slavery" [1856], in *Slavery Defended: The Views of the Old South*, ed. Eric L. McKitrick (Englewood Cliffs, NJ: 1963), 87–89; John Henry Hopkins, *A Scriptural, Ecclesiastical, and Historical View of Slavery from the Days of the Patriarch Abraham, to the Nineteenth Century* (New York: W. I. Pooley, 1864), 7–8; Charles Hodge, "The Bible Argument on Slavery," in *Cotton Is King, and Proslavery Arguments: Comprising the Writings of Hammond, Harper, Christy, Stringfellow, Hodge, Bledsoe, and Cartwright on this Important Subject*, ed. E. N. Elliott (Augusta, GA: Pritchard, Abbott & Loomis, 1860), 859.

18 Hodge, "The Bible Argument on Slavery," 847–48; Hopkins, *A Scriptural, Ecclesiastical, and Historical View*, 13–14; Stringfellow, "A Scriptural View of Slavery," 95–97.

19 Weld, *The Bible against Slavery*, 39; Bourne, *A Condensed Anti-Slavery Bible Argument*, 77. See also Angelina Grimké, *Appeal to the Christian Women of the South* (New York: New York Antislavery Society, 1836), 21–23.

20 Ceslas Spicq, *Theological Lexicon of the New Testament* (Peabody, MA: Hendrickson, 1994), 1:380–81; Carl Ludwig Wilibald Grimm, *The New Thayer's*

*Greek–English Lexicon of the New Testament with Index* (Lafayette, IN: Associated Publishers & Authors, 1981), 158.

21 Morton Smith, "Slavery," in *What the Bible Really Says*, ed. Morton Smith and R. Joseph Hoffmann (Buffalo, NY: Prometheus Books, 1989), 137–46.

22 Hopkins, *A Scriptural, Ecclesiastical, and Historical View*, 10–11; see also Stringfellow, "A Scriptural View of Slavery," 92.

23 Catherine Hezser, *Jewish Slavery in Antiquity* (New York: Oxford University Press, 2005).

24 Barnes, *An Inquiry into the Scriptural Views of Slavery*, 251–68.

25 Weld, *The Bible against Slavery*, 22–30.

26 George Barrell Cheever, *The Guilt of Slavery and the Crime of Slaveholding, Demonstrated from the Hebrew and Greek Scriptures* (Boston, MA: John P. Jewitt, 1860), 340–41, 415–17; George Bourne, *The Book and Slavery Irreconcilable* [1816] (New York: Arno Press, 1969), 21–29.

27 Fee, *The Sinfulness of Slaveholding*, 22.

28 Joseph Henry Thayer, *Greek–English Lexicon of the New Testament* (New York: Harper & Brothers, 1889), 43; Michael Marlowe, "'Make Good Use of Your Servitude': Some Observations on Biblical Interpretation and Slavery," Bible Research, accessed August 7, 2008, http://www.bible-researcher.com/slavery.html.

29 Kenneth Hughes, *Slavery* (London: George Allen & Unwin, 1975), ch. 1.

30 John Thornton, *Africa and Africans in the Making of the Atlantic World, 1400–1800*, 2nd ed. (Cambridge: Cambridge University Press, 1998), 98–102.

31 Albert Taylor Bledsoe, "Liberty and Slavery; or, Slavery in the Light of Moral and Political Philosophy," in Elliott, *Cotton Is King*, 358–59; Thornton Stringfellow, *Scriptural and Statistical Views in Favor of Slavery* (Richmond, VA: J. W. Randolph, 1856), 69.

32 Bledsoe, "Liberty and Slavery," 356–74; Hopkins, *A Scriptural, Ecclesiastical, and Historical View*, 14–16.

33 Bourne, *A Condensed Anti-Slavery Bible Argument*, 82–84.

34 Barnes, *An Inquiry into the Scriptural Views of Slavery*, 321–30.

35 Bourne, *A Condensed Anti-Slavery Bible Argument*, 53.

36 Barnes, *An Inquiry into the Scriptural Views of Slavery*, 245–47, 376–81; Grimké, *Appeal to the Christian Women*, 25; Fee, *The Sinfulness of Slaveholding*, 19.

37 John Brown, "John Brown's Speech to the Court at His Trial," National Center for Public Policy Research, accessed November 23, 2014, http://www.nationalcenter.org/JohnBrown%27sSpeech.html.

38 Harriet Beecher Stowe, *Uncle Tom's Cabin; or, Life among the Lowly* [1851] (Boston: Houghton Mifflin, 1899), 89–90.

39 Hopkins, *A Scriptural, Ecclesiastical, and Historical View*, 11–12; Stringfellow, "A Scriptural View of Slavery," 97.

40 Bledsoe, "Liberty and Slavery," 348–52.

41 Barnes, *An Inquiry into the Scriptural Views of Slavery*, 297.

42 Fee, *The Sinfulness of Slaveholding*, 21; Grimké, *Appeal to the Christian Women*, 27.

43 Bourne, *A Condensed Anti-Slavery Bible Argument*, 95.

44 Mark A. Noll, *America's God: From Jonathan Edwards to Abraham Lincoln* (Oxford: Oxford University Press, 2002), 398–400.

45 Leonard Bacon, *Slavery Discussed in Occasional Essays, 1833–1846* [1846] (New York: Arno Press, 1969), 180.

46 Hopkins, *A Scriptural, Ecclesiastical, and Historical View*, 6–7.

47 Lee Ward, *The Politics of Liberty in England and Revolutionary America* (New York: Cambridge University Press, 2004).

48 John Dickinson, Letter 7 [1768], in *Letters from a Farmer in Pennsylvania, to the Inhabitants of the British Colonies* (New York: Outlook, 1903), 77; John Adams, Essay 2 [1775], in *Novanglus; or, A History of the Dispute with America from Its Origin, in 1754, to the Present Time*, accessed July 14, 2008, http://en.wikisource .org/wiki/Novanglus_Essays/No._2; James Cannon, "Cassandra to Cato: Letter 2" [April 13, 1776], accessed December 3, 2013, http://lincoln.lib.niu.edu/cgi -bin/amarch/getdoc.pl?/var/lib/philologic/databases/amarch/.14561.

49 Cassandra Pybus, *Epic Journeys of Freedom: Runaway Slaves of the American Revolution and Their Global Quest for Liberty* (Boston: Beacon Press, 2007).

50 Eric Foner, *Forever Free: The Story of Emancipation and Reconstruction* (New York: Knopf, 2005); Manisha Sinha, "To 'Cast Just Obliquy' on Oppressors: Black Radicalism in the Age of Revolution," *William and Mary Quarterly* 64 (January 2007): 149–60.

51 As quoted in Bob Gingrich, *In Their Own Words: Founding Fathers Speak Out Regarding the Vital Role of the Bible in the Foundation of the United States of America* (Longwood, FL: Xulon Press, 2006), 160–61.

52 Paul Finkelman, *Slavery and the Founders: Race and Liberty in the Age of Jefferson* (Armonk, NY: 2001), 37–40.

53 Joanne Pope Melish, *Disowning Slavery: Gradual Emancipation and "Race" in New England, 1780–1860* (Ithaca, NY: Cornell University Press, 1998).

54 Edgar J. McManus, *Black Bondage in the North* (Syracuse, NY: Syracuse University Press, 1973).

55 Ira Berlin, *Many Thousands Gone: The First Two Centuries of Slavery in North America* (Cambridge, MA: Belknap Press of Harvard University Press, 1998), ch. 9.

56 Jordan, *White over Black*, 347.

57 William Sterne Randall, *George Washington: A Life* (New York: Henry Holt, 1997).

58 Peter Kolchin, *American Slavery, 1619–1877* (New York: Hill and Wang, 1993), 87–89, 241.

59 James D. Essig, *The Bonds of Wickedness: American Evangelicals against Slavery, 1770–1808* (Philadelphia: Temple University Press, 1982).

60 William Warren Sweet, *Methodism in American History* (New York: Abingdon-Cokesbury Press, 1933), 231–32; Lewis B. Purifoy, "The Methodist Anti-Slavery Tradition, 1784–1844," *Methodist History* 4 (July 1966): 3–16.

61 J. Manning Potts and Arthur Bruce Moss, "Methodism in Colonial America," in *The History of American Methodism* (New York: Abingdon Press, 1964), 1:74–144.

62 John Wesley, Percy Livingstone Parker, and Augustine Birrell, *The Heart of John Wesley's Journal* (New York: Fleming H. Revell, 1903), 370.

63 John Wesley, *Thoughts upon Slavery*, 4th ed. (Dublin: W. Whitestone, 1775).

64 Charles Elliott, *History of the Great Secession from the Methodist Episcopal Church in the Year 1845: Eventuating in the Organization of the New Church, Entitled the "Methodist Episcopal Church, South"* (Cincinnnati, OH: Swormstedt & Poe, 1855), 34.

65 Douglas Ambrose, "Of Stations and Relations: Proslavery Christianity in Early National Virginia," in *Religion and the Antebellum Debate over Slavery*, ed. John R. McKivigan and Mitchell Snay (Athens: University of Georgia Press, 1998), 38–39.

66 Berlin, *Many Thousands Gone*, 361–62; Kolchin, *American Slavery*, 89–90.

67 Kolchin, *American Slavery*, 95–96.

68 John G. Fee, *Non-fellowship with Slaveholders: The Duty of Christians* (New York: John A. Gray, 1851), 47. See also Donald G. Mathews, *Slavery and Methodism: A Chapter in American Morality, 1780–1845* (Princeton, NJ: Princeton University Press, 1965), 11–14.

69 Fee, *Non-fellowship with Slaveholders*, 47.

70 Mathews, *Slavery and Methodism*, 19–24.

71 Lester B. Scherer, *Slavery and the Churches in Early America, 1619–1819* (Grand Rapids, MI: William B. Eerdmans, 1975), 135–37; Ambrose, "Of Stations and Relations," 39–46.

72 Eric Burin, *Slavery and the Peculiar Solution: A History of the American Colonization Society* (Gainsville: University of Florida Press, 2005).

73 Paul Goodman, *Of One Blood: Abolitionism and the Origins of Racial Equality* (Berkeley: University of California Press, 1998), ch. 9.

74 Ibid., ch. 4.

75 Daniel Walker Howe, *What Hath God Wrought: The Transformation of America, 1815–1848* (New York: Oxford University Press, 2007), 426.

76 Goodman, *Of One Blood*, ch. 9.

77 James A. Morone, *Hellfire Nation: The Politics of Sin in American History* (New Haven, CT: Yale University Press, 2003), 183-91.

78 Amos A. Phelps, *Lectures on Slavery and Its Remedy* (Boston: New England Anti-Slavery Society, 1834), 17.

79 Harriet Martineau, *Society in America* (Paris: Baudry's European Library, 1837), 2:244.

80 John R. McKivigan, *The War against Proslavery Religion: Abolitionism and the Northern Churches, 1830-1865* (Ithaca, NY: Cornell University Press, 1984).

81 Ibid., ch. 9.

82 Calculated from the membership figures provided in ibid., 92, 96.

83 The essays are excerpted in Mason I. Lowance Jr., *A House Divided: The Antebellum Slavery Debates in America, 1776-1865* (Princeton, NJ: Princeton University Press, 2003), 12-15.

84 McKivigan, *The War against Proslavery Religion*, ch. 9.

85 Paul Kuenning, *The Rise and Fall of American Lutheran Pietism: The Rejection of an Activist Heritage* (Macon, GA: Mercer University Press, 1988), 145-49; David Lynn Holmes, *A Brief History of the Episcopal Church* (Valley Forge, PA: Trinity Press International, 1993), 80-82.

86 George M. Marsden, *The Evangelical Mind and the New School Presbyterian Experience: A Case Study of Thought and Theology in Nineteenth-Century America* (New Haven, CT: Yale University Press, 1970), 89.

87 Tamar Szabó Gendler, *Thought Experiment: On the Powers and Limits of Imaginary Cases* (New York: Garland, 2000).

88 See, for example, Gary DeMar, "Does the Bible Support Slavery?," American Vision, accessed May 11, 2014, http://americanvision.org/1249/does -bible-support-slavery-part/#sthash.Akk3Y9N0.dpbs; Rick Phillips, "The Sin of Manstealing," Reformation 21, accessed May 11, 2014, http://www .reformation21.org/blog/2007/01/the-sin-of-manstealing.php; Leland Ryken, Philip Ryken, and James Wilhoit, *Ryken's Bible Handbook: A Guide to Reading and Studying the Bible* (Wheaton, IL: Tyndale, 2005), 581; "Does the Bible Condone Slavery?," ChristianAnswers.net, accessed July 18, 2012, http://www .christiananswers.net/q-aiia/aiia-slavery.html.

89 Richard Dawkins, *The God Delusion* (Boston: Houghton Mifflin, 2006); Daniel C. Dennett, *Breaking the Spell: Religion as a Natural Phenomenon* (New York: Viking Press, 2006); Christopher Hitchens, *God Is Not Great: How Religion Poisons Everything* (New York: Twelve Books, 2007); Sam Harris, *The End of Faith: Religion, Terror, and the Future of Reason* (New York: Norton, 2004).

90 Sam Harris, *Letter to a Christian Nation* (New York: Alfred A. Knopf, 2006), 14-19. See also "Slavery in the Bible," Evil Bible, accessed August 8, 2008, http://www.evilbible.com/Slavery.htm; "Christianity and History: Bible, Race

& Slavery," About.com: Agnosticism/Atheism, accessed August 8, 2008, http://atheism.about.com/library/weekly/aa112598.htm.

91 Paul Copan, *Is God a Moral Monster? Making Sense of the Old Testament God* (Grand Rapids, MI: BakerBooks, 2011), chs. 12–14; "Why Atheists NEED the Bible to Endorse Slavery," michaelpatrickleahy.com, accessed May 14, 2014, http://www.michaelpatrickleahy.com/column_042907_bibleonslavery.html.

92 William Faulkner, *Requiem for a Nun* (New York: Random House, 1951), act 1, scene 3.

### CHAPTER THREE

1 Nathaniel Hawthorne, *The Scarlet Letter* [1850] (New York: Reinhart, 1947).

2 H. L. Mencken, *A Mencken Chrestomathy* (New York: A. A. Knopf, 1949), 624.

3 John Witte Jr., *From Sacrament to Contract: Marriage, Religion, and Law in the Western Tradition* (Lexington, KY: Westminster John Knox Press, 1997), ch. 4; Nelson Manfred Blake, *The Road to Reno: A History of Divorce in the United States* (New York: Macmillan, 1962), 40–41; Glenda Riley, *Divorce: An American Tradition* (New York: Oxford University Press, 1991), 25–29.

4 Riley, *Divorce*, 9–11.

5 Blake, *The Road to Reno*, 34–40; Riley, *Divorce*, 11–23, 44–49.

6 Benjamin Trumbull, *An appeal to the public, especially to the learned, with respect to the unlawfulness of divorces, in all cases, excepting those of incontinency. . . .* (New Haven, CT: J. Meigs, 1788), 5, 6 (capitalization in original).

7 Timothy Dwight IV, *Theology, Explained and Defined in a Series of Sermons* (London: J. Haddon, 1824), 4:259, 274.

8 This does not imply that the Old Testament is irrelevant to the discussion. A fuller treatment of the topic than is possible here would consider marriage and divorce in both the Old and New Testaments.

9 All biblical citations in this chapter are from *The Holy Bible, New International Version* (Grand Rapids, MI: Zondervan, 2011).

10 William A. Heth, "Jesus on Divorce: How My Mind Has Changed," *Southern Baptist Journal of Theology* 6 (Spring 2002): 10.

11 John Nolland, "The Gospel Prohibition of Divorce: Tradition History and Meaning," *Journal for the Study of the New Testament* 17 (1995): 19–35; Nolan Patrick Howlington, "The Historic Attitude of the Christian Churches Concerning Marriage, Divorce, and Remarriage" (ThD thesis, Southern Baptist Theological Seminary, 1948), 69–70.

12 Howlington, "Historic Attitude," 222.

13 J. Cary Laney, "No Divorce & No Remarriage," in *Divorce and Remarriage: Four Christian Views*, ed. H. Wayne House (Downers Grove, IL: Intervarsity Press, 1990), 15–54; William A. Heth and Gordon J. Wenham, *Jesus and Di-*

*vorce: The Problem with the Evangelical Consensus* (Nashville, TN: Thomas Nelson, 1984).

14 Elizabeth A. Clark, ed., *St. Augustine on Marriage and Sexuality* (Washington, DC: Catholic University of America, 1996).

15 Stephanie Coontz, *Marriage, A History: How Love Conquered Marriage* (New York: Penguin Books, 2006), 105–7.

16 Joseph Martos, "Catholic Marriage and Marital Dissolution in Medieval and Modern Times," in *Catholic Divorce: The Deception of Annulments*, ed. Pierre Hegy and Joseph Martos (New York: Continuum, 2000), 127–53.

17 Some of the relevant scholarly works include Craig S. Keener, . . . *And Marries Another: Divorce and Remarriage in the Teaching of the New Testament* (Peabody, MA: Hendrickson, 1991); Raymond F. Collins, *Divorce in the New Testament* (Collegeville, MN: Liturgical Press, 1992); William F. Luck, *Divorce and Remarriage: Recovering the Biblical View* (San Francisco: Harper & Row, 1987); Heth and Wenham, *Jesus and Divorce*; House, *Divorce and Remarriage*.

18 Riley, *Divorce*, 34–49.

19 Ibid., 62–67.

20 Horace Greeley, *Recollections of a Busy Life* (New York: J. B. Ford, 1868), 571.

21 As quoted in Blake, *Road to Reno*, 84.

22 Ibid., 130–33.

23 As quoted in James P. Lichtenberger, "Divorce: A Study in Social Causation" (PhD diss., Columbia University, 1909), 474, 464.

24 "Resolution on Divorce" [May 1904], Southern Baptist Convention, accessed January 29, 2008, www.sbc.net/resolutions/amResolution.asp?ID=441.

25 *Dill v. People*, 19 Colorado 469, in *The American State Reports Containing the Cases of General Value and Authority* (San Francisco: Bancroft-Whitney, 1895), 41:262.

26 Louis Aloisius Lambert, *Tactics of Infidels* (Buffalo, NY: Peter Paul & Brother, 1887), 195.

27 Elizabeth Kingsbury, *Thoughts on Marriage* (London: Simpkin, Marshall, 1882), 111.

28 Morgan Dix, *Lectures on the Calling of a Christian Woman* (New York: D. Appleton, 1883), 98.

29 "A Record of Broken Vows; Marriage Is Very Often a Failure," *New York Times*, March 31, 1889, 16.

30 Blake, *Road to Reno*, 134–36; Riley, *Divorce*, 79–81, 86–87.

31 Lichtenberger, "Divorce," 123.

32 Blake, *Road to Reno*, 139–40.

33 Ibid., 141–45.

34 Ibid., 145–51; Riley, *Divorce*, 134.

35 Kimberly A. Faust and Jerome N. McKibben, "Marital Dissolution: Divorce, Separation, Annulment, and Widowhood," in *Handbook of Marriage and the Family*, 2nd ed., ed. Marvin B. Sussman, Suzanne K. Steinmetz, and Gary W. Peterson (New York: Plenum Press, 1999), 475-77.

36 M. C. Weersing, "The New Testament Statement Concerning Divorce and Remarriage: Especially as It Applies to Twentieth Century Church Polity" (master of theology thesis, Columbia Theological Seminary, 1937-1938), 56-57.

37 Ibid., 44.

38 Pierre Hegy, "Disputed Biblical Interpretations about Marriage and Divorce," in Hegy and Martos, *Catholic Divorce*, 62-63.

39 As quoted in Jack Bartlett Rogers, *Jesus, the Bible, and Homosexuality: Explode the Myths, Heal the Church* (Louisville, KY: Westminster John Knox Press, 2006), 42.

40 Ibid., 42-43.

41 Kyle D. Fedler, *Exploring Christian Ethics: Biblical Foundations for Morality* (Louisville, KY: Westminster John Knox Press, 2006), 161-62.

42 Daniel R. Heimbach, *True Sexual Morality: Recovering Biblical Standards for a Culture in Crisis* (Wheaton, IL: Crossway Books, 2004), 204-5.

43 *The Doctrines and Discipline of the Methodist Episcopal Church* (New York: Phillips & Hunt, 1884), 33.

44 *The Doctrines and Discipline of the Methodist Episcopal Church* (New York: Methodist Book Concern, 1932), 63.

45 *The Doctrines and Discipline of the Methodist Church* (Nashville, TN: Methodist Publishing House, 1964), 159.

46 Howlington, "Historic Attitude," 233-34; Blake, *Road to Reno*, 230-31.

47 Howlington, "Historic Attitude," 203.

48 Bill J. Leonard, *Baptists in America* (New York: Columbia University Press, 2005), 238-39.

49 Pierre Hegy, "Catholic Divorce, Annulments, and Deception," in Hegy and Martos, *Catholic Divorce*, 9-25.

50 Herbert Jacob, *The Silent Revolution: The Transformation of Divorce Law in the United States* (Chicago: University of Chicago Press, 1988).

51 James Dobson, *Marriage under Fire: Why We Must Win This War* (Sisters, OR: Multnomah, 2004), 37-38.

52 Mary Ann Glendon, *The Transformation of Family Law: State, Law, and Family in the United States and Western Europe* (Chicago: University of Chicago Press, 1989), 188.

53 James C. Garand, Pamela A. Monroe, and Denese Vlosky, "Do No Fault Divorce Laws Increase Divorce Rates in the American States?" (paper presented

at the 1998 annual meeting of the American Political Science Association, Boston, MA).

54 David Popenhoe, "The Future of Marriage in America," in *The State of Our Unions: 2007* (Piscataway, NJ: National Marriage Project, 2007); Dan Hurley, "Divorce Rate: It's Not as High as You Think," *New York Times*, April 19, 2005.

55 "The Tricky Business of Estimating Divorce" [November 15, 2006], Council on Contemporary Families, accessed November 23, 2014, https://contemporaryfamilies.org/tricky-business-estimating-divorce.

56 David Snowball, *Continuity and Change in the Rhetoric of the Moral Majority* (New York: Praeger, 1991), 16.

57 Snowball, *Continuity and Change*; John Kater Jr., *Christians on the Right: The Moral Majority in Perspective* (New York: Seabury Press, 1982).

58 "Pat Robertson is Back," *St. Petersburg Times*, May 26, 1990, 3E.

59 Justin Watson, *The Christian Coalition: Dreams of Restoration, Demands for Recognition* (New York: St. Martin's Press, 1997).

60 Ralph Reed, *Active Faith: How Christians Are Changing the Soul of American Politics* (New York: Free Press, 1996). Reed's statements on divorce occur on pages 5 and 42.

61 Katharine Q. Seelye, "Christian Coalition Plans Inner-City Program," *New York Times*, January 31, 1997, A21.

62 Watson, *The Christian Coalition*, 189.

63 Available at the website of the Family Research Council at http://www.frc.org/content/about-frc-1 (accessed July 18, 2012).

64 See, for example, Randall Balmer, *Thy Kingdom Come: How the Religious Right Distorts the Faith and Threatens America, An Evangelical's Lament* (New York: Basic Books, 2006).

65 Accessed July 18, 2012, on the website of the Family Research Council (http://www.frc.org/get.cfm?i=FQ04H47).

66 These e-mails are titled *Tony Perkins' Washington Update*. A much smaller group of e-mails asks members and supporters to contact government officials over particular matters currently under discussion.

67 Of those eight items, three addressed the efforts of organizations like Marriage Savers to prevent divorce; two focused on a report finding that no-fault divorce laws increased the incidence of divorce; and one each covered a Florida county which allows couples to file for divorce online, a report claiming that divorce hurts the environment by creating more households, and a decision by Rhode Island courts to refuse to grant a divorce to a same-sex couple married in Massachusetts. Another twenty-one e-mails mentioned divorce with only a passing reference—for example, in noting that a certain person in the story was divorced.

68 The Family Research Council used to archive its op-eds (including those that did and did not make it into print) at its website (http://www.frc.org/get.cfm?c =OPED_PRESS, accessed July 18, 2012).

69 Coontz, *Marriage*.

70 Ibid.; Lawrence Stone, *Road to Divorce: England, 1530–1987* (Oxford: Oxford University Press, 1990).

71 Coontz, *Marriage*.

72 J. Herbie DiFonzo, *Beneath the Fault Line: The Popular and Legal Culture of Divorce in Twentieth-Century America* (Charlottesville: University Press of Virginia, 1997).

73 Gerhard Falk, *Stigma: How We Treat Outsiders* (Amherst, NY: Prometheus Books, 2001).

74 Tom W. Smith, Peter Marsden, Michael Hout, and Jibum Kim, *General Social Surveys, 1972–2012* [machine-readable data file] (Chicago: National Opinion Research Center, 2013).

75 To classify people into these seven traditions, I use the method sociologist Brian Steensland and his collaborators devised. Steensland's article, which won an award from the American Sociological Association, uses religious doctrines and histories to identify the seven traditions. On the basis of people's answers to several questions about their religious affiliations and denominations, Steensland places them into one of the groups. See Brian Steensland et al., "The Measure of American Religion: Toward Improving the State of the Art," *Social Forces* 79, no. 1 (September 2000): 291–318.

76 See, for example, Dobson, *Marriage under Fire*, 54.

77 John P. Bartowski, *The Promise Keepers: Servants, Soldiers, and Godly Men* (Piscataway, NJ: Rutgers University Press, 2004).

78 Accessed November 23, 2014, on the website of Promise Keepers (https:// promisekeepers.org/about/7-promises).

79 See, for example, "Marriage: Love and Life in the Divine Plan," US Conference of Catholic Bishops, accessed July 5, 2012, http://www.usccb.org/issues -and-action/marriage-and-family/marriage/love-and-life/upload/pastoral-letter -marriage-love-and-life-in-the-divine-plan.pdf.

80 "Legislative Issues for the 112th Congress,". US Conference of Catholic Bishops, March 2011, accessed July 5, 2012, http://www.usccb.org/about/government -relations/legislative-issues/legislative-issues-for-the-112th-congress.cfm.

81 Greenberg Quinlan Rosner Research, Inc., "Memorandum to Religion and Ethics Newsweekly, 'Faith and Family in America,'" Public Broadcasting System, October 19, 2005, accessed November 23, 2014, http://www-tc.pbs.org /wnet/religionandethics/files/2005/10/ReligionAndFamily_Summary.pdf.

82 Question IDs USGALLUP.01MAY10, R481, and USGALLUP.02MA006, R561,

ipoll Databank, Roper Center for Public Opinion Research, accessed November 23, 2014, http://www.ropercenter.uconn.edu/data_access/ipoll/ipoll.html (hereafter cited as iPoll Databank).

83 The best-known study is probably Judith S. Wallerstein, Julia Lewis, and Sandra Blakeslee, *The Unexpected Legacy of Divorce: A Twenty-Five Year Landmark Study* (New York: Hyperion, 2000).

84 Paul Amato, "Children of Divorce in the 1990s: An Update of the Amato and Keith (1991) Meta-analysis," *Journal of Family Psychology* 15 (2001): 355-70; E. Mavis Hetherington and John Kelly, *For Better or For Worse: Divorce Reconsidered* (New York: Norton, 2002).

85 Question ID USYANKP.20012, Q27, iPoll Databank.

86 Question IDs USROPER.84-2, R25B, and USROPER.640019, Q18A, iPoll Databank.

87 See, for example, "BW/Harris Poll: He Said, She Said," *Business Week*, August 3, 1998, accessed December 29, 2007, http://www.businessweek.com/1998 /31/b3589005.htm.

88 Question ID USNORC.GSS06A, Q0215A, iPoll Databank.

89 Question ID USTIPP.031202, R30, iPoll Databank.

90 Steven L. Nock, James D. Wright, and Laura Sanchez, "America's Divorce Problem," *Society* (May/June 1999): 43-52.

91 Katherine Shaw Spacht, "The Modern American Covenant Marriage Movement: Its Origins and Its Future," in *Covenant Marriage in Comparative Perspective*, ed. John Witte and Eliza Ellison (Grand Rapids, MI: William B. Eerdmans, 2005), 239-64.

92 Katherin Shaw Spacht, "Why Covenant Marriage May Prove Responsive to the Culture of Divorce," in *Revitalizing the Institution of Marriage for the Twenty-First Century: An Agenda for Strengthening Marriage*, ed. Alan J. Hawkins, Lynn D. Wardle, and David Orgon Coolidge (New York: Prager, 2002), 59-67.

93 Katherine Brown Rosier and Scott L. Feld, "Covenant Marriage: A New Alternative for Traditional Families," *Journal of Comparative Family Studies* 31, no. 3 (Summer 2000): 385-94.

94 Spacht, "The Modern American Covenant Marriage Movement," 245.

CHAPTER FOUR

1 Volumes 1 to 5, covering 1900 to 1928, filled 15,734 pages. Using a random sample from throughout the period, I found that each page indexed an average of seventy-five articles, leading to a total of more than one million articles indexed from 1900 to 1928. Although some of those articles may have referred to homosexuality in passing, the compilers of the *Readers' Guide* did not perceive homosexuality as the central subject of any of them.

2 *Readers' Guide to Periodical Literature* 20 (March 1955 to February 1957): 1144–45.

3 John D. Emilio, *Sexual Politics, Sexual Communities: The Making of a Homosexual Minority in the United States, 1940–1970* (Chicago: University of Chicago Press, 1983), 41–51.

4 As quoted in Lillian Faderman, *Odd Girls and Twilight Lovers: A History of Lesbian Life in Twentieth-Century America* (New York: Columbia University Press, 1991), 164.

5 Allan Berube, *Coming Out Under Fire: The History of Gay Men and Women in World War II* (New York: Free Press, 1990).

6 US Senate, "Employment of Homosexuals and Other Sex Perverts in the US Government," reprinted (selections) in *We Are Everywhere: A Historical Sourcebook of Gay and Lesbian Politics*, ed. Mark Blasius and Shane Phelan (New York: Routledge, 1997), 241–51 (quote is from p. 251).

7 David K. Johnson, *The Lavender Scare: The Cold War Persecution of Gays and Lesbians in the Federal Government* (Chicago: University of Chicago Press, 2004), 166–69.

8 American Psychiatric Association, *Diagnostic and Statistical Manual: Mental Disorders* (Washington, DC: American Psychiatric Association, 1952), 38–39.

9 Herb Kutchins and Stuart A. Kirk, *Making Us Crazy: DSM; The Psychiatric Bible and the Creation of Mental Disorders* (New York: Free Press, 1997), 58–60.

10 Founded in Chicago in 1924, the short-lived Society for Human Rights preceded the Mattachine Society as the earliest known gay rights organization in America.

11 Mattachine Society, "Missions & Purposes," reprinted (selections) in *Homosexuals Today: A Handbook of Organizations & Publications*, ed. Marvin Cutler (Los Angeles: One, 1956), 13–14.

12 Daughters of Bilitis, "Statement of Purpose" [1955], reprinted in Blasius and Phelan, *We Are Everywhere*, 328.

13 Figure based on word searches of the *New York Times* archive, accessed November 4, 2011, http://www.nytimes.com/ref/membercenter/nytarchive.html.

14 Gary J. Gates, "How Many People Are Lesbian, Gay, Bisexual, and Transgender?" Williams Institute, UCLA School of Law, April 2011, accessed December 2, 2014, http://williamsinstitute.law.ucla.edu/wp-content/uploads/Gates-How-Many-People-LGBT-Apr-2011.pdf.

15 Hazel Gaudet Erskine, "The Polls: Morality," *Public Opinion Quarterly* 30 (Winter 1966–1967): 680. When reporting the results, Louis Harris and Associates apparently grouped the "don't knows" (i.e., the people unable to answer the question) with the people giving the substantive answer that homosexuals

"don't help or harm" America. I have thus calculated the percentage saying "don't help or harm" by subtracting an estimate of 9 percent for the "don't knows," which is the figure yielded by an identical Louis Harris and Associates survey five years later.

16 American Psychiatric Association, *Diagnostic and Statistical Manual: Mental Disorders*, 2nd ed. (Washington, DC: American Psychiatric Association, 1968), 41–46.

17 Martin Duberman, *Stonewall* (New York: Plume, 1994).

18 David Carter, *Stonewall: The Riots that Sparked the Gay Revolution* (New York: St. Martin's Press, 2004).

19 Alan Yang, "The Polls—Trends: Attitudes toward Homosexuality," *Public Opinion Quarterly* 61 (1997): 484.

20 Benjamin I. Page and Robert Y. Shapiro, *The Rational Public: Fifty Years of Trends in Americans' Policy Preferences* (Chicago: University of Chicago Press, 1992).

21 Evelyn Hooker, "The Adjustment of the Male Overt Homosexual," *Journal of Projective Techniques* 21 (1957): 18–31.

22 Judd Marmor, ed., *Sexual Inversion: The Multiple Roots of Homosexuality* (New York: Basic Books, 1965).

23 Kutchins and Kirk, *Making Us Crazy*, 67.

24 Ronald Bayer, *Homosexuality and American Psychiatry: The Politics of Diagnosis* (New York: Basic Books, 1981).

25 Robert L. Spitzer, "A Proposal about Homosexuality and the APA Nomenclature: Homosexuality as an Irregular Form of Sexual Behavior and Sexual Orientation Disturbance as a Psychiatric Disorder," *American Journal of Psychiatry* 130 (1973): 1214–16.

26 Simon LeVay, "A Difference in Hypothalmic Structure between Heterosexual and Homosexual Men," *Science* 253 (August 1991): 1034–37.

27 J. M. Bailey, M. P. Dunne, and N. G. Martin. "Genetic and Environmental Influences on Sexual Orientation and Its Correlates in an Australian Twin Sample," *Journal of Personality and Social Psychology* 78 (March 2000): 524–36.

28 R. Blanchard and P. Klassen, "H-Y Antigen and Homosexuality in Men," *Journal of Theoretical Biology* 185 (April 1997): 373–78.

29 "The Homosexual in America," *Time*, January 21, 1966, 41.

30 W. Lance Bennett, "Toward a Theory of Press-State Relations in the US," *Journal of Communication* 40 (Spring 1990): 103–25; John R. Zaller, *The Nature and Origins of Mass Opinion* (New York: Cambridge University Press, 1992).

31 Edward Alwood, *Straight News: Gays, Lesbians, and the News Media* (New York: Columbia University Press, 1996).

32 Tom W. Smith, Peter Marsden, Michael Hout, and Jibum Kim, *General Social Surveys, 1972–2012* [machine-readable data file] (Chicago: National Opinion Research Center, 2013).

33 This and all subsequent references to the General Social Survey are based on my own analyses of the raw data.

34 This figure is essentially a mirror image of one showing the percentage of people saying "always wrong."

35 In most of the graphs I present throughout the book, I use a method called "locally weighted scatterplot smoothing" (LOESS). Measures of variables over time contain both real change — of interest here — and random variations from year to year owing to factors such as sampling error. LOESS allows the analyst to smooth out the short-term fluctuations so that the eye can focus on the long-term trends. As an added benefit, which is relevant later in the chapter, LOESS allows me to present the figures from multiple religious groups on the same graph. Without this smoothing, some of my graphs would be too cluttered to read.

36 Donald P. Haider-Markel and Mark R. Joslyn, "Beliefs about the Origins of Homosexuality and Support for Gay Rights: An Empirical Test of Attribution Theory," *Public Opinion Quarterly* 72 (2008): 291–310; Gregory B. Lewis, "Does Believing Homosexuality Is Innate Increase Support for Gay Rights?" *Policy Studies Journal* 37 (November 2009): 669–93.

37 Gregory M. Herek and John P. Capitanio, "'Some of My Best Friends': Intergroup Contact, Concealable Stigma, and Heterosexuals' Attitudes toward Gay Men and Lesbians," *Personality and Social Psychology Bulletin* 22 (1996): 412–24; Paul R. Brewer, *Value War: Public Opinion and the Politics of Gay Rights* (Lanham, MD: Rowman & Littlefield, 2008), ch. 3.

38 Robert Andersen and Tina Fetner, "Cohort Differences in Tolerance of Homosexuality: Attitudinal Change in Canada and the United States, 1981–2000," *Public Opinion Quarterly* 72 (Summer 2008): 311–30.

39 William N. Eskridge Jr., *Dishonorable Passions: Sodomy Laws in America, 1861–2003* (New York: Viking, 2008).

40 Gary Mucciaroni, *Same Sex, Different Politics: Success and Failure in the Struggles over Gay Rights* (Chicago: University of Chicago Press, 2008), ch. 4.

41 "Employment Non-discrimination Laws on Sexual Orientation and Gender Identity," Human Rights Campaign, accessed March 21, 2013, http://preview.hrc.org/issues/4844.htm.

42 "Fair Housing Laws: Renters' Protection from Sexual Orientation Discrimination." FindLaw, accessed March 21, 2013, http://civilrights.findlaw.com/discrimination/fair-housing-laws-renters-protection-from-sexual-orientation.html.

43 Margot Canaday, *The Straight State: Sexuality and Citizenship in Twentieth-Century America* (Princeton, NJ: Princeton University Press, 2009), ch. 5.

44 Chad C. Carter and Anyony Barone Kolenc, "'Don't Ask, Don't Tell': Has the Policy Met Its Goals?" *University of Dayton Law Review* 31 (2005): 1–24.

45 See, for example, "A Quiet End," *Mobile Register*, December 27, 2010, A5.

46 The only exception came in Arizona in 2006, when voters rejected a constitutional amendment that would have banned both same-sex marriage and civil unions. In 2008 Arizona voters passed a constitutional amendment that banned only same-sex marriage.

47 "Same-Sex Marriage Laws." National Conference of State Legislatures, accessed November 23, 2014, http://www.ncsl.org/research/human-services/same-sex-marriage-laws.aspx.

48 The Church of England, which released its influential Wolfenden Report in 1957, acted a full decade before any American denomination. Proceeding without the official sanction of a national body, a group of British Quakers in 1963 also engaged the issue of homosexuality several years before any American denominations. See J. Gordon Melton, *The Churches Speak on Homosexuality: Official Statements from Religious Bodies and Ecumenical Organizations* (Detroit: Gale Research, 1991), 57–65 and 181–200.

49 Augustine, *Confessions*, trans. Henry Chadwick (Oxford: Oxford University Press, 1991), 3:8:15.

50 Timothy M. Renick, *Aquinas for Armchair Theologians* (Louisville, KY: Westminster John Knox Press, 2002), 87–88.

51 Sabina Flanagan, *Hildegard of Bingen: A Visionary Life* (New York: Routledge, 1999), 66–67.

52 As quoted in Ewald Martin Plass, *What Luther Says: An Anthology* (St. Louis: Concordia Publishing House, 1959), 1:134.

53 "Westminster Catechism," reprinted (selections) in Melton, *The Churches Speak on Homosexuality*, 146.

54 United Methodist Church, "Resolution on Health, Welfare, and Human Development," reprinted (selections) in Melton, *The Churches Speak on Homosexuality*, 240.

55 United Methodist Church, "Social Principles," reprinted (selections) in Melton, *The Churches Speak on Homosexuality*, 241.

56 Unfortunately, the 1970 survey did not ask detailed questions about the respondent's religious affiliation, making it impossible to know for certain how United Methodists compared to the general population.

57 Council for Christian Social Action of the United Church of Christ, "Resolution on Homosexuals and the Law," reprinted in Melton, *The Churches Speak on Homosexuality*, 203–4.

58 Wendy Cadge, "Vital Conflicts: The Mainline Denominations Debate Homosexuality," in *The Quiet Hand of God: Faith-Based Activism and the Public Role of Mainline Protestantism*, ed. Robert Wuthnow and John H. Evans (Berkeley: University of California Press, 2002), 272–73.

59 United Presbyterian Church in the United States of America, "Sexuality and the Human Community," reprinted (selections) in Melton, *The Churches Speak on Homosexuality*, 147–48.

60 Lutheran Church in America, "Sex, Marriage, and Family," reprinted (selections) in Melton, *The Churches Speak on Homosexuality*, 113.

61 Southern Baptist Convention, "On Homosexuality," reprinted in Melton, *The Churches Speak on Homosexuality*, 200.

62 The complete set of resolutions passed by the Southern Baptist Convention can be found at the group's website (http://www.sbc.net/resolutions/default.asp, accessed April 20, 2011).

63 National Conference of Catholic Bishops, "Principles to Guide Confessors in Questions of Homosexuality," reprinted in Melton, *The Churches Speak on Homosexuality*, 2–9.

64 To classify people as Catholics, mainline Protestants, evangelical Protestants, and black Protestants, I use the system developed by Brian Steensland and his collaborators. (I used the same system in my previous chapter on divorce.) See Brian Steensland et al., "The Measure of American Religion: Toward Improving the State of the Art," *Social Forces* 79, no. 1 (September 2000): 291–318.

65 Congregation for Catholic Education, "Instruction Concerning the Criteria for the Discernment of Vocations with regard to Persons with Homosexual Tendencies in View of Their Admission to the Seminary and to Holy Orders," The Vatican, accessed April 20, 2011, http://www.vatican.va/roman_curia/congregations /ccatheduc/documents/rc_con_ccatheduc_doc_20051104_istruzione_en .html.

66 *The Book of Discipline of the United Methodist Church* (Nashville, TN: Abingdon Press, 2009), par. 2702.1.

67 Jerald Hyche and Pat McCaughan, "Bishops Affirm Openness of Ordination Process," Episcopal News Service, July 14, 2009, Episcopal Church, accessed November 23, 2014, http://library.episcopalchurch.org/sites/default /files/daily07_071409.pdf; "ELCA Assembly Opens Ministry to Partnered Gay and Lesbian Lutherans," *The Lutheran*, August 21, 2009, Evangelical Lutheran Church in America, accessed November 23, 2014, http://www.thelutheran.org /blog/index.cfm?person_id=194&blog_id=1324.

68 "Presbyterian Church (USA) Approves Change in Ordination Standard," Presbyterian Church (USA), accessed May 11, 2011, http://www.pcusa.org/news /2011/5/10/presbyterian-church-us-approves-change-ordination.

69  "On Homosexuality and the United States Military" [June 2010] and "On Biblical Sexuality and Public Policy" [June 2009], both available at the Southern Baptist Convention's website (http://www.sbc.net/resolutions/default.asp, accessed June 12, 2011).

70  Dave Bohon, "Black Pastors Challenge NAACP's Support for Same-Sex Marriage," *New American*, July 17, 2012, accessed July 19, 2012, http://www.thenewamerican .com/culture/faith-and-morals/item/12094-black-pastors-challenge -naacp percentE2 percent80 percent99s-support-for-same-sex-marriage.

71  "Churchgoers Disapprove of Gay and Lesbian Pastors," Rasmussen Reports, June 30, 2006, accessed April 20, 2011, http://www.rasmussenreports.com /public_content/politics/general_politics/june_2006/churchgoers_disapprove _of_gay_and_lesbian_pastors.

72  I identified the titles through WorldCat, a database that compiles the collections of 70,000 libraries around the world. For the subjects under investigation here, books published in the United States constitute a clear majority. The data in figure 4.5 include all books the Library of Congress classifies under the subjects of "homosexuality—religious aspects—Christianity," "homosexuality—religious aspects—biblical teaching," "homosexuality in the Bible," and "homosexuality—biblical teaching." Most of the titles are traditional books bearing the imprint of commercial, university, or nonprofit presses, but some are reports from advocacy groups, denominations, and other religious bodies.

73  Marion L. Soards, *Scripture and Homosexuality: Biblical Authority and the Church Today* (Louisville, KY: Westminster John Know Press, 1995), 24.

74  Bruce Hilton, *Can Homophobia Be Cured? Wrestling with Questions that Challenge the Church* (Nashville, TN: Abingdon Press, 1992), 75.

75  Joe Dallas, *A Strong Delusion: Confronting the "Gay Christian" Movement* (Eugene, OR: Harvest House, 1996), 187–88.

76  Victor Paul Furnish, "What Does the Bible Say about Homosexuality?" in *Caught in the Crossfire: Helping Christians Debate Homosexuality*, ed. Sally B. Geis and Donald E. Messer (Nashville, TN: Abingdon Press, 1994), 59.

77  Soards, *Scripture and Homosexuality*, 16.

78  Dallas, *A Strong Delusion*, 191–92. Biblical quotations in this chapter are taken from *The Holy Bible, New Revised Standard Version* (Grand Rapids, MI: Zondervan, 1989).

79  Dallas, *A Strong Delusion*, 92–93.

80  Hilton, *Can Homophobia Be Cured?*, 70.

81  James B. De Young, *Homosexuality: Contemporary Claims Examined in Light of the Bible and Other Ancient Literature and Law* (Grand Rapids, MI: Kregel, 2000), 189–95.

82  Dallas, *A Strong Delusion*, 198.

83 Furnish, "What Does the Bible Say about Homosexuality?," 61; John Boswell, *Christianity, Social Tolerance, and Homosexuality: Gay People in Western Europe from the Beginning of the Christian Era to the Fourteenth Century* (Chicago: University of Chicago Press, 1980), 341-53.

84 Robin Scroggs, *The New Testament and Homosexuality* (Philadelphia: Fortress Press, 1983), 107-109.

85 De Young, *Homosexuality*, 198-99.

86 Dallas, *A Strong Delusion*, 194.

87 Soards, *Scripture and Homosexuality*, 20-23.

88 Victor Paul Furnish, *The Moral Teachings of Paul*, 2nd ed. (Nashville, TN: Abington Press, 1985), 52-82.

89 Boswell, *Christianity, Social Tolerance, and Homosexuality*, 109.

90 Stanley J. Grenz, *Welcoming but Not Affirming: An Evangelical Response to Homosexuality* (Louisville, KY: Westminster John Knox Press, 1998), 60.

91 Tom Horner, *Jonathan Loved David: Homosexuality in Biblical Times* (Philadelphia: Westminster Press, 1979).

92 Hilton, *Can Homophobia Be Cured?*, 75-76.

93 Jeffrey S. Siker, "Gentile Wheat and Homosexual Christians: New Testament Directions for the Heterosexual Church," in *Biblical Ethics & Homosexuality: Listening to Scripture*, ed. Robert L. Brawley (Louisville, KY: Westminster John Knox Press), 145-50.

94 Dallas, *A Strong Delusion*, 203-206.

95 The most obvious example is Troy Perry, founder of the Metropolitan Community Church. Perry has written several books that discuss, with varying degrees of detail, questions of the Bible and homosexuality. Other examples include David Day, *Things They Never Told You in Sunday School: A Primer for the Christian Homosexual* (Austin: Liberty Press, 1987); and Samuel Kader, *Openly Gay, Openly Christian: How the Bible Really Is Gay Friendly* (San Francisco: Leyland, 1999).

96 Siker, "Gentile Wheat and Homosexual Christians," 146; Paul R. Smith, *The Bible and Homosexuality: Affirming All Sexual Orientations as Gifts from God* (Kansas City, MO: Paul Smith, 1998), 28.

97 Jack Bartlett Rogers, *Jesus, the Bible, and Homosexuality: Explode the Myths, Heal the Church* (Louisville, KY: Westminster John Knox Press, 2006), xviii.

98 Barry D. Adam, *The Rise of a Gay and Lesbian Movement*, rev. ed. (New York: Twayne, 1995), ch. 6.

99 "Resolution on Homosexuality" [June 1977], Southern Baptist Convention, accessed August 4, 2011, http://www.sbc.net/resolutions/amResolution.asp?ID=607; "Resolution on Commendation of Anita Bryant" [June 1978], Southern

Baptist Convention, accessed August 4, 2011, http://www.sbc.net/resolutions /amResolution.asp?ID=744.

100 Anita Bryant, *The Anita Bryant Story: The Survival of Our Nation's Families and the Threat of Militant Homosexuality* (Old Tappan, NJ: Fleming H. Revell, 1977), 62.

101 Ibid., 78, 114.

102 Morton Kondracke, "Anita Bryant Is Mad about Gays," *New Republic*, May 7, 1977, 13–14.

103 John Kenneth White, "Terrorism and the Remaking of American Politics," in *The Politics of Terror: The US Response to 9/11*, ed. William Crotty (Boston: Northeastern University Press, 2004), 55.

104 Family Research Council, *Tony Perkins' Washington Update*, e-mail newsletter. The arguments appeared in the following editions: "Ignore Amos?" November 8, 2010; "GOP Clips Senate's (Left) Wing," December 1, 2010; "DADT Defeat Doesn't Mean Conservative Surrender," December 20, 2010."

105 Family Research Council, *Tony Perkins' Washington Update*, e-mail newsletter. The arguments appeared in the following editions: "Harry Knuckles . . . Under," November 18, 2010; "Lame Ducks Talk Turkey," November 19, 2010; "Repeal Loses Appeal among Troops," November 30, 2010; and "Mullen: Don't Like 'Don't Ask?' Don't Serve!" December 2, 2010.

106 "Marriage Talking Points." National Organization for Marriage, accessed April 20, 2011, http://www.nationformarriage.org/site/c.omL2KeN0LzH/b.4475595 /k.566A/Marriage_Talking_Points.htm.

107 Transcript of Vice-Presidential Debate at Washington University in St. Louis, October 2, 2008, The American Presidency Project, The University of California, Santa Barbara, accessed April 20, 2011, at http://www.presidency.ucsb.edu /ws/index.php?pid=84382#axzz1K5ts1oNv.

108 A full transcript of Pope Francis's remarks can be found in "A Memorable In-Flight Press Conference," *Inside the Vatican*, August 2013, accessed November 4, 2013, https://insidethevatican.com/lead-story/a-memorable-in-flight -press-conference.

109 See, for example, "Pope Francis: Who Am I to Judge Gay People," BBC News, July 29, 2013, accessed November 4, 2013, http://www.bbc.co.uk/news/world -europe-23489702.

110 Antonio Spadaro, S.J., "A Big Heart Open to God: The Exclusive Interview with Pope Francis," *America: The National Catholic Review*, September 30, 2013, accessed November 4, 2013, http://www.americamagazine.org/pope-interview.

111 Ibid.

### CHAPTER FIVE

1 Didache 2:2, accessed September 20, 2011, at www.thedidache.com.

2 The Epistle of Barnabas 19:5, trans. J. B. Lightfoot, accessed September 20, 2011, http://www.earlychristianwritings.com/text/barnabas-lightfoot.html.

3 Aaron L. Mackler, *Introduction to Jewish and Catholic Bioethics: A Comparative Analysis* (Washington, DC: Georgetown University Press, 2003), 123.

4 John Connery, *Abortion: The Development of the Roman Catholic Perspective* (Chicago: Loyola University Press, 1977), 17–19.

5 Carol A. Tauer, "The Tradition of Probabilism and the Moral Status of the Early Embryo," in *Abortion and Catholicism: The American Debate*, ed. Patricia Beattie Jung and Thomas A. Shannon (New York: Crossroad, 1988), 57–58.

6 Donald DeMarco, "The Roman Catholic Church and Abortion: An Historical Perspective," *Homiletic & Pastoral Review*, July 1984.

7 Connery, *Abortion*, 149–50.

8 Joseph Donceel, "Immediate Animation and Delayed Hominization," *Theological Studies* 31 (1970): 76–105.

9 John T. Noonan Jr., "An Almost Absolute Value in History," in *The Morality of Abortion: Legal and Historical Perspectives* (Cambridge, MA: Harvard University Press, 1970), 1–59.

10 Anthony Nathan Cabor, "History of Abortion Law," *Arizona State Law Journal* 67 (1980): 88.

11 Louis M. Guenin, *The Morality of Embryo Use* (Cambridge: Cambridge University Press, 2008), 157.

12 Cabor, "History of Abortion Law," 88–91.

13 Edward Coke, *The Third Part of the Institutes of the Laws of England* [1644] (London: W. Clarke and Sons, 1817), 50.

14 William Blackstone, *The Commentaries of Sir William Blackstone, Knight, on the Laws and Constitution of England* [1769] (Chicago: American Bar Association, 2009), 9–10.

15 Joseph Dellapenna, *Dispelling the Myths of Abortion History* (Durham, NC: Carolina Academic Press, 2006), ch. 4.

16 Marvin Olasky, *Abortion Rites: A Social History of Abortion in America* (Wheaton, IL: Crossway Books, 1992), 37.

17 *Commonwealth v. Bangs* [1812], excerpted in Melody Rose, *Abortion: A Documentary and Reference Guide* (Westport, CT: Greenwood Press, 2008), 4–5.

18 James C. Mohr, *Abortion in America* (New York: Oxford University Press, 1978), 21.

19 Ibid., 145–56, 42–43.

20 John M. Riddle, *Eve's Herbs: A History of Contraception in the West* (Cambridge, MA: Harvard University Press, 1997), ch. 8.

21  Carole E. Joffe, "Abortion in Historical Perspective," in *A Clinician's Guide to Medical and Surgical Abortion*, ed. Maureen Paul, E. Steven Lichtenberg, Lynn Borgatta, David A. Grimes, and Phillip G. Stubblefield (Philadelphia: Churchill Livingstone, 1999).

22  Charles R. King, "Abortion in Nineteenth Century America: A Conflict between Women and Their Physicians," *Women's Health Issues* 2 (1992): 32–39.

23  Thomas Massie, "An Experimental Enquiry into the Properties of the Polygala Senega," in *Medical Theses, Selected from among the Inaugural Dissertations, Published and Defended by the Graduates in Medicine of the University of Pennsylvania, and of Other Medical Schools in the United States*, ed. Charles Caldwell (Philadelphia: Thomas and William Bradford, 1806), 203.

24  Theodric Romeyn Beck, *Elements of Medical Jurisprudence*, 2nd ed. (London: John Anderson, 1825), 142.

25  Ellen K. Rothman, *Hands and Hearts: A History of Courtship in America* (New York: Basic Books, 1984).

26  Dellapenna, *Dispelling the Myths of Abortion History*, 266.

27  "The Evil of the Age," *New York Times*, August 23, 1871, 6.

28  James S. Whitmire, "Criminal Abortion," *Chicago Medical Journal* 31 (1874): 386.

29  J. Foster Scott, "On Criminal Abortion," *Transactions of the Washington Obstetrical and Gynecological Society*, 3 (June 7, 1895): 374.

30  "Journals and Books," *Medico-Legal Journal* 24, no. 1 (June 1906): 201.

31  For descriptions of the advertising, including references to the early months of a pregnancy, see "Criminal and Obscene Quack Literature," *Medical and Surgical Reporter*, December 24, 1858, 218.

32  Scott, "On Criminal Abortion," 378.

33  Whereas scholars have not identified any statements from Protestant leaders in America from 1776 to 1857, at least one Catholic bishop took a strong stand. In 1841 Francis Kenrick published a treatise, in Latin, where he forcefully condemned all abortions. See Francisco Patricio Kenrick, *Theologiae Moralis* (Philadelphia: Apud Eugenium Cummiskey, 1841), 1:110–13.

34  Mohr, *Abortion in America*, 300n29.

35  Ibid., 182.

36  The works include Janet Farrell Brodie, *Contraception and Abortion in Nineteenth-Century America* (Ithaca, NY: Cornell University Press, 1994); Dellapenna, *Dispelling the Myths of Abortion History*; Olasky, *Abortion Rites*; and Leslie J. Reagan, *When Abortion Was a Crime: Women, Medicine, and Law in the United States, 1867–1973* (Berkeley: University of California Press, 1997).

37  Olasky, *Abortion Rites*, 34. Olasky also cites the opposition to abortion of several European religious leaders from the sixteenth to the eighteenth centuries.

38  Andrew Nebinger, "Criminal Abortion; Its Extent and Prevention," *Transactions of the Medical Society of the State of Pennsylvania*, vol. 11 (Philadelphia: Collins, 1876), 133. The article is a reprint of a report originally presented in 1869 to a meeting of the Medical Society of Pennsylvania.

39  Horatio R. Storer and Franklin Fiske Heard, *Criminal Abortion: Its Nature, Its Evidence, and Its Law* (Boston: Little, Brown, 1868), 74.

40  William M. Newman and Peter L. Halvorson, *Atlas of American Religion: The Denominational Era, 1776-1990* (Walnut Creek, CA: AltaMira Press, 2000), 69; Francis D. Cogliano, *Revolutionary America, 1763-1815: A Political History*, 2nd ed. (New York: Routledge, 2009), 32; US Bureau of the Census, *Statistical Abstract of the United States, 1992*, 112th ed. (Washington, DC: US Government Printing Office, 1992), 8.

41  Paul J. Fabrizio, "Evolving into Morality Politics: US Catholic Bishops' Statements on US Politics from 1792 to the Present," in *The Public Clash of Private Values: The Politics of Morality Policy*, ed. Christopher Z. Mooney (New York: Chatham House, 2001), 73-90.

42  Third Provincial Council of Baltimore, "Pastoral Letter" [April 22, 1837], in *Pastoral Letters of the United States Catholic Bishops*, vol. 1, *1792-1940*, ed. Hugh J. Nolan (Washington, DC: National Conference of Catholic Bishops, 1983), 85, 90.

43  Fourth Provincial Council of Baltimore, "Pastoral Letter" [May 23, 1840], in Nolan, *Pastoral Letters of the United States Catholic Bishops*, 1:133.

44  Martin Luther, *The Table Talk of Martin Luther*, trans. and ed. Alexander Chalmers (London: H. G. Bohn, 1857), 172. Scholars have uncovered one other reference by Luther to abortion, from a lecture Luther delivered in 1540. For Calvin's views, see John Calvin, *Commentaries on the Last Four Books of Moses, Arranged in the Form of a Harmony*, trans. Charles William Bingham (Edinburgh: Calvin Translation Society, 1854), 3:41-42.

45  Some people think that Numbers 5:11-31 uses coded language to describe a priest giving a potion to induce abortion in a woman who committed adultery, but this point is disputed.

46  Nebinger, "Criminal Abortion; Its Extent and Prevention," 128-29.

47  Mohr, *Abortion in America*; Brodie, *Contraception and Abortion in Nineteenth-Century America*, ch. 8.

48  Neil Schlager and Josh Lauer, eds., *Science and Its Times: Understanding the Social Significance of Scientific Discovery* (Detroit: Gale Group, 2001), 5:155.

49  "Report of the Special Committee on Criminal Abortion," *Ninth Annual Report of the Secretary of the State Board of Health of the State of Michigan for the Fiscal Year Ending Sept. 30, 1881* (Lansing, MI: W. S. George, 1882), 165.

50 Mohr, *Abortion in America*.

51 "Report on Criminal Abortion," *Transactions of the American Medical Association* 12 (1859): 75–78.

52 Nebinger, "Criminal Abortion; Its Extent and Prevention," 131.

53 "Report of the Committee on Criminal Abortion," *Transactions of the American Medical Association* 22 (1871): 255.

54 Nebinger, "Criminal Abortion; Its Extent and Prevention," 137.

55 Mohr, *Abortion in America*, 186–91.

56 *Minutes of the General Assembly of the Presbyterian Church in the United States of America* (Philadelphia: Presbyterian Board of Publication, 1869), 937.

57 Montrose A. Pallen, "Foeticide, or Criminal Abortion," *Medical Archives* 3 (April 1869): 196.

58 O. S. Fowler, *Sexual Science; Including Manhood, Womanhood, and Their Mutual Interactions* (Philadelphia: National Publishing Company, 1870), 899–900.

59 *Minutes of the General Assembly of the Presbyterian Church in the United States of America*, 937.

60 "Report of the Special Committee on Criminal Abortion," 167.

61 Pallen, "Foeticide, or Criminal Abortion," 195.

62 Todd Timmons, *Science and Technology in Nineteenth-Century America* (Westport, CT: Greenwood Press, 2005).

63 Mohr, *Abortion in America*, 187.

64 Ibid., chs. 8–9.

65 Andrea Tone, ed., *Controlling Reproduction: An American History* (Wilmington, DE: SR Books, 1997).

66 Reagan, *When Abortion Was a Crime*.

67 "Abortion Comes Out of the Shadows," *Life*, February 27, 1970, 20B.

68 American Law Institute, "Model Penal Code" [1959], in Rose, *Abortion*, 38–39.

69 Gerald N. Rosenberg, *The Hollow Hope: Can Courts Bring about Social Change?* (Chicago: University of Chicago Press, 1991), 184.

70 National Conference of Catholic Bishops, "Abortion (1969)," in J. Gordon Melton, *The Churches Speak on Abortion: Official Statements from Religious Bodies and Ecumenical Organizations* (Detroit: Gale Research, 1989), 7.

71 Some state groups of Congregationalists adopted positions on abortion, but Congregationalists — owing to their tradition of local church governance — did not unite in a national body.

72 United Presbyterian Church in the United States of America, "Sexuality and the Human Community (1970)," in Melton, *The Churches Speak on Abortion*, 90.

73 Rosemary Skinner Keller and Rosemary Radford Ruether, eds., *Encyclopedia of Women and Religion in North America* (Bloomington, IN: Indiana University Press, 2006), 1:378.

74 62nd General Convention of the Episcopal Church, "Resolution on Abortion (1967)," in Melton, *The Churches Speak on Abortion*, 48.

75 United Methodist Church, "Statement on Responsible Parenthood (1968)," in Melton, *The Churches Speak on Abortion*, 162–63.

76 Southern Baptist Convention, "Resolution on Abortion (1971)," in Melton, *The Churches Speak on Abortion*, 153.

77 Mary C. Segers and Timothy A. Byrnes, "Introduction: Abortion Politics in American States," in *Abortion Politics in American States*, ed. Segers and Byrnes (Armonk, NY: M. E. Sharpe, 1995), 5.

78 *"Roe v. Wade,"* in Rose, *Abortion*, 91–113.

79 Lawrence Van Gelder, "Cardinals Shocked—Reaction Mixed," *New York Times*, January 23, 1973, A1.

80 National Conference of Catholic Bishops, "Pastoral Plan for Pro-Life Activities (1975)," in Melton, *The Churches Speak on Abortion*, 12.

81 Elliott Wright, "Protestants Split on Abortion Edict," *Washington Post*, January 26, 1973, B7.

82 Southern Baptist Convention, "Resolution on Abortion (1974)," in Melton, *The Churches Speak on Abortion*, 153–54.

83 Southern Baptist Convention, "Resolution on Abortion (1980)," in Melton, *The Churches Speak on Abortion*, 154.

84 Kristin Luker, *Abortion and the Politics of Motherhood* (Berkeley: University of California Press, 1984), ch. 6.

85 Amy Fried, "Abortion Politics as Symbolic Politics: An Investigation into Belief Systems," *Social Science Quarterly* 69 (1988):137–54.

86 Luker, *Abortion and the Politics of Motherhood*.

87 Southern Baptist Convention, "Resolution on Abortion (1980)," in Melton, *The Churches Speak on Abortion*, 154.

88 Assemblies of God, "A Biblical Perspective on Abortion (1985)," in Melton, *The Churches Speak on Abortion*, 28–33.

89 United Methodist Church, "Statement on Responsible Parenthood (1976)," in Melton, *The Churches Speak on Abortion*, 163–64; 69th General Convention of the Episcopal Church, "Resolution on Abortion (1988)," in Melton, *The Churches Speak on Abortion*, 48–49; Presbyterian Church (USA), "Covenant and Creation: Theological Reflections on Contraception and Abortion (1983)," in Melton, *The Churches Speak on Abortion*, 91–131.

90 16th General Synod of the United Church of Christ, "Sexuality and Abortion: A Faithful Response (1987)," in Melton, *The Churches Speak on Abortion*, 159–60.

91 Cornelia B. Horn and John W. Martens, *Let the Little Children Come to Me: Childhood and Children in Early Christianity* (Washington, DC: Catholic University Press, 2009), 214–15.

92  John B. Cobb, ed., *Progressive Christians Speak: A Different Voice on Faith and Politics* (Louisville, KY: Westminster John Knox Press, 2003), 42.

93  Randy Alcorn, *ProLife Answers to ProChoice Arguments*, rev. ed. (Colorado Springs, CO: Multnomah Books, 2000), 313.

94  Unless otherwise noted, all quotations from the Bible in this chapter use *The Holy Bible, New American Bible Revised Edition* (Charlotte, NC: Saint Benedict Press, 2011).

95  Wayne A. Grudem, *Politics According to the Bible: A Comprehensive Resource for Understanding Modern Political Issues in Light of Scripture* (Grand Rapids, MI: Zondervan, 2010), 158.

96  Dennis R. Di Mauro, *A Love for Life: Christianity's Consistent Protection of the Unborn* (Eugene, OR: Wipf & Stock, 2008), 7–8.

97  Larry L. Lewis, "Bible Answers to Abortion Questions," in *Proclaiming the Pro-Life Message: Christian Leaders Address the Abortion Issue* (Hannibal, MO: Hannibal Books, 1997), 120.

98  Allen Verhey, *Reading the Bible in the Strange World of Medicine* (Grand Rapids, MI: William B. Eerdmans, 2003), 204.

99  John R. Ling, *When Does Human Life Begin? Christian Thinking and Contemporary Opposition* (Newcastle upon Tyne, England: Christian Institute, 2011), 9.

100  Di Mauro, *A Love for Life*, 7.

101  Christine Ammer, *The Encyclopedia of Women's Health*, 6th ed. (New York: Facts on File, 2009), 293.

102  Anne Eggebroten, "The Bible and Choice," in *Abortion: My Choice, God's Grace; Christian Women Tell their Stories*, ed. Eggebroten (Pasadena, CA: New Paradigm Books, 1994), 209–34.

103  Stephen M. King, *God and Caesar: The Biblical Keys to Good Government and Community Action* (Fairfax, VA: Xulon Press, 2002), 102.

104  T. Desmond Alexander and David W. Baker, eds., *Dictionary of the Old Testament Pentateuch: A Compendium of Contemporary Biblical Scholarship* (Downers Grove, IL: InterVarsity Press, 2003), 93–94; Peter Enns, *The NIV Application Commentary: Exodus* (Grand Rapids, MI: Zondervan, 2000), 446.

105  I ignore here the controversies over the Septuagint, the translation in ancient times of the Hebrew Bible into Greek. The Greek text, along with its distinction between a "formed" and "unformed" fetus, was important historically but carries little if any weight today among people on either side of the abortion debate.

106  Robert Woods, *Death before Birth: Fetal Health and Mortality in Historical Perspective* (Oxford: Oxford University Press, 2009), 19, 210.

107  James Hastings, ed., *Dictionary of the Bible* (New York: Scribner's Sons, 1909), 221.

108 John Wycliffe's translation, Wesley Center Online, accessed January 29, 2012, http://wesley.nnu.edu/fileadmin/imported_site/biblical_studies/wycliffe/Exo .txt.

109 The dates in parentheses all refer to the first publication of either Exodus or the Old Testament as a whole; the New Testament and the complete Bible some-times appeared at different times.

110 David Daniell, *The Bible in English* (New Haven, CT: Yale University Press, 2003), 439-43.

111 Available online at Study Bible, accessed January 29, 2012, http://studybible .info/Bishops.

112 These publication dates, again, refer to Exodus or the Old Testament, with the complete Bible sometimes appearing at different times.

113 The wording of these verses is slightly different in the 2011 edition of the NIV, which revised the entire translation to make it gender inclusive. However, the 2011 edition preserved the key phrase "she gives birth prematurely."

114 The introductory pages of Bibles commonly list the names and institutional af-filiations of the translators.

115 Mark W. Foreman, *Christianity & Bioethics: Confronting Clinical Issues* (Joplin, MO: College Press, 1999), 102.

116 The 1995 version of the NASB is widely available online, including at www.bible .com, www.biblegateway.com, and www.biblestudytools.com (accessed Janu-ary 30, 2012).

117 Robert N. Congdon, "Exodus 21:22-25 and the Abortion Debate," *Bibliotheca Sacra* 146 (1989): 132-47; H. Wayne House, "Miscarriage or Premature Birth: Additional Thoughts on Exodus 21:22-25," *Westminster Theological Journal* 41 (1978): 108-23.

118 Tom W. Smith, Peter Marsden, Michael Hout, and Jibum Kim, *General Social Surveys, 1972-2011: Cumulative Codebook* (Chicago: National Opinion Research Center, 2011), 397-99.

119 Author's analysis of the General Social Survey data.

120 As I do for my public opinion graphs in the rest of the book, I categorize people into the Christian groups according to the method of Brian Steensland and his colleagues, which the Association of Religion Data Archives calls "the most widely accepted way of accounting for differences in religious tradition." See the website of the Association of Religion Data Archives (http://wiki.thearda.com /tcm/concepts/denominationalism, accessed July 20, 2012). Steensland's team describes the method in Brian Steensland et al., "The Measure of American Religion: Toward Improving the State of the Art," *Social Forces* 79, no. 1 (Sep-tember 2000): 291-318.

121 Ted G. Jelen and Clyde Wilcox, "Causes and Consequences of Public Attitudes toward Abortion: A Review and Research Agenda," *Political Research Quarterly* 56 (2003): 489–500.

CHAPTER SIX

1 Richard L. Abel, *American Lawyers* (New York: Oxford University Press, 1989), chs. 3–4.

2 Jane M. Friedman, "Myra Bradwell: On Defying the Creator and Becoming a Lawyer," *Valparaiso University Law Review* 28, no. 4 (1994): 1287–88.

3 Ibid., 1291.

4 *Bradwell v. State of Illinois*, 83 US 130 (1873).

5 Justice Joseph Bradley, concurring opinion in *Bradwell v. State of Illinois*, 83 US 130 (1873).

6 Except where otherwise noted, all quotations in this chapter are from *The Holy Bible, New King James Version* (Nashville, TN: Thomas Nelson, 1982). My quotations do not, however, include the italics that the translators applied to certain words.

7 *Matthew Henry's Commentary on the Whole Bible* (Peabody, MA: 1991), 14.

8 Ibid., 2335, 2317.

9 Ibid., 2353.

10 Ibid.

11 *George Whitefield's Journals*, ed. Jay P. Greene Sr. (Lafayette, IN: Sovereign Grace, 2000), 40.

12 Charles Hodge, *An Exposition of the First Epistle to the Corinthians* (New York: Robert Carter & Brothers, 1857), 305.

13 Albert Taylor Bledsoe, *An Essay on Liberty and Slavery* (Philadelphia: J. B. Lippincott, 1856), 225.

14 Kathryn Cullen-DuPont, *Encyclopedia of Women's History in America*, 2nd ed. (New York: Facts on File, 2000), 232.

15 Ken Burns and Geoffrey C. Ward, *Not for Ourselves Alone: The Story of Elizabeth Cady Stanton and Susan B. Anthony* (New York: A. A. Knopf, 1999).

16 Beverly Wilson Palmer, ed., *Selected Letters of Lucretia Coffin Mott* (Urbana: University of Illinois Press, 2002).

17 Anthony's diary revealed her disbelief in "special providences." See Ida Husted Harper, *The Life and Work of Susan B. Anthony* (Indianapolis: Hollenbeck Press, 1898), 1:388. Stanton said Anthony was an agnostic. See Elizabeth Cady Stanton, "Susan B. Anthony," in *Our Famous Women: An Authorized Record of the Lives and Deeds of Distinguished American Women of Our Times* (Hartford, CT: A. D. Worthington, 1884), 59.

18 Harper, *The Life and Work of Susan B. Anthony*, 2:631.

19 Elizabeth Cady Stanton, "Has Christianity Benefitted Women?," in *North American Review* 140 (1885): 389.

20 Elizabeth Cady Stanton, *Eighty Years and More* (New York: European Publishing Company, 1898), 26.

21 Elizabeth Cady Stanton and Harriet Stanton Blatch, *Elizabeth Cady Stanton as Revealed in Her Letters, Diary and Reminiscences* (New York: Harper & Brothers, 1922), 1:239.

22 Elizabeth Cady Stanton, *The Woman's Bible*, vol. 1 (New York: European Publishing Company, 1895), 7, 8, 10, 12. I will address and quote only those parts of *The Woman's Bible* that Stanton herself wrote.

23 Ibid., 7, 15, 21.

24 Elizabeth Cady Stanton, *The Woman's Bible*, vol. 2 (New York: European Publishing Company, 1898), 113, 185.

25 Kathi Kern, *Mrs. Stanton's Bible* (Ithaca, NY: Cornell University Press, 2001), 216.

26 Morgan Dix, *The Calling of a Christian Woman* (London: Richard D. Dickinson, 1884), 15.

27 Reprinted in Stanton, *The Woman's Bible*, 2:215.

28 Lucretia Mott, "Religious Instinct in the Constitution of Man," in *Lucretia Mott: Her Complete Speeches and Sermons*, ed. Dana Greene (New York: Edwin Mellen Press, 1980), 242–43.

29 Lucretia Mott, "The Laws in Relation to Women," in Greene, *Lucretia Mott*, 215.

30 Sarah M. Grimké, *Letters on the Equality of the Sexes, and the Condition of Woman* (Boston, Isaac Knapp, 1838), 4, 6–7, 8, 115–16 (emphasis in original).

31 Ibid., 35, 24, 98, 91, 114.

32 Elizabeth Wilson, *A Scriptural View of Woman's Rights and Duties in All the Important Relations of Life* (Philadelphia: Wm. S. Young, 1849), 177, 176 (emphasis in original).

33 Ibid., 154, 159–60.

34 Ibid., 67, 37, 144.

35 Carolyn Williams, "The Female Antislavery Movement: Fighting against Racial Prejudice and Promoting Women's Rights in Antebellum America," in *The Abolitionist Sisterhood: Women's Political Culture in Antebellum America*, ed. Jean Fagan Yellin and John C. Van Horne (Ithaca, NY: Cornell University Press, 1994), 159–78.

36 Hannah Whitall Smith, *The Christian's Secret of a Happy Life*, rev. ed. (Chicago: Fleming H. Revell, 1888), 95.

37  Rev. Charles Duren, "Woman's Place in Religious Meetings," in *The Congregational Review* (Boston: M. H. Sargent, 1868), 8:22.

38  Horace Bushnell, *Women's Suffrage: The Reform against Nature* (New York: Charles Scribner, 1869), 81.

39  Duren, "Woman's Place in Religious Meetings," 26–7.

40  Ebenezer Platt Rogers, *The Obligations and Duties of the Female Sex to Christianity* (Augusta, GA: James McCafferty, 1849), 5.

41  Rev. Hubbard Winslow and Mrs. John Sanford, *The Lady's Manual of Moral and Intellectual Culture* (New York: Leavitt and Allen, 1854), 20. Winslow wrote part 1 of the book and Sanford wrote part 2.

42  George W. Burnap, *The Sphere and Duties of Woman* (Baltimore: John Murphy, 1861), 114, 115.

43  Dix, *The Calling of a Christian Woman*, 22.

44  "Declaration of Sentiments and Resolutions," in *Encyclopedia of Women in American Politics*, ed. Jeffrey D. Schulz and Laura Van Assendelft (Phoenix, AZ: Oryx Press, 1999), 258.

45  Carole Shammas, "Re-assessing the Married Women's Property Acts," *Journal of Women's History* 6 (1994): 9–30.

46  Glenda Riley, *Divorce: An American Tradition* (New York: Oxford University Press, 1991).

47  Regina E. Werum, "White Women's Higher Education: Coeducation and Gender Role Expectations, 1870–1890," in *Women and Work: A Handbook*, ed. Paula J. Dubeck and Kathryn Borman (New York: Garland, 1996), 227.

48  Mark Chaves, *Ordaining Women: Culture and Conflict in Religious Organizations* (Cambridge, MA: Harvard University Press, 1997), 16.

49  Susan Hill Lindley, *You Have Stept Out of Your Place: A History of Women and Religion in America* (Louisville, KY: Westminster John Knox Press, 1996), 331–37.

50  Chaves, *Ordaining Women*, 17.

51  Pope John Paul II, *Ordinatio Sacerdotalis* [encyclical letter], par. 1, 2, 11, The Vatican, accessed February 24, 2013, http://www.vatican.va/holy_father/john_paul_ii/apost_letters/documents/hf_jp-ii_apl_22051994_ordinatio-sacerdotalis_en.html.

52  "Resolution on Ordination and the Role of Women in Ministry" [June 1984], Southern Baptist Convention, accessed February 24, 2013, http://sbc.net/resolutions/amResolution.asp?ID=1088.

53  General Presbytery of the Assemblies of God, "The Role of Women in Ministry as Described in Holy Scripture" [August 2010], Assembles of God, accessed February 24, 2013, http://ag.org/top/Beliefs/Position_Papers/pp_downloads/PP_The_Role_of_Women_in_Ministry.pdf.

54 Southern Baptist Convention, "Resolution on Ordination and the Role of Women in Ministry."

55 Assemblies of God, "The Role of Women in Ministry as Described in Holy Scripture," 2, 4.

56 Betty Friedan, *The Feminine Mystique* (New York: Norton, 1963).

57 Linda Greenhouse and Reva B. Siegel, *Before* Roe v. Wade: *Voices that Shaped the Debate before the Supreme Court's Ruling* (New York: Kaplan Pub., 2010), 36–38.

58 Stephanie Gilmore, ed., *Feminist Coalitions: Historical Perspectives on Second-Wave Feminism in the United States* (Urbana: University of Illinois Press, 2008).

59 Leslie Heywood, ed., *The Women's Movement Today: An Encyclopedia of Third-Wave Feminism*, 2 vols. (Westport, CT: Greenwood Press, 2006).

60 Casey Miller and Kate Swift, *The Handbook of Nonsexist Writing* (New York: Lippincott & Crowell, 1980), 8.

61 C. Wright Mills, *The Sociological Imagination* (New York: Oxford University Press, 1959), 3, 5.

62 Miller and Swift, *The Handbook of Nonsexist Writing.*

63 Amy Einsohn, *The Copyeditor's Handbook: A Guide for Book Publishing and Corporate Communications* (Berkeley: University of California Press, 2000), 361–62.

64 Friedan, *The Feminine Mystique.*

65 Mary Daly, *The Church and the Second Sex* (New York: Harper and Row, 1968).

66 When Daly, in 1975, published a revised edition of *The Church and the Second Sex*, she included a "Feminist Postchristian Introduction."

67 Mary Daly, *Amazon Grace: Re-Calling the Courage to Sin Big* (New York: Palgrave Macmillan, 2006); Mary Daly, *Outercourse: The Be-Dazzling Voyage* (San Francisco: Harper San Francisco, 1992); Mary Daly, *Quintessence . . . Realizing the Archaic Future: A Radical Elemental Feminist Manifesto* (Boston: Beacon Press, 1998).

68 Susan Bridle, "No Man's Land: An Interview with Mary Daly," *What Is Enlightenment?*, Fall–Winter 1999.

69 Mary Daly, *The Church and the Second Sex*, rev. ed (New York: Harper and Row, 1975), 6.

70 Sharon James, "An Overview of Feminist Theology" (blog post), Theology Network, accessed February 22, 2013, http://www.theologynetwork.org/theology-of-everything/an-overview-of-feminist-theology.htm; Censor Librorum, "What Happened to Mary Daly," *Nikil Obstat* (blog), January 23, 2010, accessed February 22, 2013, http://nihilobstat.info/2010/01/23/what-happened-to-mary-daly.

71 Margaret Elizabeth Köstenberger, *Jesus and the Feminists: Who Do They Say He Is?* (Wheaton, IL: Crossway Books, 2008), 42.

72  Letha Scanzoni and Nancy Hardesty, *All We're Meant to Be: A Biblical Approach to Women's Liberation* (Waco, TX: Word Books, 1974).

73  Ibid., 27–28, 72, 69. On Jesus as "woman's best friend," see ch. 5.

74  Pamela D. H. Cochran, *Evangelical Feminism: A History* (New York: New York University Press, 2005), chs. 2–3 (on founding and activities), 4 (on split).

75  "Statement of Faith," Christians for Biblical Equality, accessed February 25, 2013, http://www.cbeinternational.org/?q=content/statement-faith.

76  "Men, Women and Biblical Equality," Christians for Biblical Equality, accessed November 24, 2014, http://www.cbeinternational.org/sites/default/files/english_0.pdf.

77  "Mission & Vision," Council on Biblical Manhood and Womanhood, accessed November 24, 2014, http://cbmw.org/mission-vision.

78  "Core Beliefs," Council on Biblical Manhood and Womanhood, accessed November 24, 2014, http://cbmw.org/core-beliefs.

79  All Gallup numbers reflect my analyses of various Gallup polls archived at the iPoll Databank, Roper Center for Public Opinion Research, accessed November 23, 2014, http://www.ropercenter.uconn.edu/data_access/ipoll/ipoll.html.

80  I have calculated these and the following figures from the General Social Survey, 1972–2012. Tom W. Smith, Peter Marsden, Michael Hout, and Jibum Kim, *General Social Surveys, 1972–2012* [machine-readable data file] (Chicago: National Opinion Research Center, 2013).

81  I have combined the percentage of people saying they "agree" and "strongly agree."

82  As in figure 6.2, figure 6.3 combines the numbers for "agree" and "strongly agree."

83  Sally K. Gallagher, *Evangelical Identity and Gendered Family Life* (New Brunswick, NJ: Rutgers University Press, 2003), 134.

84  "The Baptist Faith and Message" [2000], Southern Baptist Convention, accessed February 25, 2013, http://www.sbc.net/bfm/bfm2000.asp.

85  Gallagher, *Evangelical Identity and Gendered Family Life*, 69–77.

86  Gallagher, *Evangelical Identity and Gendered Family Life*; Cristel J. Manning, *God Gave Us the Right: Conservative Catholic, Evangelical Protestant, and Orthodox Jewish Women Grapple with Feminism* (New Brunswick, NJ: Rutgers University Press, 1999); Julie Ingersoll, *Evangelical Christian Women: War Stories in the Gender Battles* (New York: New York University Press, 2003); and R. Marie Griffith, *God's Daughters: Evangelical Women and the Power of Submission* (Berkeley: University of California Press, 1997); Nancy Ammerman, *Bible Believers: Fundamentalists in the Modern World* (New Brunswick, NJ: Rutgers University Press, 1987); Susan M. Shaw, *God Speaks to Us, Too: South-*

*ern Baptist Women on Church, Home, and Society* (Lexington: University Press of Kentucky, 2008).

87 W. Bradford Wilcox, *Soft Patriarchs, New Men: How Christianity Shapes Fathers and Husbands* (Chicago: University of Chicago Press, 2005).

88 Manning, *God Gave Us the Right*, 10.

89 Gallagher, *Evangelical Identity and Gendered Family Life*, 83.

90 Manning, *God Gave Us the Right*, 142, 124, 94 (emphasis in original).

91 Ibid., vii. On evangelical perceptions of feminism, see ch. 8. On the feminist ideas evangelicals accept, see ch. 4.

92 Division of Christian Education of the National Council of the Churches of Christ in the United States of America, *New Revised Standard Version Bible* (Grand Rapids, MI: Zondervan, 1989), xi.

93 Ibid.

94 David Dewey, *A User's Guide to Bible Translations: Making the Most of Different Versions* (Downers Grove, IL: InterVarsity Press, 2004), 162.

95 Susan Olasky, "The Stealth Bible: The Popular New International Version Is Quietly Going 'Gender-Neutral,'" *World*, March 29, 1997, 12–15.

96 Vern S. Poythress and Wayne A. Grudem, *The Gender-Neutral Bible Controversy: Muting the Masculinity of God's Words* (Nashville, TN: Broadman & Holman, 2000), 20, 306. On Focus on the Family's translation guidelines, see pages 299–319.

97 Marty King, "LifeWay Trustees Vote to Continue Selling '11 NIV," *Baptist Press*, February 15, 2012, accessed February 25, 2013, http://www.bpnews.net/bpnews .asp?id=37181.

98 Olasky, "The Stealth Bible," 12.

99 "CBA Best Sellers through December 29, 2012," Christian Booksellers Association, accessed January 28, 2013, http://www.cbaonline.org/nm/documents/bsls /bible_translations.pdf. Data from Amazon.com compiled by the author on January 28, 2013.

100 "The Presbyterian Panel: Listening to Presbyterians" [August 2006], Presbyterian Church (USA), accessed February 26, 2013, http://www.pcusa.org/media /uploads/research/pdfs/08-06fullreportwithappendix.pdf.

101 "Daily Bible Reading," Evangelical Lutheran Church in America, accessed November 24, 2014, http://www.elca.org/en/Faith/DailyBible.

102 "Does the United Methodist Church Designate an 'Official' Version of the Bible?" United Methodist Church, accessed November 24, 2014, http://www .umc.org/what-we-believe/does-the-united-methodist-church-designate-an -official-version-of-the-bible.

103 Wayne Grudem, *Systematic Theology: An Introduction to Biblical Doctrine* (Grand Rapids, MI: Zondervan, 1994). Information about Wayne Grudem can

be found at his website (http://www.waynegrudem.com, accessed February 26, 2013).

104 Wayne A. Grudem, *What's Wrong with Gender-Neutral Bible Translations?* (Libertyville, IL: Council on Biblical Manhood and Womanhood, 1997); Poythress and Grudem, *The Gender-Neutral Bible Controversy*; Vern S. Poythress and Wayne A. Grudem, *The TNIV and the Gender-Neutral Bible Controversy* (Nashville, TN: Broadman & Holman, 2005).

105 Poythress and Grudem, *The Gender-Neutral Bible Controversy*, 117–24.

106 Wayne Grudem, *Politics According to the Bible: A Comprehensive Resource for Understanding Modern Political Issues in Light of Scripture* (Grand Rapids, MI: Zondervan, 2010).

107 Figures based on word searches at Google Books of *Politics According to the Bible*.

108 See, for example, the Right Wing Watch program sponsored by People for the American Way (www.rightwingwatch.org, accessed January 8, 2012).

109 James C. Dobson, *What Wives Wish Their Husbands Knew about Women* (Carol Stream, IL: Tyndale, 1975); James C. Dobson, *Straight Talk: What Men Need to Know, What Women Should Understand* (Nashville, TN: Word Publishers, 1991).

110 James C. Dobson, *Bringing Up Girls: Practical Advice and Encouragement for Those Shaping the Next Generation of Women* (Carol Stream, IL: Tyndale, 2010), 136–39, 67 (emphasis in original).

111 As quoted in Andrew Malcolm, "With Sarah Palin Aboard, John McCain Gets Official Nod from Major Evangelical Leader Dobson," *Top of the Ticket* (blog), October 6, 2008, accessed January 8, 2012, latimesblogs.latimes.com /Washington/2008/10/mccain-palin-do.html.

112 Sarah Pulliam Bailey, "James Dobson Interviews Sarah Palin," *Christianity Today Politics Blog*, October 22, 2008, accessed January 8, 2012, http://blog .christianitytoday.com/ctpolitics/2008/10/james_dobson_in.html.

113 E. J. Dionne Jr., *Souled Out: Reclaiming Faith and Politics after the Religious Right* (Princeton, NJ: Princeton University Press, 2008), 70.

114 Jennifer Baumgardner and Amy Richards, *Manifesta: Young Women, Feminism, and the Future* (New York: Farrar, Straus and Giroux, 2000), 17.

CHAPTER SEVEN

1 Abby Goodnough, "Student Faces Town's Wrath in Protest against a Prayer," *New York Times*, January 26, 2012.

2 *Ahlquist v. Cranston*, United States District Court for the District of Rhode Island, C.A. No. 11-138L (January 11, 2012), 39.

3 Laura Crimaldi, "RI School Officials to Discuss Prayer Banner Case," *Boston Globe*, February 15, 2012.

4 Goodnough, "Student Faces Town's Wrath in Protest against a Prayer."

5 Paul Davis, "Cranston School Prayer Banner: Crowd Jams Hearing on Whether to Appeal Its Removal," *Providence Journal*, February 16, 2012.

6 Greta Christina, "Why Is an Atheist High School Student Getting Vicious Death Threats?," AlterNet, January 18, 2012, accessed June 27, 2012, http://www.alternet.org/belief/153803/why_is_an_atheist_high_school_student_getting_vicious_death_threats?page=entire.

7 Billy Hallowell, "'Teen Atheist Behind Prayer Mural Ban Threatened with Rape: 'We Will Get You—Look Out!'" The Blaze, April 12, 2012, accessed June 27, 2012, http://www.theblaze.com/stories/teen-atheist-behind-prayer-mural-ban-threatened-with-rape-we-will-get-you-look-out.

8 Penny Egell, Joseph Gerteis, and Douglas Hartmann, "Atheists as 'Other': Moral Boundaries and Cultural Membership in American Society," *American Sociological Review* 71 (2006): 211–34.

9 Jeffrey M. Jones, "Some Americans Reluctant to Vote for Mormon, 72-Year-Old Presidential Candidates," Gallup, February 20, 2007, accessed April 19, 2012, http://www.gallup.com/poll/26611/some-americans-reluctant-vote-mormon-72yearold-presidential-candidates.aspx, accessed April 19, 2012.

10 Will M. Gervais, Azim F. Shariff, and Ara Norenzayan, "Do You Believe in Atheists? Distrust Is Central to Anti-atheist Prejudice," *Journal of Personality and Social Psychology* 101 (December 2011):1189–1206.

11 "An Argument against Abolishing Christianity," in *The Prose Works of Jonathan Swift*, ed. Temple Scott (London: George Bell & Sons, 1898), 3:19.

12 Fyodor Dostoyevsky, *The Brothers Karamazov*, trans. Constance Garnett (New York: Random House, 1950), 78.

13 David Aikman, *The Delusion of Disbelief* (Carol Stream, IL: SaltRiver, 2008), 96–97.

14 Dinesh D'Souza, *What's So Great about Christianity* (Washington, DC: Regnery Publishing, 2007), 226.

15 William Lane Craig, "The Kurtz/Craig Debate: Is Goodness without God Good Enough?" in *Is Goodness without God Good Enough?*, ed. Robert K. Garcia and Nathan L. King (Lanham, MD: Rowman & Littlefield, 2009), 38; Aikman, *The Delusion of Disbelief*, 100.

16 C. S. Lewis, *Mere Christianity*, rev. ed. (New York: Macmillan, 1960), 17–21.

17 D'Souza, *What's So Great about Christianity*, 237.

18 Kenneth Richard Samples, *Without a Doubt: Answering the 20 Toughest Faith Questions* (Grand Rapids, MI: Baker Books, 2004), 237.

19 Mark F. Rooker, *The Ten Commandments: Ethics for the Twenty-First Century*

(Nashville, TN: B&H Publishing Group, 2010); David Hazony, *The Ten Commandments: How Our Most Ancient Moral Text Can Renew Modern Life* (New York: Scribner, 2010), 7.

20  William Lane Craig, *Reasonable Faith: Christian Truth and Apologetics*, 3rd ed. (Wheaton, IL: Crossway Books, 2008), 84–86.

21  Josh McDowell and Sean McDowell, *The Unshakeable Truth: How You Can Experience the 12 Essentials of a Relevant Faith* (Eugene, OR: Harvest House, 2010), 63.

22  As quoted in Stephen Law, *The Philosophy Gym: 25 Short Adventures in Thinking* (New York: St. Martin's Press, 2003), 104.

23  Jeff Jacoby, "Created by God to Be Good," *Boston Globe*, November 14, 2010.

24  Michael Novak, *No One Sees God: The Dark Night of Atheists and Believers* (New York: Doubleday, 2008), 53.

25  Walter Sinnott-Armstrong, *Morality without God* (Oxford: Oxford University Press, 2009); Greg Epstein, *Good without God: What a Billion Nonreligious People Do Believe* (New York: William Morris, 2009).

26  Sam Harris, *The End of Faith: Religion, Terror, and the Future of Reason* (New York: Norton, 2004).

27  Phil Zuckerman, *Society without God: What the Least Religious Nations Can Tell Us about Contentment* (New York: New York University Press, 2008); Gregory S. Paul, "The Chronic Dependence of Popular Religiosity upon Dysfunctional Psychosociological Conditions," *Evolutionary Psychology* 7 (2009): 398–441.

28  Bertrand Russell, "Why I Am Not a Christian," in *Why I Am Not a Christian and Other Essays on Religion and Related Subjects* (New York: George Allen & Unwin, 1957), 21.

29  Voltaire to Frederick II of Prussia, April 6, 1767 [letter 160], in *Letters of Voltaire and Frederick the Great*, trans. Richard Aldington (New York: Brentano's, 1927), 5.

30  "Medieval Sourcebook: Fourth Lateran Council: Canon 3 on Heresy 1215," Fordham University Center for Medieval Studies, accessed March 29, 2012, http://www.fordham.edu/halsall/source/lat4-c3.asp.

31  Michael C. Thomsett, *The Inquisition: A History* (Jefferson, NC: McFarland, 2010).

32  Brian P. Levack, *The Witch-Hunt in Early Modern Europe*, 3rd ed. (New York: Pearson Longman, 2006).

33  William Nicholls, *Christian Antisemitism: A History of Hate* (Lanham, MD: Rowman & Littlefield, 1993).

34  Jonathan Riley-Smith, *The Crusades: A History*, 2nd ed. (New York: Continuum, 2005), 19–25.

35 Marvin Perry and Frederick M. Schweitzer, *Antisemitism: Myth and Hate from Antiquity to the Present* (New York: Palgrave Macmillan, 2002), 79–81.

36 Martin Luther, *On the Jews and Their Lies*, trans. Martin H. Bertram, parts 11 and 12, accessed November 24, 2014, http://www.ccjr.us/dialogika-resources /primary-texts-from-the-history-of-the-relationship/273-luther-1543.

37 Dan Barker, *Godless: How an Evangelical Preacher Became One of America's Leading Atheists* (Berkeley, CA: Ulysses Press, 2008), 166.

38 Ruth Hurmence Green, *The Born Again Skeptic's Guide to the Bible*, 4th ed. (Madison, WI: Freedom From Religion Foundation, 1999), 109–16.

39 Elizabeth Anderson, "If God Is Dead, Is Everything Permitted?" in *The Portable Atheist: Essential Readings for the Nonbeliever*, ed. Christopher Hitchens (Philadelphia: Da Capo Press, 2007), 336–37.

40 Biblical quotations in this chapter are from the *The New Jerusalem Bible* (New York: Doubleday, 1985).

41 Joseph C. Sommer, "Some Reasons Why Humanists Reject the Bible," American Humanist Association, accessed June 27, 2012, http://www.americanhumanist .org/humanism/Some_Reasons_Why_Humanists_Reject_the_Bible.

42 Cyndi Banks, *Criminal Justice Ethics: Theory and Practice*, 3rd ed. (Thousand Oaks, CA: Sage, 2013).

43 Barker, *Godless*, 175.

44 Ibid., 185.

45 Sam Harris, *Letter to a Christian Nation* (New York: Alfred A. Knopf, 2006), 14.

46 Bill Maher, from the film *Religulous*, as quoted by Internet Movie Database (IMDb) , accessed January 14, 2012, www.imdb.com/title/tt0815241/quotes.

47 Émile Durkheim, *The Elementary Forms of Religious Life* [1912], trans. Carol Cosman (New York: Oxford University Press, 2001).

48 David W. Moore, "Three in Four Americans Believe in Paranormal," Gallup, June 16, 2005, accessed April 2, 2012, http://www.gallup.com/poll/16915/three -four-americans-believe-paranormal.aspx.

49 Patricia U. Bonomi, *Under the Cope of Heaven: Religion, Society, and Politics in Colonial America* (New York: Oxford University Press, 1986); Thomas J. Curry, *The First Freedoms: Church and State in America to the Passage of the First Amendment* (New York: Oxford University Press, 1986).

50 Pope Pius IX, "The Syllabus," EWTN Global Catholic Network, accessed April 2, 2012, http://www.ewtn.com/library/PAPALDOC/P9SYLL.HTM.

51 Chris Beneke, *Beyond Toleration: The Religious Origins of American Pluralism* (New York: Oxford University Press, 2006).

52 Steven Waldman, *Founding Faith: Providence, Politics, and the Birth of Religious Freedom in America* (New York: Random House, 2008).

53  Francis Graham Lee, *Church-State Relations* (Westport, CT: Greenwood Press, 2002).

54  Pope Paul VI, "Declaration on Religious Freedom" [December 7, 1965], The Vatican, accessed April 2, 2012, http://www.vatican.va/archive/hist_councils /ii_vatican_council/documents/vat-ii_decl_19651207_dignitatis-humanae_en .html.

55  Jerome A. Chanes, *Antisemitism: A Reference Handbook* (Santa Barbara, CA: ABC-CLIO, 2004), 56–64.

56  Kevin B. Spicer, ed., *Antisemitism, Christian Ambivalence, and the Holocaust* (Bloomington: Indiana University Press, 2007).

57  Pope Paul VI, "Declaration on the Relation of the Church to Non-Christian Religions" [October 28, 1965], The Vatican, accessed April 2, 2012, http://www .vatican.va/archive/hist_councils/ii_vatican_council/documents/vat-ii_decl _19651028_nostra-aetate_en.html.

58  Helen P. Fry, ed., *Christian-Jewish Dialogue: A Reader* (Chicago: University of Chicago Press, 1996).

59  "Public Opinion on the Death Penalty," Pew Forum on Religion and Public Life, September 23, 2011, accessed April 19, 2012, http://www.pewforum.org /Death-Penalty/Public-Opinion-on-the-Death-Penalty.aspx.

60  Patrick J. Buchanan, "1992 Republican National Convention Speech," accessed November 24, 2014, http://buchanan.org/blog/1992-republican-national -convention-speech-148.

61  Patrick J. Buchanan, "The Aggressors in the Culture Wars," WND Commentary, March 8, 2004, accessed September 6, 2012, http://www.wnd.com/2004 /03/23626.

62  James Davison Hunter, *Culture Wars: The Struggle to Define America* (New York: Basic Books, 1991).

63  Alan Wolfe, *One Nation, After All: What Middle-Class Americans Really Think about God, Country, Family, Racism, Welfare, Immigration, Homosexuality, the Right, the Left, and Each Other* (New York: Viking, 1998); Morris P. Fiorina, with Samuel J. Abrams and Jeremy C. Pope, *Culture War? The Myth of a Polarized America* (New York: Pearson Longman, 2005). See also Paul DiMaggio, John Evans, and Bethany Bryson, "Have Americans' Social Attitudes Become More Polarized?" *American Journal of Sociology* 102 (November 1996): 690–755; Nancy J. Davis and Robert V. Robinson, "Are the Rumors of War Exaggerated? Religious Orthodoxy and Moral Progressivism," *American Journal of Sociology* 102 (November 1996): 756–87; and Wayne Baker, *America's Crisis of Values: Reality and Perception* (Princeton, NJ: Princeton University Press, 2005). For contrary views, see Alan I. Abramowitz, *The Disappearing Center: Engaged Citizens, Polarization, and American Democracy* (New Haven, CT: Yale

University Press, 2010); David C. Barker and Christopher Jan Carman, *Representing Red and Blue: How the Culture Wars Change the Way Citizens Speak and Politicians Listen* (New York: Oxford University Press, 2012); and William G. Jacoby, "Is There a Culture War? Conflicting Value Structures in American Public Opinion," *American Political Science Review* 108 (November 2014):754-71.

64 Wolfe, *One Nation, After All*; Fiorina, *Culture War?*

65 Untitled resolution [May 1898], Southern Baptist Convention, accessed July 1, 2012, http://www.sbc.net/resolutions/amResolution.asp?ID=47. The Southern Baptist Convention passed seventeen similar resolutions during its regular meetings from 1886 to 1932.

66 Laurence R. Iannaccone, "Why Strict Churches Are Strong," *American Journal of Sociology* 99 (1994):1180-1211; Dean M. Kelley, *Why Conservative Churches Are Growing* (New York: Harper & Row, 1972).

67 See, for example, Rob Kerby, "Have Americans Lost Their Faith . . . Or Just their Trust in Old 'Mainline' Churches?," BeliefNet, July 2012, accessed September 30, 2013, http://blog.beliefnet.com/news/2012/07/have-christians-lost-confidence-in-church-officials.php; and Lewis Willis, "The Denominations Have Been Hijacked," *Guardian of Truth*, March 7, 1991, 142.

68 Francis A. Schaeffer, *The Great Evangelical Disaster* (Westchester, IL: Crossway Books, 1984), 38, 28, 36, 150, 60, 138.

69 Ibid., 133, 137.

70 Ibid., 64, 65.

71 "Divorce—the Scandal of the Evangelical Conscience," AlbertMohler.com, September 30, 2010, accessed July 6, 2012, http://www.albertmohler.com/2010/09/30/divorce-the-scandal-of-the-evangelical-conscience.

72 R. Albert Mohler Jr., *Desire and Deceit: The Real Cost of the New Sexual Tolerance* (Multnomah, OR: Multnomah Books, 2008), chs. 6-14.

73 Abby Day, *Believing in Belonging: Belief and Social Identity in the Modern World* (New York: Oxford University Press, 2011).

74 Christian Smith, *American Evangelicalism: Embattled and Thriving* (Chicago: University of Chicago Press, 1998).

75 I owe the metaphor to Graham Wilson, who used it to describe public policies in economically developed countries. See Graham K. Wilson, *Only in America? The Politics of the United States in Comparative Perspective* (Chatham, NJ: Chatham House, 1998).

76 Ross Douthat, "The Persistence of the Culture War," *New York Times*, February 7, 2012.

# Index

The letter *f* following a page number denotes a figure; the letter *t*, a table.